THE GUV'NOR
THROUGH THE EYES OF OTHERS

THE GUV'NOR

THROUGH THE EYES OF OTHERS

Lenny McLean was a living legend. These are the true
stories of the people whose lives he touched.

Anthony Thomas

with Foreword by Valerie McLean

JOHN BLAKE

Published by John Blake Publishing Ltd,
3, Bramber Court, 2 Bramber Road,
London W14 9PB, England

www.blake.co.uk

First published in hardback in 2006

ISBN 1 84454 216 5

British Library Cataloguing-in-Publication Data:

A catalogue record for this book is available from the British Library.

Design by www.envydesign.co.uk

Printed in Great Britain by
CPD Wales, Ebbw Vale

1 3 5 7 9 10 8 6 4 2

Papers used by John Blake Publishing are natural, recyclable products
made from wood grown in sustainable forests. The manufacturing processes
conform to the environmental regulations of the country of origin.

Dedication

This book is dedicated to my Guv'nor, my late father
Edwin Charles Thomas, always in our thoughts; and also to the
late Alfie Hayes, who sadly passed away on 23 May 2005 during
the writing of this book – a true gentleman with a heart of gold.

Edwin Charles
Thomas

Alfie Hayes

Acknowledgements

I'd like to thank a few people without whose help I wouldn't have been able to complete this book:

Lenny's favourite cousin Martin Rogers, Alfie Hayes, Mr Stellakis Stylianou, Jimmy Andrews… Thanks for your help, lads.

Valerie McLean – thanks for your blessing, it means a lot.

My girlfriend Anne Marie, for all she's done to help me with this book.

John Blake for giving me the chance.

Richard Camp, Rosie Hayes, Terry Currie, Julian Davies, Lee Crystal, Chris Chapman, Graham Noble and Bernard Driscoll.

My brother Steve, Michael Clayden and Dav Owens for their time and patience in writing this book, and to all the people who have contributed to it.

Also, big thanks to all the people who have contributed to the website throughout the years, including my brother Steve, who keeps the memory alive through thick and thin. Keep up the good work, Steve. And thanks to our newest member, site designer Lyn Williams, for his hard work.

Last but not least, thanks to the Guv'nor himself, Lenny McLean.

The Official Lenny McLean Website: www.lennymclean.co.uk

Contents

Foreword   ix

Introduction   xv

1   Hoxton Born and Bred   1

2   Best of Friends   29

3   Gloved Up   79

4   Respect   115

5   Stir Crazy   147

6   Role Model   163

7   Life and Soul   203

8   Door Rage   219

9   To Bexley and Back   237

10   Meeting the Guv'nor   257

11   The Legend Lives On   287

12   The Show Must Go On   293

Foreword By Valerie McLean

Lenny died on 28 July 1998, but it seems like it was just yesterday. Not a day passes that my children, Jamie and Kelly, and I don't talk about him, think about him and remember him with the true love that only a husband and father can inspire. We all miss him terribly. But Lenny left a legacy that lives on to this day, one that makes his whole family proud that a man from such poor, humble beginnings achieved so much and won the hearts and respect of ordinary people the world over.

The day he died, his book, *The Guv'nor*, went to number one, just like he always knew it would. It wasn't arrogance that told him that, just a knowledge that, in a world where men like him were a dying breed, there would be real interest in the amazing story of his life. I wonder if he had any idea, though, that, so many years on, people would still be talking about him, writing books about him, remembering his exploits and telling stories about his life that mean that, even though he's gone, he never seems far away. It would make him proud, certainly, and I sometimes imagine him looking down on us and having a good laugh at how it all turned out. 'What did I tell you, Val?' he'll be chuckling. 'I told you that book would be a good 'un.'

Many people remember Lenny as a tough guy, and he was certainly that. Being tough was just part of his profession – he was a man who was never afraid to do what he had to do in order to make sure that his family, the most important thing in his life, had everything they wanted. And it was his family that drove everything he did, because he learned very early on in life that, if you don't look after those people closest to you, you never know who's just around the corner ready to do them harm.

He might have been a strong man, but he used to have a lump in his throat when he remembered the day his mum gathered him up in her arms and told him that his dad had gone to heaven to be an angel. Some time later, she married again. Jim Irwin, Len's stepfather, was a bully. The first time he slapped Len across the face was for spilling a cup of tea and, from that moment on, he made their lives nothing but a misery. He beat their mum for giving them too much food, and sent the children to school with bruises on their faces as punishments for the slightest misdemeanours.

The final straw, though, came when he beat Len's younger brother Raymond for wetting the bed. Four years old, and beaten raw. That same night, as he cuddled his little brother and heard him whisper, 'I'm sorry I wet meself, Lenny,' he knew that the time had come for him to take action. He sneaked Raymond out of the house and over to his grandmother's, who called her brother, Jimmy Spinks. Now

Jimmy was one of the old school, one of the strongest men to come out of the East End of London, a fighter and a hard man. His way of dealing with the situation would probably be frowned upon by some people nowadays, who would like to give monsters like Irwin the benefit of the doubt. But the East End was Jimmy's manor, and he wouldn't tolerate that kind of thing happening to anyone, least of all his family. And he certainly got the result he wanted. He went round to Lenny's house in a flash and burst through the door, and the only reason he didn't do Irwin some serious harm was because Len's mum begged him not to. But Irwin – who found it easy to bully a few defenceless children, but crumbled when faced with a real man – never laid a finger on them again.

Lenny learned a valuable lesson that day – the only way to deal with a bully is to stand up to him. And that's what he spent his life doing. He couldn't bear to see anyone pick on someone smaller, weaker or less intimidating than themselves, and God forbid if anyone was rude to a lady in his company – it would be something they would always regret.

They call Lenny a hard man, and there's no denying that, in the ring, he was a violent man. Even now I can't bear to look at pictures of him fighting but, deep down, I know he was almost untouchable. And there's no denying that the day he beat Roy Shaw was one of the most important of his life.

But to be a real hard man you have to have respect, and you don't earn that through random acts of violence on the street. Lenny always said that there was a difference between two powerful men, each with respect for the other, fighting in the ring and some lowlife mugging old ladies or bullying those weaker than him. The only time you'd find Lenny brawling was when, as he put it, he was 'cleaning the rubbish off the streets'. And just as I knew that fighting was something in him, something he just had to do in order to make a decent living for his family, I also knew that he had just as strong an urge to help people and protect them. If someone went to Lenny with a problem, it became his problem, and he used to take pride in sorting it out in whatever way he saw fit.

Despite the steel core at the heart of Lenny, he was a long way from being just the stereotypical tough guy. He was sharp as a nail, and he lived his life according to that one watchword – respect. He demanded respect, but he gave it out, too, wherever it was deserved. That was what made him the Guv'nor.

Sometimes, this led him into dangerous situations – more than once, he found himself looking down the barrel of a gun – but he was a man of honour, not somebody who would turn around and walk away when things became difficult. It was that quality that earned him respect in whatever he did from everyone who knew him, and it was that quality that made him the best father and husband anyone could wish for. If there were a few more real men like Lenny around today, perhaps the world would not be the place that it is.

Reading this book brings back so many memories for me. I'll never forget the first time I saw Lenny all those years ago, or the sparkling McLean charm that won my heart; it's been lovely to read so many of the memories of others for the first time, and to be reminded of why he was held in such high regard. And as I leaf through these pages, it brings home to me how many lives Lenny touched. The people who knew him either respected him or feared him, but the fantastic success of his autobiography showed that he was an inspiration to all sorts of people from all walks of life – young or old, rich or poor, literally hundreds of thousands of people have found something about Lenny's story that moves them. And even though, in his youth, Len was not always on the right side of the law, even though he had his collar felt by the Old Bill on more than one occasion, I have no doubt that he is a great role model for so many people today.

You can tell the quality of a man by how he acts in difficult situations. God knows, Lenny faced a few of those in his time, but, whenever the going got tough, his main thought was never for himself but for others around him. When he found himself on remand facing the possibility of a 24-year sentence for a crime he hadn't committed, his first thoughts were not for himself but for the family he'd leave behind on the outside – who was going to put 'steam on the table' for them while he was behind bars? And when he was told that the cancer in his brain was likely to defeat him in four to six months, and his close friends found themselves crying at the news, more often than not it was Lenny himself who had to comfort them. 'Come on,' he'd say, putting his arm round them, 'you've got to be strong.'

Lenny loved stories; he loved telling them and he loved hearing them. That's why he would have loved this book. As I read it, I imagined him sitting next to me, laughing at the funny memories, growling at the thought of more difficult times. He wasn't much of a one for looking back – even at the end he was looking forward to all the things he would achieve when he 'shook off' his illness. But he knew he had a past to be proud of and, now that he's gone, his family feel that sense of pride for him. We love him and miss him so much. The world is a poorer place now he's not here.

Thank you, Anthony, for writing a fantastic book and giving

us all another way to remember this giant among men. Thank you to everyone who took the time to contribute their memories. And thank you, above all, to Lenny. You were so many things to so many people. You will never be replaced.

Valerie McLean, February 2006

Introduction by Anthony Thomas

The Guv'nor – Lenny McLean. The name will stay with me forever.

What started out as a hobby became a fixation. A number of years back, I borrowed a video from a mate containing footage of the man himself: I was determined to get more material of the Guv'nor in action.

Not long afterwards, the bestselling book *The Guv'nor* was released and I borrowed it from another of my mates. I finished the book in 24 hours and rushed out to buy my own copy so that I could read it again. I was hooked.

Around this time, sadly, Lenny passed away and the newspapers were full of stories about him. I didn't even know the bloke but, like so many others who'd read the book, I felt like I'd known him for years. I wanted to attend the funeral with a couple of mates, but we were unable to make it and caught it on the television instead.

A couple of weeks later, my brother went out and bought a

computer. The first thing to come into mind was to put Lenny's name into the search engines on the internet. I searched for days and days, but found nothing. I also tried boxing magazines and various other sources to get articles and footage, but with no joy. I knew they were out there, it was just a case of finding them. I then began to think about setting up some web pages on Lenny and to try and get hold of a few videos and articles.

A mate of mine had quite a few articles, so we started scanning them and within a few weeks we had about ten pages. Then came the hardest part: getting the website advertised with the search engines. We spent weeks advertising it on forums and trying to get it on to as many search engines as possible. We had put a guestbook on the website as well and all of a sudden people started leaving messages from all over the world. The next thing I knew people were emailing me saying they had some footage of a fight or an article and, all of a sudden, we were finally up and running.

Every day, my obsession with Lenny was growing. I needed to know more about him all the time. I then saw the email address of Lenny's co-author Peter Gerrard on the internet. I knew this was my big chance to get closer to someone who knew Lenny well, so I gave it a go and within a couple of days Peter had answered my email and told me he would bookmark the site and check it often. I was chuffed that he'd taken the time to answer my message and I now knew he would be checking the site out.

The site grew and grew; messages started coming from places as far afield as Australia, the USA and even Africa. We had finally done it, we had passed 1000 hits. We were happy with what we had achieved. We'd hit the big 1000.

It wasn't long before I started getting emails from people who had met the Guv'nor and wanted to post their stories or photos on the site. The articles and videos were still coming in but I now needed more. I needed to know stories. I tried to get in touch with Len's wife, even sending letters to all the Val McLeans in England, but I couldn't get an answer. So it was now time to get out of Wales and get up to London and start asking questions.

A good fighting mate of mine had given me his tickets to a launch party for the channel 5 documentary *Natural Born Fighters*. So I headed up to London for the day with a mate who used to run an unlicensed boxing website. We then went on to the party in the evening. We had been at the party for a while when who should walk in but none other than Roy Shaw, Joey Pyle and Nosher Powell. After a few more drinks, I built up the courage and introduced myself to Roy Shaw. He was great and started telling us about the fights he'd had with Lenny. You could still feel his presence and he looked like he could still explode any minute even though he had turned 60. I left that night with some more comments from Nosher and the great Joe Pyle.

The number of visitors to the website kept increasing and the comments were coming in thick and fast, and before we knew it we had 10,000 hits. Just when everything was going OK, somebody sabotaged our guestbook, over one hundred comments and contacts disappeared, just like that. So we changed the guestbook and the comments started rolling in again.

Peter Gerrard was now in contact with us through regular emails and was really happy with the way the site was developing. I then received an email from Len's wife Val. I was over the moon. So I asked Peter Gerrard if Val would make us the official website. There were a couple of small websites around but nothing special and we now had over seventy pages and were still growing. Peter got back to me and told us he'd ask her at a later date. I suppose she thought we were out to make money on her late husband's name, but that was the last thing going through our minds.

Then one day, I missed a phone call from Val McLean and got a message that she wanted a word with me. I was absolutely gutted that I'd missed the call and she hadn't left a number. The following day she rang again, and then said she would ring later that night. I was now on pins, thinking about what I would say to her. This was Val, wife of the Guv'nor Lenny McLean. I couldn't get any closer than this. I prayed that she could understand my Welsh accent and that I didn't make a fool of myself.

When she did call me back, she sounded upset that I had obtained photos of her and her family, photos she hadn't even seen. She also wanted to know about some other things on the website. I gave her all the details and she thanked me. I then asked her if she was happy with the site and she said that she was and that was it, she was gone. I was still a bit gutted this had been my big chance to talk to Lenny's wife and it was over in minutes. I suppose at the end of the day she was new to the computer game and I was just someone on the end of the phone with a funny Welsh accent!

I thought about it the next day and realised how upset she must have been, and who could blame her? I emailed her all the details she needed to know in order to sort things out.

We then received an email from a computing magazine called *Station* asking if they could run a review of our website with photos in their magazine. We didn't need long to think about the answer to that one. We had finally got some recognition, everything had been worthwhile.

I think it's about time I brought my brother Steve into this story. Without Steve, there wouldn't be a Lenny McLean website. He's the brains behind it all. Whenever there's a page to go up, he's the one who does it – I wouldn't know where to start. The way I've nagged him these last couple of years, it's a wonder he's still talking to me. He enjoys it, though and it's a challenge for him to keep improving it.

Then, about three years ago, I was contacted by film producer Clinton Montague who told me he was making the film of *The Guv'nor*. Right from the start, this bloke said he was going to get the film to the big screen and at present he is on his way. Meanwhile, the website continued to attract even more visitors and we topped 50,000 hits. Peter Gerrard contacted us saying Val was happy with the site and that it should become the official Lenny McLean website. I should have been chuffed with this but it had got to the stage where we didn't care if we were 'official' or not. After what we had built over the last couple of years, we knew we had the best website dedicated to the Guv'nor. Now don't get me wrong, we were happy, but it came a bit late. We now knew that Val and Peter must have been regularly looking at the site.

Then the big problems started. Our server was preventing us from uploading new material to the site. We came to a standstill for a few months. Steve had started a new job and just didn't have the time to update the website. I realised I needed to learn how to do the work myself, but in all honesty there was more hope of me learning Chinese. I started to get really depressed, when fate stepped in. Poor Steve got the sack from his new job, which was very bad luck for him, but it meant he had time to concentrate on the site. He changed its appearance completely and made it look more professional and up-to-date. Throughout all this, the hits counter went flying past the big 100,000 mark. TV companies were now contacting us about documentaries and other things. Just when things were looking up, the guestbook was sabotaged a second time. To make matters worse, this time it happened as Peter Gerrard was showing the website to some reps from a book company. God knows how he must have felt.

By this time, I'd had a gutful and nearly packed it in. I started wondering if I had upset anyone. OK, Lenny was no angel, but, in his day and living the life that he led, you couldn't be. He must have made a lot of enemies as well as friends. I thought I'd give it one last chance, we'd got this far, why quit now? Our local newspaper then wanted to do a feature on our website and ended up giving us nearly a whole page.

After a long couple of years, we finally met Peter Gerrard. Steve and I had gone along to one of the roadshows for *The Guv'nor* film and Peter was there. After all the time we had spent virtually 'chatting' over the internet, I still felt nervous. He came and met us and, when the documentary cameras were filming him, he spoke very highly of us! We were finally acknowledged for the work we had done over the years. We also had the chance to meet the film producer.

I then started to think about what else we could add to the website. We already had things like chat rooms and competitions, etc. It was then that I first came up with the idea of doing a page called 'Meeting the Guv'nor', containing people's stories about times when they had met Lenny. I'd travelled around the UK with my mate when he wrote his book called *Street Fighters* and had picked up his interview technique. We met quite a few people who had encoutnered Lenny and I started writing down their stories. At this time I'd bought a laptop and had started writing some of my own stories about working on the doors for a book called *Bouncers*.

I then thought to myself, Why don't I write a book on the subject? There are thousands of people out there who had met Lenny, and it would be a real challenge. Now I know a lot of people are going to say, 'He's that bloke who never met Lenny but wrote a book on him.' True. I can't turn back the clock, but there's no one on this planet who would have liked to have met Lenny more than me.

I started putting the word about that I was doing a book. I mentioned it on the website and a few people contacted me. I also got in touch with a few well-known people, but for some strange reason they didn't want to contribute to the book.

The website got sabotaged for the third time and we lost over one hundred messages. After what had happened in the past, I was now saving the messages every couple of weeks. So in the end we only lost one or two.

I was then contacted by a Sky TV channel who wanted to do a segment about Lenny in their programme. I put them in touch with Peter Gerrard and he did a good interview for the programme.

I put a message on the website advertising for people who had met Lenny to get in touch and contribute to a new book. About six weeks later I contacted two book publishers to see if they were interested in publishing a book about Lenny McLean. Within a few hours I had a reply from one saying that they would love to publish my book. I was over the moon that the publisher was interested, even though I knew I had a big task ahead of me.

Around this time, my father suddenly became ill and was diagnosed with lung cancer. It struck me as ironic that, here I was, writing a book about Lenny and my father had the same illness that Lenny had. I continued. Ten months later, my father passed away. It hit me hard and I couldn't think straight for a while. I now know how Lenny's family had felt, losing him to the same bastard of a disease.

After a while I pulled myself back together and got the urge to keep on going. It was then back to months and months of late nights, typing away, and travelling thousands of miles up and down the motorways, pretending to be Mike Peters of The Alarm or Van Halen's Sammy Hagar.

Then, on the day I finished this book, I received a phone call from Alfie Hayes's son, Rob, telling me that his dad had passed away the day before. I was absolutely gutted and just couldn't get my head around it. I'd only spoken to Alfie four days earlier and we'd had a cracking little chat about the book. He had told me that he was looking forward to reading it. The man was a true gentleman and will be sadly missed. I hope Alfie's family enjoy his contribution as much as I enjoyed writing it.

Not long after finishing this book, I received a phone call from Len's wife Val.

It turned out she didn't even know I was writing a book and she was quite upset. Yet again, who could blame her? We talked for quite a while and I explained a few things; she gave me her blessing and even offered me help with the book. It was nice to finally be in touch with the wife of the Guv'nor.

Finally, after two-and-a-half years of sheer hard work, my

project is finished and, apart from some minor corrections, the stories remain in the words of the people who told them. This book you are holding now is the result of all that hard work. I hope you think it's worth it. I would like to think that Val and her family and close friends are reading this book and, while going through the many stories in it, they are nodding their heads saying, 'Yes, that's our Lenny allright.' Someone once asked me what I could write about Lenny that hadn't already been written. Well, for that person (he knows who he is) here's your answer... enjoy. I'll leave the rest up to all of you and hope you enjoy reading the stories as much as I've enjoyed writing them.

1
Hoxton Born and Bred

Where do you start writing about Lenny's past? What has not already been written about in the bestselling autobiography *The Guv'nor*? I packed my bags and made my way right into the heart of it, the place where Lenny was born – Hoxton. I got in touch with a relative of Lenny's – Martin Rogers – over the internet and, as the saying goes, the rest is history. Lenny's father and Martin's mother had been brother and sister and Lenny used to call Martin his favourite cousin.

After speaking to Martin over the phone, I knew straight away I had to travel up to London to interview him. Martin had worshipped the bloke and really looked up to him, and had been through a tough time himself after getting brain damage while in prison. He then offered for me to go and stay with him for a few days and show me a few sights.

After eight hours of travelling, I finally arrived in the vicinity of Hoxton and Martin was there to pick me up. Within ten minutes of being in his company, I could see he was a right character, just like his cousin Lenny. We then made our way back to the day centre where Martin went every day, and where the list of illustrious visitors included the boxer Michael Watson. You could see that Martin loved being there helping the other people out.

Martin showed me his framed Lenny photo, signed with the message: 'To my favourite cousin Martin, The Guv'nor'. After a while, we made our way to a quiet room so I could interview Martin. He then told me a little about his life before we got started with Lenny, and I thought to myself that there's probably enough material for a book on Martin's life given what he's been through. He then started to tell me about Lenny.

MARTIN ROBERT ROGERS

From a young age, I have always looked up to Lenny (Boy) McLean. There's always been something about him which used to make the hairs on the back of my neck stand on end.

I was born and bred in Hoxton. My earliest memories of being with Lenny was when myself, Lenny and a couple of our other cousins used to visit our nan's. My nan, named Frances, used to live across the street from where I was brought up. My nan had seven daughters and two brothers; we were a bit of a huge family, and we all used to visit our nan's flat and play. Lenny always used to call me his favourite cousin. I remember my nan saving the old PG Tips cards for me as I was her favourite grandson.

My other cousin Tony McLean – 'Carrots' – was also living with my nan at the time. I remember my mother telling me stories about Lenny's stepfather who used to beat him when he was a kid. Lenny once said to his stepfather, 'When

2

I get big, I'm going to bash your fucking head in,' and, when Lenny did get big, he had fucked off. I used to do a few driving jobs for my cousin Tony when I was younger, just to make a living.

I remember the first time I saw Lenny fighting bare-knuckle on the street; I'm not just saying this because he's belonging to me, but he's the meanest fucker I have ever seen fighting. I also remember going to see him fight in Tottenham with the gloves on. My brother, my mother and father and I went along, and Lenny done a right job on the geezer, smashed him to pieces. Every time I went to see Lenny fight he never lost, he just used to smash fuck into people.

I remember one night me, my parents, Lenny and a few of his family went to see Roy Shaw fight. Shaw had smashed this bloke right up and was offering challenges after the match. Next thing I remember is Lenny ripping his jacket off and getting in the ring. Within seconds, a fight had been arranged.

I remember when Lenny was bouncing in this nightclub called Jovies (in the Barbican) and he got shot in the back. Two young kids pulled up on a scooter and shot him from behind; he never found out who they were. But, like he said, they wouldn't dare go at him head on.

I used to go up to one club and Lenny would be on the front door with a couple of others working with him, and he used to let me in for nothing all the time. A couple of my other cousins would walk in and Lenny would call them back and make them pay. I also used to go down to the Camden Palace and Lenny would look after me all night. I seen him chuck some people out of there; they didn't just go out, they flew out. He was so strong.

I was really young when my mother and father took me to see Lenny fight against Roy Shaw. Shaw had already beaten Lenny once and Lenny had challenged him to a rematch. We had a table near the front row for all the family, and I'd had a bit to drink as well. Lenny smashed him to pieces. What a day it was for me! I was trying to get in the ring to congratulate Lenny, and my mother and father were going nuts and loved it, too. I remember looking at Shaw and he didn't know where he was; we didn't half celebrate that night after the fight.

I saw Lenny challenge a few boxers after that fight. We then had another table at the third fight between Shaw and Lenny. Shaw was still going round saying he was going to do Lenny. The fight went more or less like their second fight and it was another good night for us as well.

There was also this other bloke, I can't quite remember his name now, who was a self-made millionaire from working in the meat market. He fought on the same bill as Lenny, too, and he would turn up in his Rolls-Royce. He didn't need the money, he just loved it.

By now my life was hectic and I was up to all sorts. I saw Lenny training around Victoria Park quite a lot and he'd tell me all these stories. He'd even add a bit on sometimes, but I didn't care as I just loved being with him and listening to him. We'd spar up and mess about and that. He loved his kids and always went on about them.

Then, in 1986, I got into a serious bit of trouble over a family matter and ended up in Brixton Prison. I heard that, when Lenny was in nick, they used to drug him up like a zombie because they were all scared of him and that was the only way they could control him.

4

While in prison, I got seriously beaten up by some prison guards and was left in a coma for months. Some of the guards were eventually charged for this and were imprisoned themselves. I was then sent to hospital for a couple of years and I was finally let out to go home and try and pull my life back together. The doctors said I'd never walk or talk again. One side of my body was paralysed and I just felt like a cabbage. I then started receiving regular visits from a couple of my cousins. At the time, I didn't want to see anybody, but Steve and Dave would come and tell me stories and cheer me up. Lenny and my other cousin Johnny Wall – 'Boot Nose' – used to visit me as well. Johnny, who used to train with Lenny, was an ex-pro boxer. He also used to do a bit of bouncing with Lenny as well, lovely bloke. He and Lenny would go to the West End together collecting money from the arcades.

They would pop round and Lenny would start telling me and my mum stories about smashing gypsies up. He would start showing us how he'd knock them out and what happened in the fights. Lenny and Johnny would play hell with me. They would tell me jokes and stories and have me in stitches laughing. I was begging them to stop, sometimes, as I felt like I was going to piss myself. They then started taking me out and trying to get my head working again. My mother nursed me for years through all the bad times. It also made Lenny's day seeing me on the mend, as he knew how much I liked him.

I then started fighting back and, before long, I was walking and talking again. I used to like a bit of a tear-up myself, having tranied as a boxer when I was younger. I used to do a bit in the Repton Boys' Club, but I didn't like getting beat, so I'd do them outside.

I then met this girl and I decided to move up north. I had a word with Lenny and he put a party on in his Guv'ner's pub for me. He brought the food up, and I put £1,000 over the bar and we had a good drink up; I'm sure he even dipped into his own pocket that night.

Lenny always used to say to me, 'If you ever get any problems, come and see me, Mart, and you only have to say the word.' I had to once or twice, and it was always nice knowing the big man was there for you.

Then, one day, I had a phone call from my mother saying that Lenny had passed away. I jumped in a car and brought a few friends down from up north. They'd never seen nothing like it in their lives. There were a few people there with guns keeping things in order in case anyone had come to mess things up. Everyone was there – my cousins, brothers. I'd never seen anything like it and it was a hell of a send-off for Lenny.

I still see some of Lenny's brothers and sisters now and again. Lenny's sister, Boo, is a lovely woman and Len's brother, Kruger – now he can fight – he has his own window cleaning business around here.

I then mentioned to Martin some of the not so complimentary stuff I'd heard people saying about Lenny and he said, 'When Lenny was alive, no one opened their mouths because he'd go round and smash their heads in. I think that proves a point.'

After the interview, Martin showed me some photos of his life. We had a bit of food and then we started on my own private tour of Hoxton. We first stopped off at Martin's mother's house, where he asked her a few questions about Lenny, but she seemed very reluctant to talk about him. She then mentioned to Martin that I looked like a young Lenny McLean. Martin's mum and dad had been to a few of Lenny's fights when they were younger, and Martin recalls how his mother used to go nuts when Lenny fought. But, for some reason, they just weren't talking today. And who was I to blame them? Here I am, a Welshman in their house, asking questions about their nephew. I could have been anyone. Anyway, we didn't push it and Martin looked as surprised as me that they were so quiet. I said my goodbyes and we then resumed our tour.

Martin was by now pulling up in the street and introducing me as the boy who was doing a book on Lenny Boy. He'd wind the window down and people were telling me all sorts of stuff. I was trying to remember all this as the tape recorder was in my bag. We then went round a mate of Martin's, Richard Camp, who had been to a few of Lenny's fights and knew Lenny well. He went upstairs and pulled out a couple of extremely rare programmes from Lenny's fights. I then got the tape recorder out of the car and listened, fascinated, to what he had to say.

RICHARD CAMP

I had heard loads of stories about Lenny when I was growing up from my mate Martin, who was Lenny's cousin. I remember Martin and his brother telling us all about the fight that Lenny had with Roy Shaw. We all went and bought tickets for their third fight in the Rainbow Theatre in Finsbury Park. I was only young at the time and I'd never seen anything like it. Lenny battered him. The seconds jumped in and were trying to pull them apart; there was also fighting in the crowd. I remember Boot Nose being Lenny's corner man.

7

I then remember Lenny snatching the microphone and shouting out to us, 'Who's the Guv'nor? I'm the Guv'nor!'

I then heard that Lenny was going to fight the big bloke who was the referee in the fight, Cliffy Fields. So I bought some tickets to Lenny's next fight against Cliffy.

I remember Lenny just going for it and hammering Cliffy. Cliffy didn't throw a punch, he was just covering up and taking everything. Cliffy was smothered in blood and close to defeat. The headbutts were going in and the bell went. By now, though, Lenny had punched himself out and his stamina had gone. Cliffy then come out for round two and knocked Lenny down.

Lenny was a bit shocked that he lost. I heard they had a rematch, but I couldn't make it. A while later, I seen him fight this black bloke named Tshaku who had beaten Cliffy Fields. Lenny Boy battered him.

I also remember Lenny fighting Steve 'Columbo' Richards on one bill, and Lenny also challenged John L Gardner as well, but he didn't want to know. I then saw him fight the King of the Gypsies and Lenny demolished him.

I remember Lenny moving to a flat in Roman Road years ago. A mate of mine was living on the same landing as him. On the landing, there was this big corridor of flats. In this one flat, a gang of blokes had moved in and they were playing their music quite loud. At the time, Lenny had been working nights, so he goes around the next day and kicks their door in. He then goes in the flat and says to them, 'Look, lads, I've been working all night and I beat people up for a living. If you play another fucking record, I'm going to come back in here and smash the lot of you up.' Lenny never heard another word after that.

I met Lenny loads of times through Martin. I chatted with him at some of the fights and I went up the Camden Palace a few times drinking. Steve Strange was running the Camden Palace at the time and it was full of these real weirdos. Lenny used to say to me, laughing, 'None of these people are trouble, it's the likes of your lot...' He knew what we were all like.

This one time, Martin and I went down to this fruit and veg stall Lenny had. Lenny turned up and we had a good chat with him. Both of his hands were smashed in because he had been fighting the night before in one of the nightclubs with a pile of jocks from Scotland. Lenny had smashed them right up going by the state of his hands.

My younger brother ended up in Belmarsh at the same time as Lenny was in. They were drugging Lenny in the prison to calm him down but he still managed to take my brother under his wing and keep an eye out for him.

This other time I was in the Camden Palace and this big bloke had smashed one of those big chunky pint glasses that people used to drink out of and was going to use the handle to glass someone. Lenny went at him and demolished him, he was in a right mess. Another time, this bloke had been playing up in the club, so Lenny took him outside in front of everyone and pulled his trousers down and smacked his arse; he was a bit of a joker like that.

Richard's wife then came in the room and had a cup of tea with us and told a few stories about Lenny. She recalled how Lenny had always been a gentleman to her. 'Richard and I used to go up to the Camden Palace and Lenny would see us and pull us right to the front of the queue and let us in.

He would then take us upstairs to the champagne bar, push everyone out of the way and then tell the girl to look after us for the night; he would put it on his bill and we wouldn't pay for anything.'

She recalled how a few times there would be fights, but you'd hardly see Lenny moving from the front door. 'He had a good team of boys with him who could usually handle the situation. But, once, Lenny came walking past us and he was putting his black leather gloves on, so we knew there was going to be trouble and just to get out of the way. The speed on Lenny was amazing for a big man like him.'

Richard rang his mate up on the phone for me, and Kenny Lawson gave me an interview, too.

KENNY LAWSON

I knew Lenny for years. I used to have a pub in Hackney called The Duke of Marlborough and Lenny used to come in with his aunt and his nephew who was an up-and-coming boxer from Scotland.

Lenny was a very funny man and always joking around. I remember bumping into him this one night while he was outside the Venus restaurant in Bethnal Green Road. The unlicensed scene was all the go at the time and I fancied having a go at it myself. I had done a bit of boxing when I was a kid, but nothing special. I then got offered to fight this bloke who was supposed to have been a bit of a farmer. I was right up for the fight and was telling Lenny about it. I mentioned to Lenny that his name was Cliffy Fields. Lenny, laughing loudly, says to me, 'Are you mad or what? Cliffy will destroy you.' Lenny then started explaining to me about

Cliff's past record in the boxing ring. He then said to me, 'Cliffy could probably do you in about ten seconds, but he will just go to your body and arms and torture you until you are tired, and then take you out.'

A few weeks later, I went and saw the fight between Lenny and Cliffy in which Lenny had lost in the first couple of rounds. So, if Cliffy beat Lenny, God knows what he would have done to me. I think I owe Lenny one for saving my bacon.

I also used to do a lot of work for charity. I was helping Bart's Hospital in the children's cancer ward. We were organising a night for all the kids. We'd hold pool and darts competitions and loads of other stuff to raise money. I was then chatting to Lenny one night and I was telling him about it. He said to me that he would fight anyone on a show for the charity. He then said to me to go ahead and sort it out. I was over the moon that Lenny was helping and I was sure it was going to be a sell-out.

I then mentioned it to the Sister who was working on the ward where the kids were. All of a sudden, she didn't want any of it. She didn't want the charity having anything to do with violence. I was now stuck with the awkward task of breaking the news to Lenny. I then caught up with Lenny and had a chat with him. I said to him, 'Len, they want to stop tax on whatever money is raised.' He replied, 'Fuck that, I'm not paying tax to them to have a fight.' Lenny and I were both gutted that the show didn't come off.

I also used to see Lenny a lot when he was working in club land on the doors. The bloke was like a superstar. He had this aura about him; when people would pass him, you could hear them saying to each other, 'There's Lenny McLean there.' He was easily recognised.

Kenny then gave me one of his mate's numbers, Johnny Fisher, who also had some stories to tell.

JOHNNY FISHER

I remember Lenny from when he was a kid. I had known his mother Rosie Campion and all the McLean family really well. I used to run my own fruit stall down Tottenham Road and I gave Lenny a job with me when he was about 14 years of age.

He picked the job up really easy and he used to juggle the apples and the oranges. Another thing he was good at was picking up people's characteristics. People would come in the shop and, within minutes of them leaving, he would have them down to a tee. He was really good at doing impressions and taking them off. Lenny must have worked for me for about two years before he decided to leave. He then ended up working for his uncle Johnny Collis as a window cleaner.

We left Richard's house and Martin and I went back to the flat for some food. After Martin had left, I had a good read of the programmes and thought about the day's events. It had been worth the trip just from what I had already. By now, I must have had a Lenny McLean overdose. All this information was coming in and I was trying to remember it all.

After finally getting to sleep that night, I was up nice and early the next morning, looking forward to meeting Martin's cousin Steve. Steve's mother was another of Len's father's sisters. Martin took me to a café in Hoxton, which Lenny used to frequent. Martin explained to the owner and a few of his mates that I was writing a book about Lenny. They all start winding this one bloke up about the day Lenny had knocked him out. The owner of the café then started recounting a few stories about Lenny.

> This one day, Lenny had got a new job window cleaning. There must have been around 40 people in this room and Lenny walks in. He then starts asking, 'Who's the foreman here?' This bloke walks up to Lenny and says, 'I am.' Lenny knocks him spark out, and starts shouting at everyone, 'I'm the foreman now.' Lenny then went and took a fiver out of everyone's pay packet each week.
>
> You could never have the last word with Lenny. He'd have an answer for everything. He'd rib you with jokes, and you just couldn't beat him. When we used to go out drinking in the pubs, he'd start singing Elvis songs; he used to do a brilliant rendition of Dean Martin as well. The one thing Lenny did regret was when he had a fight over in this pub with one of our mates, and Lenny bit his cheek. He used to say to me a lot that he regretted that.

Another bloke then joined in laughing and told a story about when Lenny had this sweet shop. 'Lenny used to do raffles and every month he would put the name of the winner in the window; the only thing is, all the people who were winning didn't exist, but who was going to tell him?'

As I ate my breakfast, all the women were saying how much of a gentleman Lenny was. Everyone was now talking about Lenny and recalling incidents. Eventually, Martin's cousin Steve turned up and I could see straight away he was another character. Steve began laughing as he was remembering some of his antics with Lenny. After a cup of tea, Steve phoned his older brother Dave and we went and met him in another café, run by another of Lenny's cousins. By now, it was starting to look like a family reunion. Everyone was telling little stories about Lenny in weddings, fighting and on the door.

After a while, everyone had to go back to work and wished me well with the book. Martin then took me back on the tour around Hoxton. He parked the car up near this shop and we went into a pub right next to the entrance to Hoxton Park. Martin went up to this bloke who wanted to remain anonymous and said to him, 'You knew Lenny, didn't you?'

'Of course I did,' the bloke replied, 'I saw you at the funeral, didn't I?'

Martin explained to him that I was writing a book and was looking for some stories. The bloke then started explaining a few things to me. 'Lenny got a couple of things mixed up in that book *The Guv'nor*. I was hanging around with Lenny in my teens and he mentions one story. I was actually there with him but he put one of our other friends' names in there instead of me. I used to go round window cleaning with Lenny; I taught him everything he knew.'

The bloke then started coming out of his shell and you could see he was really enjoying himself telling the stories. He told me about his drinking days with Lenny and the pubs they went to.

Lenny always had something about him... the littlest of things would upset him. I remember this one day, me, Lenny and a couple of others were walking down this street to go to the pub and Lenny clocked this little bit of silver paper, a bit like a Kit-Kat wrapper, on the floor. Now me and the boys knew he had a habit of picking things up. All of a sudden, you could see he was looking back at the wrapper and by now he was starting to twitch. We then went in the pub and Lenny says to us, 'I've got to go out a minute.' We knew where he'd gone, but we weren't going to say anything to him.

We went to his mum's one day and his mother comes in and pulls all these small bits of silver and wrappers out of his pocket and asks him, 'What are these for, Len?' His face was a hell of a picture. You could notice the change in Lenny after his mother died; he became like a different person, a lot nastier.

He then explained how he and Lenny and a couple of others would go up to the West End after a few beers and go into a club.

This one night, though, Lenny had knocked this big bloke out cold; the bloke had started it, and was then chucked out of the club. We were leaving a while later, when Lenny noticed about 20 men outside. He said, 'Stay in here, I'll be back shortly.'

He then went outside on his own. We made our way out behind him. He then starts screaming at them, 'Come on, who's your best, who's your Guv'nor?' This big bloke then goes at Lenny and Lenny knocks him out first punch. Another one follows and he gets the same. Lenny must have knocked about five of them out and you could see the others didn't want to know. They all got back up and started shaking Lenny's and our hands.

Another time, Lenny had been given this suit and it was a couple of sizes too small but he still wore it. He still thought it looked good on him, though, as his muscles were bulging out of it.

I also remember the time Lenny went to the gym for the first time. He went up the gym to see his cousin Johnny Wall sparring. A couple of the boys then wound Lenny up and, after a while, he gave in. He got in and sparred with one of the trainers of the gym. He gave the trainer a hell of a punch and dropped him. The trainer later told me that it was the hardest he'd ever been hit. He then went on to spar with Johnny Wall regularly after that.

I used to play fuck with him in beer, but I also knew when to stop. I seen him fighting one of the owners of this pub once and Lenny smashed him right in.

I did have one bad run-in with him once; something happened and I had a serious word with him and then we were all sorted. Lenny would be out drinking and then just flip at the slightest of things. I seen him knock out many a man, a lot of big men as well, he didn't give a shit.

I went to jail a few years later and Lenny visited me with a couple of our other mates. I then heard he had got shot and was lucky to be alive after minding this one club. I remember when he started seeing Val and the trouble he was having.

Another thing Lenny liked was his big breakfasts. We went to this café one day and he ordered a breakfast three times the normal size. He had half a loaf of bread to go with it. Now, like I said earlier, the littlest of things would piss Lenny off and get to him. So this one day, I was picking my nose while he was eating his breakfast, he looks up at me and goes completely fucking nuts. He then warned me never to do it again.

After talking to me for a while, the bloke then drank up and moved on to another pub. It would have been nice speaking to him for a bit longer as he obviously knew many more stories, but we had to move on as well.

At the next pub, Martin knew this old bloke in the corner who remembered Lenny. The bloke then said to me, 'I remember Lenny McLean. He was a fucking animal.' He then repeated himself while shaking his head, thinking back to some fight Lenny had been in.

That was the end of my Hoxton tour and, as I left, I thanked Martin for his help and for putting me up for two days. He was over the moon that I'd got in touch with Lenny's favourite cousin.

I also came across another good friend of Lenny's through a contact on the internet. This bloke had been neighbours with Lenny and even went to the same school as him when they were kids.

VICTOR NUTLEY

I first met Lenny McLean when I was a kid. We went to the Shoreditch Comprehensive School in Bow and we become good friends from that day on.

Even in those early days, it didn't take long to realise what kind of man Lenny was. Even back then, Lenny was a giant, with hands as big as shovels. There was something about Lenny that told you he meant business; he could make your blood run cold with just a stare.

I remember one day at school, Lenny was having a fight with this big lad in the playground. It didn't take long before Lenny got the upper hand and smashed the kid to the ground. Lenny turned to walk away – after all, the job was done, and the boy was down. But, as soon as his back was turned, the lad punched Lenny straight in the back of the head, knocking him down. You can bet your life that kid paid the price the next day, but this time Lenny didn't stop when the boy went down, he was like a raving lunatic. I can't help but think that this may have something to do with Lenny's not knowing when to stop attitude, which became more apparent in later life.

When I was about 16, I moved to Jeffery Court in Hoxton. I moved next door to a bloke named Johnny Wall, who happened to be Lenny's cousin and, on the other side of him, lived Lenny McLean.

When I left school, I got a job with Lenny working for this towel company called Initials. We would have to collect the dirty towels from hotels, hospitals and such like, and replace them with clean ones. I remember that at a push I could lift four towels at a time; we'd then throw them into a large trolley. When it was full with about 25 rolls in it, two or three of us would lift the trolley into the back of the lorry. One day, Lenny was giving it the big one and fucking about, saying, 'Make me right, but I reckon I can lift that on my fucking own, without you mugs!' Next thing we knew, Lenny was grunting, groaning and throwing this trolley straight into the back of the lorry saying, 'Piece of piss!'

A few years later, Lenny and I moved and we lost touch. I'd bump into Lenny every now and then because I was a minicab driver at the time and Lenny was, by this time, minding several doors across London.

Then in 1983, I moved to Tate Court, St Stephen's Road in Bow. You can imagine my surprise when I came out of my front door one morning to hear, 'Fuck me, you following me or what?' How could anyone mistake that voice? It turned out that Lenny lived a few doors down from me on the same landing. Our kids ended up going to the same school and, as kids do, would often end up fighting other kids and even each other at times.

It was here at Tate Court that my wife Linda noticed that one morning one of our pints of milk went missing off the doorstep. We checked with the milkman and he assured us that he had delivered two pints that morning, so we knew that some little piece of shit was nicking our milk. Well, fuck me, if the same thing didn't happen the next morning as well.

By Wednesday, I was getting really pissed off with it, so, as soon as the milkman had called, me and the wife kept an eye out of the window and waited. It wasn't too long, either; this guy from down the landing came out of his door and went straight for our milk. I threw my tea in the sink and I made for the door. I think the bloke heard the commotion, because he had it on his toes and was halfway down the landing by the time I got to the front door. Unfortunately for him, Lenny was just coming out of his front door, so I shouted, 'Grab him, Len!' Well, Lenny, as calm as you like, gave this bloke a lovely right hook which sent him crashing to the ground. Lenny then picked up the bottle of milk and said, 'Is this yours, Vic?' Lenny then walked off as if nothing had happened. Funnily enough, the milk didn't go missing any more.

Now Lenny, as big as he was, used to drive this beaten-up old mini. Don't get me wrong, he could afford any motor he wanted, but he was never really that big on cars and absolutely hated the idea of cleaning them. Me, being a minicab driver, used to have to clean my car every week, so whenever I was doing mine you could almost guarantee that Len would ask me to give his one a quick clear out. You would not believe the amount of tobacco that would be lying on the floor of that car. Well, you can imagine Lenny trying to roll a little fag with those massive sausage fingers.

A good friend of Lenny's in those early years was Johnny Rolly. He told me once about a time when Lenny was in the Adam and Eve café in Hoxton. These three CID officers came in to arrest Len over something or other. Lenny was only about 17 at the time and these three blokes were well into their thirties. But, nonetheless, Lenny made them an offer they couldn't refuse. By the side of the café was an alleyway. Lenny said that he would take a walk with them down the alley and, if they were able to walk out, then he would go with them to the station, but, if he walked out, he would be a free man. They didn't have to think about the offer for too long and agreed. Twenty minutes later, a cut and bruised Lenny walked out of that alley, followed half-an-hour later by two of the cops carrying the third in their arms. Even from that young age, Lenny could fight.

Lenny was a man's man, he was respectful and polite. You always knew where you stood with him. Len's temper was like an on-off switch and it didn't matter who you were – if you pissed him off, you'd better beware. In all the years I knew Lenny, I would still find myself choosing my words wisely in his company. He was a great dad to his son Jamie and daughter Kelly and loved his Val to the end.

A bit later on in life, Lenny came round the house one day. It was my grandson's first birthday party. The camera was rolling and caught me and Lenny sparring up on tape. At one stage, someone was trying to film the baby and Lenny's head was in the way. I shouted to Lenny, 'Lenny, move your head, it's the baby's birthday, not a horror movie…' Lenny jumped out of the way of the camera laughing.

Some hard men are bullies and get a kick out of preying on the weak; Lenny was the opposite to this. He would often be seen helping the underdog and, as we all learned later from Val and Lenny's books, he didn't tolerate bullies, because he knew only too well what it was like on the receiving end of a bully. If there is any one out there who has read Lenny's book and says, 'What a load of bollocks… he was just a big fucking bully!' well, what I'd say to that is that they were obviously people that had crossed him and upset him and, if they were stupid enough to do that, then they deserved a good slap!

Growing up as a teenager, Lenny had got himself into a spot of bother and ended up spending some time in Borstal, some of his memories from that era being retold in his book *The Guv'nor*. I received a phone call from Kevin who had spent some months in the same dormitory as Lenny in 1967. After talking on the phone several times, I decided to go and meet this man in person.

Kevin well remembers his time in the presence of Lenny McLean.

KEVIN

Just before Christmas 1966, I had got locked up; I was 17 at the time. I'd had a bit too much to drink, come into a scene of a crime and joined in. I then got arrested at three o'clock in the morning while I was sleeping at home. I was then locked up for a month in Norwich Prison, waiting to go to court.

I went to court and was given Borstal training for six months to two years. A month later, I was taken to Wormwood Scrubs to be assessed for which Borstal I would be put into. You would have to spend about six weeks in the first wing under psychologists and various people, who would then assess you.

Wormwood Scrubs at the time was a fairly run-down prison; there was no hot water on the wings and you'd have a hot bath once a week. This night, someone in one of the cells had chucked some shit at the screws below and they all went nuts. As they didn't know who had done it, they took it out on all of us. I found out later on that Lenny had also passed through Scrubs, but I was never aware of him.

I was then allocated to Hollesley Bay colony. Everybody called it the 'Stackers' Borstal, meaning that you would do closer to two years there and would never get out in six months.

Once there, I was put in a unit called St George's. This house had about 20 boys in it. One day, I was bored and put some silver paper in one of the light fittings and blew all the lights in the whole building. They weren't impressed by this and then someone went and grassed me a couple of days later, and I ended up in the punishment block on bread and water. I did about two weeks in there.

I went back and they put me in a house called St Patrick's. After a while there, I was moved on to St Andrew's, which was one step from home – a couple of months there and you would get a home-leave date. My mate and I got moved in one afternoon and that's when I first came across Lenny McLean.

Our beds were more or less opposite each other. In the

bed close to him was his cousin Tony. Throughout the time in Borstal, you never got to know the first name of most of the people in there. You were usually called by your surnames, but with Lenny and his cousin Tony, both being McLean, everyone got to call them by their first name. At night-time, when the lights had gone off, you could hear Lenny saying, 'Goodnight, Tony,' and vice versa. Their names started sticking straight away.

That first night we were there, me and my mate were talking and I could hear Tony saying, 'Hey, Lenny, can you hear them two college boys opposite… where are they from? What are they doing here?'

Lenny replied, 'I don't know, Tony, I'll check it out in the morning.'

The banter after lights out was quite funny most nights; someone would break wind or shout things out, but eventually you'd be off to sleep as you'd be so tired and we'd be up early the next morning for a hard day's work.

The next day, Lenny comes up to me and says, 'Hello, college boy.' Lenny was used to hearing London accents and mine sounded really funny to him as he hadn't heard it before. He was very intrigued about it. He then said to me, 'Where are you from?' I replied, 'I'm from Norfolk.' He then said, 'You're a bloody swede basher… carrot cruncher.' From then on, every time he passed my bed, he'd say, 'All right, swede basher or carrot cruncher…' It broke the ice and, from there on, we got on really well.

This one day I was in my bed and I was reading the magazine *Titbits*. It had featured an article on my late dad and I felt a bit down. Lenny came past and said, 'What you reading about?' I then explained to him what had happened.

Lenny then said, 'Most of us might as well not have dads... watch today when it's visiting time.' He then consoled me and persuaded me to go down and have a game of cards with him and a few others.

It was then I got to learn a lot of their Cockney rhyming slang and other tricks. There was another person in the next bed to Tony who was also good mates with them. I'm sure he was from the same area as them.

We were all then given different jobs in the day. I had a job in the carpenter's shop and Lenny had a job out on the land. I used to see Lenny in the mornings with his barrow. He used to leave before breakfast and be back before us. We used to pull his leg sometimes when he came back dirty. Other times, we would see him pushing his barrow full of pig swill. We'd always try and get him to put his arm up and wave at us and the barrow would tip over.

I remember Lenny and Tony showing me this trick one day. We used to have these mattresses which were made of something like horsehair. Now, if you laid on it every night, it would mould to the shape of your body. To stop this from happening, they used to have a pen and write on the top of it either 'o' for odd, or underneath, 'e' for even (corresponding with the number in the date), just to make sure you turned it every day. The screw would then come along and ask you to pull your covers off to see either the 'e' or the 'o'. Lenny then said, 'What you want to do is write "e" in one corner and "o" in the other corner, but what you've got to do is remember which day odd or even it is, and just pull that corner of the blankets off each time he wants to see it... saves you turning your mattress every day.'

This one day we were taken to the swimming pool and

issued each with a canoe; we were to practise capsizing and using the oar to correct the canoe.

In turn, we went over, but I let go of the oar and remained upside down for some time. Lenny seemed to be the only one who noticed and came alongside giving the bottom of the canoe one hell of a bang with his fist. I immediately fell out and came to the surface. All the class were laughing and Tony shouted, 'Hey, look, carrot cruncher thinks he is Jesus and can walk on water.'

I was never sure if it was the pressure of his blow that had shifted me out or the sudden loud noise that made me jump out of the canoe. Later, when we had a look, there was a large dent in the canoe.

We used to go and watch programmes on a Saturday afternoon. We all watched *The Monkees* and *Top of the Pops* in the week. There was never really any trouble there; if it did happen, then it would be over very quickly in case anybody got caught and get more time added to their sentence.

Lenny's cousin Tony was also a character; he'd always have a smile on his face and be laughing. I liked Tony a lot, his grin cheered us up.

I got on well with Lenny; he picked his friends, and he knew he could trust me. I had made some wine one day outside, and I came back and offered it to Lenny. I remember him now, laughing, and saying to me, 'I'm not touching that bloody firewater, you carrot cruncher.' Lenny was quite head-down serious and just got on with his time.

I remember him chatting to me one day and then he went off. One of his mates then came up to me and said, 'That's Lenny, he can't half march on, just remember that.' I thought, I don't need telling; I could see that he could fight, he was a strapping lad, no waste on him at all, but I got on well with him. You had this feeling that, if there was trouble, then this was the man to look for, to have on your side.

Lenny was a good marcher and he could drill. I can see him now in his striped shirt, sleeves rolled up, braces and a boiler jacket on. He looked long and narrow for his age, head and shoulders above most of us.

We all had to have medicals and it was then found that I had a hernia. One day, they just came into the dormitory and told me to get my kit together and I was then whisked off to a hospital within the grounds of Wormwood Scrubs for an operation. After a while, I moved back into the same dormitory as Lenny for a week and he and his cousin then got moved on to the last discharge.

I still saw them out and about and Lenny asked me to come up to the West End of London and have a drink with him when we got out. I never made that drink and life moved on for all of us. I did think to myself a few times, I wonder what Lenny and Tony are doing these days.

Then, about 30 years later, I'm watching the film *Lock, Stock and Two Smoking Barrels* and I'm looking at this Barry the Baptist character, and I just didn't catch on this was Lenny.

Not long after watching the film, I came across a documentary on some channel about bouncers, and I'm watching this programme and I thought to myself, I know this person... as I watched one of the geezers and the faces he was pulling... it reminded me of Lenny, who had a way of squeezing his forehead together. I could do this as well and, one day, I did it to him, I squeezed my forehead together and said, 'What's up, Lenny?' He replied, 'Don't take the piss,

Kev.' And it just came flooding back to me. I thought, that's Lenny McLean. I know him.

The following day, I was on a trip down to London and went and asked in a book shop whether they had heard of him. I was then given this paperback with the title *The Guv'nor*. I started reading it straight away and there it was. Lenny was mentioning the Borstal we had been in together. I was amazed at the path his life had taken and really enjoyed his book.

The Lenny I remember was quite jovial, he wasn't mouthy or a bullyboy. We were all there for each other and cheered each other up. Lenny had quite a lot to say to me when I wasn't happy. They were good memories, considering the place we were in.

2
Best of Friends

There's no doubting that Lenny had made many good friends throughout his life and I spoke to quite a few of them while writing this book. Some of them, for whatever reason, were reluctant to speak about their friendship, while others were quite happy to talk to me and tell me their stories. I caught up with four of these people who enjoyed telling me the stories as much as I enjoyed listening to them. The first one of them was one of Lenny's old schoolmates named Alfie Hayes. Alfie was one of about 12 kids who lived upstairs above Lenny when he was a youngster. Lenny mentioned his mate Alfie numerous times in *The Guv'nor*.

I finally caught up with Alfie in his home in North London after his son contacted me via the internet. After numerous phone calls recalling past moments he had spent with Lenny, he then invited me up to meet him. After a five-hour journey,

I finally arrived and Alfie welcomed me into his house. We then sat down and chatted for hours.

A few months later, Alfie offered me the chance of a guided tour of his and Lenny's old haunts. After another long journey, I arrived with my mate Michael in Hoxton Street. It was nice to put a picture to some of the places I had been reading about for the past couple of years. We met up with Alfie in a pie and mash shop and he began his tour. Here's what he had to say about growing up in Hoxton, and the time he had spent with Lenny McLean.

ALFIE HAYES

I first met Lenny when we were really young kids when my family and I were living above him in the Godwin House flats in Bethnal Green. On the top floor there was a fire exit which me and Lenny always used to meet on and have a chat. Lenny's father then died, which I can vaguely remember, and my mother took them all in for a few weeks.

Lenny had an older sister called Linda who then went to live with Lenny's Nanny Campion who we called Aunt Poll; she was a lovely woman and was the sister of another East End legend named Jimmy Spinks.

I used to love big Jim, he was a lovely man, he was like Lenny's double. Len was a little taller then him; I know Lenny's family was McLean but you could see Lenny was a Spinks. Jimmy's wife Mary was my mum Rose's best friend. My older sister Rosie then moved in with Lenny's mother for three years when Len's father died, helping out with the kids. Rosie moved back and forth between houses as only a set of stairs separated them.

I can remember Jim Irwin then moving in with Len's

mother. To be honest with you, I found Jim all right; we was always a little dubious as he used to belt Lenny around the ear. But it was only in later years that I found out about him and what he got up to. You don't really know what's going on behind closed doors, do you? I know he used to belt Lenny's mother Rose, as my mum went down after him a few times, and my Timmy and Billy went down a few times with my mother as well. I remember Lenny one day telling me that his uncle Jimmy was going to do big Jim Irwin. Lenny was round my house all the time and we ended up like brothers rather than friends.

We didn't have much in those days and we had to make do with what we had. Outside Godwin House flats was our cricket field, our running track was around the block, and inside was our little football field. One day, this builder came with a couple of wheelbarrows filled with sand. He'd piled them on the grass outside the flats and we had a nice sandpit to play in. At the back of the flats we had a boiler room, and me and Len used to help out and the bloke would treat us.

We used to go to Hagerston Swimming Pool together; it saved having a bath, we'd go swimming instead. We used to go in at ten in the morning and come out at four in the afternoon, all withered up.

There was a little park around the corner from where we lived. When we first moved there, it was a cemetery and there was a church there. It got hit by a bomb and they had to move all the graves. Me and Lenny used to shit ourselves around there; we would say to each other, 'I'm not going around there, there are still dead people down there.' My father took a photo of us one day up against the fence; there's me, Len and a few of my brothers and sisters in it.

Another day, Lenny and I were in the park and he had a fight with this other boy. This boy had two brothers. Me and Lenny were about nine years old. The boy's brothers were about 15 and 17, a right horrible family who were always bullying kids. The younger brother was our age and used to walk around with the strut and thought he was something.

Me and Lenny were with a few of our mates; it ends up me and this boy were going to have a fight. The rest of our mates run but Lenny stayed there and said, 'I'm not fucking going… go on, Alf, smash his fucking face in, go on, fucking kill him.' Lenny then runs and gets Freddie, my brother. Our Fred has then gone over and grabbed the boy's older brother who doesn't want to know. It was all calming down and, the next thing you know, Lenny's smashed the one right in the ear; there was a hell of a noise. They then all left not wanting to know any more.

When we were kids, about six or seven, me and Lenny used to go round to a pub called Shaggy Lill's. Now my brothers and sisters said it was called Shaggy Lasses, but I'm sure it was called Shaggy Lill's. All the villains used to be there, the cream of the East End. The Twins used to go there, as well as Lenny's uncle Jimmy Spinks. Now Lenny's dad had died when Lenny was really young so he didn't remember a father as such and looked upon Jim as a kind of father figure to him, he idolised him.

Jimmy, who was a notorious villain from the East End, could fight, and he used to work for my grandfather who was also a notorious villain before the war, him and Dodger Mullins. So you had Timmy Hayes, Dodger Mullins and Jimmy Spinks, the three of them. They were even mentioned in John Pearson's book *The Profession of Violence – The Rise and*

Fall of the Kray Twins. We were so close in them days I even called Jimmy 'Uncle Jimmy'. Also, Jack Spot's been in there, Billy Hill… you name it and they have been in there.

So the way me and Lenny were earning money in them days was by singing. So we have gone to the pub and the woman who had run the pub was built like a brick shithouse, she looked like Tug Boat Ann, but I'm sure she had one leg or a gammy leg and she used to rest it on the chair. She was a lovely woman and her husband was half her size. We never had any money and we used to poke our head in there and she would give us a biscuit and a glass of lemonade if her husband wasn't there.

Anyway, we started going round there and Jimmy and a couple of the others would make us sing them a song. Lenny and I were getting good money from going there, but in the end we finally drove them all mad.

Also, on this one occasion, Lenny and I went in and my grandfather was there with Dodger Mullins and Jimmy Spinks. Now my grandfather used to wear this trilby which he never took off. The landlady I just mentioned has gone and knocked his hat off and he's turned round and knocked her straight out cold on the floor.

Another time, we were standing outside Shaggy Lill's and young Jimmy Spinks was there, too. Johnny Ray's new song 'Just A Walking in the Rain' had come out at the time. Jimmy then asked me and Lenny to sing it. We sang it to him and he wouldn't give us any money because he reckoned we hadn't done it tidy. He then said, 'You haven't done it tidy as you haven't done the whistling part.' I then said to Jimmy, 'We can't whistle, Jim, me and Lenny haven't got any front teeth.' They then really teased us and gave us some money.

Another way we used to get a bit of pocket money for ourselves was to stand on the bottom of the stairs of the flats. There was this family called the Foxes on the middle floor that had three beautiful daughters who were all courting these blokes from Hoxton. Now their boyfriends always used to give us a bit of money. We used to come down the stairs singing as the boys were picking the girls up. It always worked and we would make a nice bit of cash.

At one time, a story was going round about Jimmy Spinks, which was also going around about Lenny and also going round about the Kray Twins as well. Jimmy Spinks was standing outside either a café or pub and a little weedy city gent was going to work in a bowler hat and a briefcase and, as he walked past Jimmy Spinks, Jimmy's had a go at him. The bloke's said, 'I beg your pardon, what did you say?' and Jimmy's had a go at him again. The bloke then says, 'Say that again and I'll do you up.' The bloke then is supposed to have put his briefcase and hat down, took his coat off and bashed Jimmy Spinks up.

The same story was supposed to have happened to Lenny and Ronnie Kray, but it's so ridiculous, and that was East End folklore and you always bump into someone who knows someone that's done it, but it's usually when they are dead that they come out.

You used to hear stuff like this from time to time. I was down this pub and this bloke was saying that he knew someone who had smashed the shit out of Lenny. So I said, 'When was this?' and the bloke said, 'He done Lenny outside this club,' so I asked, 'What, did he shoot him?' and the bloke goes, 'Nah, he done him with his hands.' I then said to the bloke, 'You're a fucking liar, and go and tell your mate he's a

34

fucking liar.' This other bloke come up to me before and said, 'Reggie and Ronnie, yeah, I know a bloke that done them,' so I said, 'What, and he's still alive?' Do us a favour, these people lived on their reputations.

We used to go boxing down a little club in Hagerston Road near our flats when we were about eight, which was run by a lovely man named Joey Moss. He used to have a big pot belly and three teeth and he used to take the kids boxing. It was such a poor little club that we used to have no punch bags and we'd used to punch Joey in the belly. Lenny hit him up the derby one day and he nearly went over, so he went and got an old potato sack and filled it up with things for us to hit.

My older brother Billy then took me and Lenny up to Repton Boys Boxing Club when we were about ten years old. Lenny had everything going for him but he had no discipline. Billy used to say to him when he was a kid, 'Stand back and pick your punches... you have got the size and weight.' But, even in later life, Lenny liked throwing the big punches and, up against someone good, Lenny would run out of steam after a couple of rounds.

There was this time me and Lenny went in this pub when we were kids and the old boxer Old Man Andretti, whose son went on to become world champion, was in there. Old Man Andretti jumped on the floor and challenged Lenny to a press-up competition. He must have been nearly 70 by now and he still beat Lenny.

I used to go to a school named St Gregory's, which was one side of Bethnal Green Road, and Lenny first went to Randolph Creemer Infants' School and then on to Daniel Street School, which later got changed to Danteford, which was on the opposite side of Bethnal Green Road. Danteford was a mix of Daniel Street and Mansfield Street School. Some of the good old boys from Daniel Street School by the way were Reggie and Ronnie Kray, but yet again they used to go to my school as well. Near the school, Reggie Kray's wife Franny Shaw lived. Reggie would pull up in this big American car a few times.

Another friend of Lenny's, Micky Wall, who was no relation to Lenny's cousin Johnny Wall, used to come and meet me and, because we had finished early, we would go and walk across Bethnal Green Road and stand outside and wait for Lenny. The amount of times Lenny's come out of school and said, 'I'm going to have it off.' Now Micky, who's a nice bloke who could handle himself, turns to me and says, 'I don't need this, Alf, every time I come here, Lenny's having a fight with someone.'

But this one time, Lenny's come flying out and says, 'I'm going to do this Georgie, and he's got some mates as well.' I couldn't say no. Now with this Georgie were these twins and they were a bit tasty. Anyway, Micky Wall has bashed one of the twins up and I've bashed the other one up. Lenny then did this Georgie as well. Georgie was quite tasty but he was out of his league with Lenny; I felt quite sorry for this Georgie after Lenny had smashed him up.

Lenny and I then went over and Micky was still having a cracking fight with the taller twin, so Lenny and I watched to make sure no one jumped in. Lenny and I stood there laughing as I said to Lenny, 'Fucking good fight this, the best I have seen for ages.'

I remember when we were about 11, Lenny and I were playing on this bit of grass and this boy come along who was about 16, a big horrible bully, and he throws a stone at us. We told him to fuck off and he says, 'I'll smash your face in now.' So we said, 'Yeah, all right then.' It was right next to Shaggy Lill's, we must have been fighting for ages, up and down the grass.

My Freddie then came around the corner and the boy looked at him, he paused for a split second and I've caught him with a big haymaker. Me and Len had taken turns at fighting him; if we had any brains, we would have both jumped on him straight away. We finally beat him, though.

Another time, Lenny had a fight with this boy. Lenny had now moved into a block of flats named Geoffrey Court. Micky Wall also lived there. He had now left school and was about 16 and we used to go up to the Tottenham Royal which was a dance hall. Anyway, I went to Lenny's house one day and he says to me, 'I'm going to do this boy.' I said to Lenny, 'Are you mad? He must be about 20.' Lenny then said, 'He's the Guv'nor of the flats and I'm going to do him and be the new Guv'nor.' Lenny was stubborn.

About two or three weeks later, I met up with Micky Wall and we were going up to the Tottenham Royal. As I walked into the block of flats where Micky lived, I thought, What's happened here, it looks like someone's thrown themselves off the top of the building or something. Now, Lenny lived on the ground floor and Micky lived on the first floor. I've knocked on Micky's door and he's come out and says, 'Come in, Alf, there's been fucking murders around here… Lenny's only done that boy.' I said, 'You're joking.' He said, 'I'm not, he's fucking killed him, he's hit him and he's gone over the fence.' I said, 'He's fucking mental.' Micky then says, 'There's been Old Bill everywhere around here.'

Anyway, we get ready to go up to the Tottenham Royal and, as we are passing Lenny's flat, the door is open. The next thing I can hear is Lenny shouting, 'Alfie, Alfie…' I look round and Lenny says, 'I fucking done him… I told you I was going to do him.' I said, 'You're fucking mental.' Lenny then says, 'I told you I was going to do him, so I went and said to him, "You had a go at my little brother and told my brother to fuck off." I then said to Lenny, laughing, 'To be honest with you, Lenny, I've felt like telling your little brother Kruger to fuck off sometimes.' Lenny then said, 'Anyways, I've done him.'

Lenny turned to me one day while he was posing his muscles and said, 'I'm like a fucking Greek Adonis.' I said, 'Lenny, I'm not being funny, but you're one of the ugliest fuckers I have ever seen.' He then said, 'Bollocks, I have got rugged good looks.' I thought to myself, laughing, You cocky fucker.

A couple of years later, I went up to a club by the meat market with a mate of mine to see Lenny and, as we were getting out of the car, there was some hassle there. So I walks up to Lenny and he says, 'Do us a favour, Alfie, keep an eye on my back, these are a right bunch of pricks.' Lenny then steams into them and smashes fuck into them; he's pole-axed this one bloke and he's gone straight down, he wasn't moving and looked dead. The rest of them have run away.

Now, my mate with me had never seen anything like it in his life. I said to Lenny, 'For fuck's sake, Len.' Lenny then told me to go with my mate before the Old Bill turned up.

I picked up the daily newspapers the next day expecting to read 'man killed' or 'man murdered' or something like that. I was a bit worried for my family because I'd been there and they were a naughty mob of people, but he didn't half give it to them.

I remember this one night I was passing The Green Man pub in Hoxton. It was run by a mate, Archie Joyce. So I thought I'd pop in to see Lenny who had been working the door there that night. This other doorman then says to me, 'You're not coming in, you're trouble.' I looked at him and said, 'My mate owns the pub... are you sure you have got the right person?' He then said, 'You're not coming in, you're trouble.' As I went to walk off, I could hear someone giggling behind the door. I went to walk away and I could hear someone shouting, 'Alfie! Alfie!' Lenny then popped his head out, laughing. He was always playing practical jokes like that.

I then bumped into a friend of mine in the pub and we were having a laugh and a joke. Now I'd grown up with Lenny since we were kids and I could say things to Lenny not many people could get away with. Anyway, we were all having a laugh and I went to the toilet. I then came back, and my mate who I'd met in there was a funny ashen colour. So I said to Lenny, 'What's the matter with him?' and Lenny just shook his head and said, 'I don't know.'

When I saw the bloke later, he told me Lenny had gone over to him while I was in the toilets and grabbed him by his hand and squeezed it really hard. Lenny then said to him, 'I can take it off my mate Alfie, but, if you carry on, I'll put you right through that fucking window.'

This other time, my uncle, who was also named Alfie Hayes, the person I was named after, was the chairman of the Union of Spitalfields Market. Now, there was this bloke who worked there who was pulling a couple of strokes, so my uncle pulled him in and finished him. My uncle was going to suspend him for a bit. Anyway, he's gone and told his son, who was a bit of a villain, not the greatest villain in the world, but frightened of no one. So the bloke has come to the market asking for Alfie Hayes, and they have pointed me out to him. He comes over to me and says, 'Do you run the union in here?' I then says to him, 'That's my uncle, mate, I'm his nephew.' Now I didn't have a clue what was going on.

The next day, I'm in the café in the market and Lenny comes in, he must have been about 21 by now, and you could see the stamp he had around there. He then says to me, 'I want you.' I says, 'Come and have a cup of tea.' He then says, 'Fuck the tea, I want you, come here. Who's this fucker that's going to do you? I've been told this bloke's come round to do you.'

I explained to Lenny that I was OK and that no one was going to sort me out. My uncle then came in the café and says to Lenny, 'Hi, Lenny, what you doing here?' Lenny then says, 'Someone is supposed to have threatened Alfie.' My uncle then said, 'They didn't threaten him, they threatened me. It's all been sorted now.' But again, this is the stamp of the bloke – he's heard that someone is going to do me and he's come all the way to the market to sort it out. He then said to me, 'If you get any problems, then come and see me.'

Another time, there was this little firm down the market and they were having a bit of trouble with their staff. The guv'nor was a bit of a lairy boy, ducking and diving. A few people had tucked him up on a few bills, so he got a minder in. Now this bloke was a bit notorious, I didn't really like him. I've had a bit of a run-in with this minder one day and we had a few words.

Anyway, this minder had smashed this bloke up who's a friend of Lenny's. A couple of days later, a mate of mine says, 'I've just seen Lenny pull up outside in the car,' so I goes over and Lenny passes me on the way in. So I says, 'All right, Len.' He just nods to me and doesn't say a word; I could see he was there on business. Turns out he's gone in there and given the guv'nor a mouthful. The guv'nor then calls in the minder who pops his head round slowly. The minder then says, 'Hello, Len.' Lenny then says, 'What are you doing here?' The minder replies, 'I do a bit of work here.' Lenny then turns to the guv'nor, laughing, and says, 'You'll need about another five of them.' The minder's attitude had changed so quickly and he's even offered to make Lenny a cup of tea.

A lot of people were frightened of Lenny. He had upset a lot of people but they didn't have the courage to go and see him so they done someone who knew him or they would smash his car up which happened quite a few times. But, in all fairness, he was the most violent man I'd ever seen. I haven't seen anyone who could come near him.

I saw Lenny bash this bloke up one night in the Royal Standard. Lenny said to me, 'I'm going to do this geezer.' I said, 'You fucking ain't, Len, I'm here, I've just walked in.' Well, he's done him anyway. I then said to him, 'I only came in for a quiet drink, Len.' Some quiet drink that was.

This one night, Lenny was working in this club and there was this bloke who worked at Spitalfields Market, a right arsehole who couldn't keep his mouth shut. He's up this club one night with a couple of his mates and they must have had about three brain cells between them all. Now sone is trying to pull a bird and the bird didn't want to know, so he's called her all the slags going and the bird's gone over and told Lenny. So Lenny's gone over to the bloke and all he's said is, 'Keep your trap shut,' and he's walked off.

A little while later, the bloke's done the same again so Lenny's gone over to him and gone – bang – 'Hold that for Christmas,' and he's then thrown him out. A mate of mine then told me the next day that Lenny had given him a backhander and he's lucky he didn't hit him on the chin or he'd had gone through the fucking window. I then saw the bloke Lenny had hit the next day and he had a black eye. I said to him, 'Who done that? Don't tell me, did the boy go to school the next morning?' He then says to me, 'You're fucking flash, mate... that flash fucker Lenny McLean took a liberty and hit me from behind.' I then said, 'Why would he take a liberty with you? He could blow you over, an idiot like you.'

I bumped into Lenny and he told me that he had given this bloke a backhander for abusing this woman. He was a silly little drug addict who he had chucked out.

I then bumped into the bloke again in this café and I said to him, 'I was talking to Lenny McLean the other day and, funny enough, I'm seeing him again today and I'm going to tell him you called him a prick.' The bloke jumped up shouting, 'Don't be silly, I was only mucking about.' So, in his mind, Lenny was a bully, but, if you look at it from Lenny's point of view, it was totally different.

Lenny said to me once, 'I'm going to have you in the corner with me, Alfie, one day.' I said to him, laughing, 'You go and fuck yourself... you have got no chance.'

Lenny had then moved on and we hadn't seen each other much. Then, one day, I was waiting for a bus to go to the

Tottenham Royal when Lenny was on the way to the Royal Standard and he introduced me to his girlfriend Val. I said, 'How do you do?' and wound her up a little about Lenny. A while later, I found out Lenny had got married and had a few kids and he was now living in St Stephen's Road.

Lenny had by now started boxing unlicensed as well as having bare-knuckle fights for money. I remember Lenny asking me once to run him to a gypsy camp to have a fight. I said to him, 'There must be an easier way to make a living Len,' but he then tried telling me about side stakes. One day, I was talking to his cousin Johnny Wall and he told me some of the places they had been to fighting, and it had frightened the fucking life out of him.

Lenny's greatest trick when he was a kid was, if he was a little bit dubious of someone, he would go up to them and tell them, 'My mate will bash you up, he will fucking kill you.' They would then say to Lenny, 'You tell your mate to come round here,' so I was going round there not knowing nothing about it and these people wanted to fight me, and, if I ever bashed one of them up, Lenny would say, 'I knew I could do him.' I'd say, 'What do you mean, you done him?' Lenny then would say it was because we were 'tie-fighters' – meaning, if you draw or if you are neck and neck, then you become tie-fighters, so, if I could beat him, then Lenny could – and this was a joke we held all our lives.

I think the tie-fighters thing came from back when big Jimmy Spinks and his son little Jimmy Spinks used to say to me and Lenny, 'Who's the best fighter out of you two?' and we used to put our arms around each other and say we were tie-fighters.

When he beat Roy Shaw in their rematch, I saw him over

in Victoria Park. I was going for a run and this filthy, horrible dog came along, I think it was a white dog with a black eye. Up it comes and I looked at the dog and I thought, Only one person can own a dog like that, and, sure enough, who comes running along but Lenny. He then says to me, 'Well, did you hear about it then, Alf?' I said, 'Hear about what, Len?' I knew what he was on about but acted dull just to wind him up. He then says, 'Well, I'm British Champion, I beat that Roy Shaw.' So I says, 'Oh, that...' and I acted like I wasn't bothered. He then goes, 'Get away, you fucker,' while laughing. He then says, 'Come over the house and I'll show you the film of it.'

So Lenny and I goes to his house and little Jamie comes flying out. Len says to him, 'Will you be here for a while?' Jamie replies, 'Yes, Dad.' Lenny then takes a pound note out and says to Jamie, 'See that... if you're still here when we come out [Jamie's eyes had by now lit up], I'll leave you have another look at it.' We then went into the house laughing.

So we watched the video and Len says, 'What do you think then, Alf?' I thought I'll wind him up again and put on a straight face and I said to him, 'The truth, Len... I'd do him.' He looks at me with this face you wouldn't believe, so I said, 'It's like going back to the days about when we were tie-fighters, Len... if you could do him, then I can do him, too.' He then walked over to me and kissed me on the forehead; I won't say what he called me then, though.

Lenny asked me once if I had a job for his son on the market. I said to him, 'Lenny, you don't want him getting up at 3.30 in the morning.' I think Lenny had him a job up in the City in the end in stocks and shares. I'd pop over his way now and again and have a drink in the Duke of York with him, although Lenny wasn't a big drinker.

44

I remember going up Woody's when he done Man Mountain York. I remember him telling me, 'I've got a fight up at Woody's… I'm going to fucking do him.' So I said, 'What do you want to fight for now, Len?' Lenny then replied, 'He thinks I'm an old fucker and that I'm past it, and he's been going around saying this, that and the other, so I'm going to fucking do him.'

Anyway, I popped in to see Lenny before the fight and he was right up for it. The bloke come out and must have been a six-foot-six giant. I don't think the bloke wanted to know. Lenny hit him a couple of times in the stomach and, next thing you know, he was on the floor.

Another time, I went to see him fight and he pole-axed the bloke in about 20 seconds and his boy got in the ring to congratulate him. Lenny lent me a tape of most of his fights. I wasn't that interested in going to the fights as I didn't like that kind of scene they were bringing with them.

Lenny was telling me one day that he was going to be a bearer for Ronnie Kray's funeral at St Matthew's Church and he was asking me if I was going to go. My Timmy went as he knew the Twins, but I had something on that day.

He used to say to me, 'I've got a fight coming up, Alf, and I'll give you and your brothers some tickets.' I'd say, 'Len, you're in the hardest game in the world, what the hell do you want to give tickets away for? If we want to go, we will pay at the door.'

I once asked Lenny what was his hardest fight, and he said, 'Roy Shaw was hard, he was a right hard fucker. People don't realise how hard he was.'

I went over Victoria Park quite a lot when Lenny was training for some of his fights.

Lenny was telling me about the fight he had over in America one day. Lenny had flown out with his cousin Johnny Wall. Lenny told me, 'These blokes met us at this airport and they had these suits on and sunglasses and they took us to this hotel. Next thing I knew, they were knocking on the door and they asked me to go with them. They then drove us into this meat-packing factory and I took on one of their guv'nors there. I done him and they gave me my money and they took us back to the hotel. Me and Johnny headed back to the airport and stayed there all night; there was no way they were going to get a chance to shoot me.'

But Lenny wasn't the greatest of trainers; he was like Two-Ton Tony Gallento, the old heavyweight who used to train with a cigar in his mouth. Lenny had the same attitude as him and that was, if I don't finish them in two rounds, then they are going to beat me anyway.

I used to pop up The Guv'ner's pub but Lenny wasn't there much and I'd talk to Jamie. I was talking to Lenny's daughter Kelly once at the pub. I'd gone up there with my son Steve, and Kelly was making a right fuss of him. She was then saying to me that, every time she met a boy and they found out Lenny was her dad, they didn't want to know her.

I was talking to Lenny one day and I mentioned it was my mother's birthday coming up. He invited us up there and we had a cracking night. Lenny offered the champagne as soon as we got there. He looked after us all night. He always used to call my mother 'Mrs Hayes'. Lenny then said to my mother, laughing, 'Remember when I was a kid, I always used to say that, when I grow up, I'm going to marry you, but now I'm fucking glad I never.' I won't tell you what she said back to him.

Lenny kept asking me to bring my wife up to The Hippodrome but I never made it. The last time I went out with Lenny was just after he had come out of prison. Stringfellow had said to Lenny that he was too much of a high profile at that moment and he put Lenny on the door of one of his smaller clubs named Cairo Jack's in Soho. Lenny told me that, when I come up, to go straight to the front of the queue. So I've gone to the front of the queue with my wife and this bouncer turns to me and says, 'What's that?' So I've said to him, 'I don't know,' and he goes, 'It looks like a queue, don't it?' So I've turned to him and said, 'Can you tell Lenny I'm here please... Alfie's here.' The bloke soon changed his attitude and says to me, 'Excuse me, sir, would you like to come in please... you can use the private staircase if you want.'

Lenny's standing in there by the bar holding court. Lenny says to me, 'Don't buy any drinks as it's all down to expenses.' I think Lenny was doing *The Knock* at the time. Mad Frankie Fraser was also in there that night. Lenny was then telling me that he was looking to get a place in Bexleyheath. The last time I seen Lenny was just before he moved there.

Another mate of mine came and told me one day that Lenny had cancer; I couldn't get over it. A while later, I heard Lenny was signing his book up in Liverpool Street and I said to my wife, 'Shoot down and get me a signed book and get me Lenny's phone number.' The bloke then told everyone that he had gone into a coma and I found out that Lenny had sadly passed away the next day.

I went to a florist down in Hoxton to see if they were handling the flowers for the funeral; they couldn't do me a wreath as they had to do so many. They then gave me

Lenny's address and I sent a wreath to the house. I went to the funeral and it was amazing, I bumped into a lot of people I hadn't seen for years that day.

Anyone who knew Lenny personally knew him as 'Boy Boy', and when I had a wreath done for the funeral it had on there 'Boy Boy'.

At the funeral, one of Lenny's aunties, either Genie or Jody, came up to me and said, 'You knew Lenny then, did you?' She's then looked at the card and said, 'Oh, Alfie, you're one of the Hayeses, come straight in.' She then asked me how my mother Rosie was. I also seen a few of Lenny's brothers and sisters at the funeral and we had a good chat about old times.

While I was walking through the garden, a big, strapping bloke walks towards me and calls my name. I then realised it was Lenny's brother from Australia. He was as big as Lenny, if not even bigger. We had a good chat about the old days and some of the people who were at the funeral. He then said to me, 'I wonder if Lenny's looking down at all this, Alfie.' I said, 'Do you think he's up there then?' 'Of course he is,' he replied, 'I bet he grabbed the angel Gabriel on the doors of heaven and told him to fuck off as he's doing the door there now.' We both had a good laugh and we then went our separate ways.

Thinking back now, I can still hear that voice in my head, the way he used to shout, 'Alfie... Alfie.' We were best mates from a very early age and it was a pleasure to have known him.

Around this time, a mate told me about a guy named Jimmy Andrews who he'd been speaking to who knew Lenny really well. I finally got in touch with him and we had a chat on the phone for a few hours. I then invited him down to stay with me for the weekend. He showed me his personal photo album and his very own signed poster from Lenny which had been signed, 'To my Pal and Partner, my little nephew Jimmy.'

This showed me how close he and the big man had been throughout the years. Jimmy then had to shoot back and we arranged an interview for a later date.

A couple of weeks later, I travelled north and, after a five-hour journey in the pouring rain, I finally arrived in his home town. Jimmy had just wrapped up his book called *Scallywags* and he is about to star in a feature film called *The One-Armed Bandit*. Jimmy could take Lenny off to a tee and it was like watching Lenny in the flesh for the next couple of hours. I was enthralled by Jimmy's story, and he had plenty to say about the big man himself.

JIMMY ANDREWS

I first heard of Lenny McLean when I was a kid. My uncles in the East End of London and in Liverpool used to talk about him all the time. They used to go to his fights and they'd done some business with him over the years.

The first time I saw Lenny was when I was about ten years old. It was the summer holidays and we had gone down to visit my great-uncle Albert Reading in his caravan in Clacton-on-Sea. Lenny also had a caravan there and he would drive down most nights straight after work during the summer. He would spend a lot of his weekends there, too.

I moved to the East End when I was 17. Lenny took me under his wing; he tried to keep my nose clean and put me on the straight and narrow.

I then started boxing for West Ham when I was 18. My trainers had been Johnny Eames and Micky May. Lenny came to see me fight a few times. I used to go and watch Lenny training over in Slim Jim's throughout the years. This one time I seen Lenny chase a man around a gym as the bloke had gone Queen's Evidence on someone. He had grassed someone up blatantly in court. Lenny seen him in the gym and went berserk, and chased the bloke straight out of the gym.

I had moved in with my uncle Albert at the time. Lenny helped me get this little flat. I got the option on the right to buy. Lenny knew someone that was selling a rent book for this council flat. I didn't have much money at the time as I was always gambling. Anyway, Lenny lent me a few quid and I bought the rent book off this bird. I had the offer to buy the place when I got it in my name.

When I first started going around to see Lenny, he was living in a maisonette in Allen Road, Bow, where he lived with his wife Val, son Jamie and daughter Kelly. He also had a little staff bull terrier called Lady. They had the dog until it was about 17. Lenny thought the world of that dog. See, you hear all these stories about how he was a violent man and this, that and the other, but people don't see the side that I witnessed, silly little things like when I'd go in there and go in the maisonette, and Val would say, 'He's still in bed,' so I'd go downstairs and they had this big, smart, Victorian four-poster bed with all netting around it, a bit like something you'd see in a hotel room in Africa to keep the insects out. Because he was a big guy, his feet used to hang over the end of the bed and he had these massive feet – he had the biggest big toes you'd ever seen.

I'd duck down quietly and start tickling his feet. All of a sudden, he'd say, 'Who the fuck's tickling my feet?' I'd then jump up and run upstairs laughing.

He'd come upstairs and say to Val, 'Do us a cup of tea, babes.' I can see him sat in that chair now, and all he would have on was his ball-stranglers, like a tight pair of boxers, and not a care in the world. He'd sit in the chair and start flexing his muscles, he'd then start making expressions in his face, but they wasn't to make you laugh or anything, you could see he was thinking about something.

All across the front room was small, red glass squares which made the wall up. He'd then stand up and say, 'Do you think I'm looking bigger today, son? Is Uncle Len looking bigger?' He wasn't actually my blood uncle but he used to tell everybody and tell me to tell everyone that he was my uncle, because, being from Liverpool and being in the East End, you're going to come across the odd dickhead who's going to want to pick you out some time or other.

I went up to see Lenny work this one night and we had a chat. I was telling him I was going away the following Saturday because it was my birthday on the following Friday. I was about to turn 18. He then said to me, 'Come up and see me on the Friday before you go away.'

So I went up his house on the day of my birthday and he's sat in his big leather chair with cream all round his face. So I says to him, 'So, what's with all that cream?' He then starts grinning and says, 'That was your birthday cake, son. I asked Val to get it for you, but I didn't think you was coming up, so I ate it.' Anyway, he gave me 50 quid and said for me to get something for myself on holiday; that's just the way he was.

It didn't matter who Lenny was with when he was out

driving, he'd be driving along and he'd pass his pouch of tobacco over to you and say, 'Do us a roll-up, son.'

Lenny had this Mini when he lived in Allen Road flats. It had a canvas roof on it like a convertible. It was so funny watching him trying to get into it. It must have taken him about 15 minutes to get in it because of the stature of the man. When he was in the car, he had to crouch right down and the wheel would be up against his chest; a bit of his head would be stuck out of the sunroof and it looked like a bump on the canvas where it stuck out. He had to get rid of the Mini because kids kept cutting the roof open all the time. He was gutted and it upset him that he had to see it go. He then bought a black Granada off an ex-mayor; it was a lovely big car on a B-plate.

This one night, my mate Alex and I got a lift home from Lenny after work. The handbrake was a bit dodgy so we pulled in by this garage. He stopped his car on a bit of a slope and the car started to roll back; he's pulled the handbrake up but it still bumped the car behind him.

This black bloke jumps out and says, 'What the fuck you doing, you mug?' Lenny jumps out of the car and, before you know it, the bloke's jumped back in his car and shot off; it was quite comical to see.

Alex got shot and killed a few weeks later outside this pub my uncle Albert had called The Horn of Plenty. I was 18 at the time. It was all over a stupid game of pool, which was his cousin's fault and not his. I'd taken him up to the West End a few weeks earlier and Lenny had taken a liking to him. Alex had this thing like we all did at that age; we all wanted to be tough guys. Lenny told Alex, 'There's nothing good about being a tough guy, son, take it from Uncle Len.' He then dropped us at Mile End Station on the way home.

A few years later, Lenny had been working in Cairo Jack's and I went up there for my twenty-fifth birthday. We went up the West End and we went to Cairo's before moving on to the clubs. Lenny laid loads of bottles of champagne on for us and, when I went to pay for it, he had already paid for it and he wouldn't take a penny off me or the lads. I used to go and see him with my mates and he would drop us back into the East End at Mile End Station which was by his house. He only lived around the corner by then as he had moved from Allen Road.

Lenny always had a soft spot for his cousin Johnny Wall. Lenny had given Johnny a job at The Hippodrome with him. Lenny was laughing and told me once, 'John was at it again last night.' I said to Lenny, 'What do you mean?' to which he replied, 'It kicked off, and where was John? Fast asleep in the office.' But, knowing John as I did, I wouldn't have liked a slap off him, never mind a right-hander.

As you went into The Hippodrome, there was a room on the left; it was a right smart office with a couple of leather chairs in there. Lenny would stand on the front door at its busiest period when people were coming in, then, at about 11.30, Lenny would go into the office and relax. He would maybe then do the rounds about once an hour, just have a little look around the club – he used to do the same at the Camden Palace – and he'd then go back to the office. There were always people coming into the office talking to him.

Knowing of all the fights Lenny had had, I never actually saw him do anything in all the years I knew him and lived in London. The only time I ever witnessed him raise his hand was to me after he slapped me across the back of the head for telling him to fuck off in front of some of the other doormen at The Hippodrome. I'd gone up there one night and I got this feeling he wasn't himself. You see, it had become like a formality to go up there with my mates and he'd usually say, 'Go through, son, you and your mates,' but on this particular night I said, 'All right, Len,' and he said, 'Not tonight, son,' I was a bit confused as that had never happened before. So I said to him, 'Is there a problem, Len?' and he says, 'Do me a favour, son… fuck off,' so he must have had the right hump about something. I was still only young and looked at him like a dad-type figure. I was really baffled, so I told him to fuck off, to which he hit me across the back of the head and knocked me on my arse, and I felt it all right. I then got up off the floor and told him to fuck off again and I walked off. I hadn't had much to drink but I had deserved the slap for talking to him like that.

We never spoke after that for about three years and then, one day, I went around his house and it was like it had only been the day before that I seen him and it was never ever mentioned again. I never even went in to apologise. The thing about Lenny was that he was a bit like my Albert – even if he thought he was in the wrong, Lenny was one of these people, because of his pride, he wouldn't say, 'Oh listen, Jim, I'm sorry about that,' he would say, 'Anyway, it's sorted now, son, so we'll forget about it,' and that would be his way of apologising.

A couple of times I went up The Hippodrome, Lenny's mate and ex-Page 7 male model John Huntley was there. Every time I saw him, I always had a scuff under my eye after having a tear-up or something. John must have had it in his head that I was out scrapping every weekend, but it was just my luck that something had happened every time I seen him.

Sometimes, if Len had the hump with you, he could hold it for a while. I'd say to my mum or our Albert, 'Give him a call and tell him I want to go round and see him, as he will listen to you, as he respects you more.' He was very wary of people. If I went around his house with anybody, Lenny would say to me, 'Have they got a good CV, son?' I used to say to Lenny, like a mafia-type thing, really, 'I'll vouch for them... they are good people,' and he would then say, 'All right then, son,' because he knew where he was then. Lenny was a private person and a proper family man. He loved Val, Jamie and Kelly, and he lived for them, and all the stuff that he did was for them.

I was with my cousin Bobby one day and Lenny must have seen Bobby over 50 times, but Lenny got it into his head that his name was Tommy. I used to say to Lenny, 'His name is Bobby, Len, not Tommy.' Lenny would then say, 'Bobby... Tommy... what's in a letter, son?' I used to think to myself, laughing, He's not even close; it wasn't like Will or Bill.

I've been in a few arguments with Lenny face to face and over the phone, but then the air would be clear within seconds, and it would be like, 'Put the kettle on and do us a roll-up, son.' Sometimes, you'd have to watch what you said as the slightest wrong word could cause an argument.

I never used to talk about Lenny's fights much. We just used to talk about nice things, such as general day-to-day things. Lenny used to get really pissed off with people coming up to the club and bragging about who they had been fighting with or beaten up. Lenny just used to smile at them but, when they walked off, he'd call them 'fucking mugs'. Lenny would rather someone nice came up to him and talked about how they were doing or if they were having a baby or getting engaged and so on.

This is where you saw the other side of Len, as I witnessed on several occasions. He'd say to these people, 'Go to the bar, ask for a bottle of champagne, and say, "Uncle Len said it's down to him."'

I once got put on remand for wounding with intent. I had a tear-up in this Chinese and, to cut it short, I got locked up and I ended up in Pentonville nick on remand. One day, I had this visit and I was expecting to see my uncle Albert and Charlie Kray. So I'm sat there and who walks in but Albert Reading, Charlie Kray, Lenny McLean and Charlie Richardson. Basically, when I went back to my cell, I had screws asking me whether Charlie Kray was coming back again, and if he could he sign their books. My cell became like a tobacconist within 24 hours; after that, the inmates were throwing all sorts of goodies at me. When I come out, I said to Lenny, 'What was all that about?' as I knew Lenny was always thinking ten steps ahead of anyone I ever knew. Lenny then said, 'Look, son, you are still young, you're a handsome lad, but liberties can be taken. I know you're a tasty little boxer and you can have a tear-up, but the bottom line is, there's a lot of naughty people out there and I've fucking met a lot of them. So I knew by us four faces coming in to see you that you were not going to be getting any bother.'

So much stuff happened in them early years when I was a teenager; life was so fast in them days. A few weeks down the line, the charges were dropped and I was a free man again. Years later, I gave Val a few letters when Lenny was in prison to make sure he got them.

I went to his house one day and he was always singing the song 'Lean on Me' by Bill Withers. He used to love that song and wouldn't stop singing it all the time. It was one of his most favourite songs. Val was there one day when I said to him, 'Len, you're wasted working on the doors and minding people and stuff like that. You could make a load of money doing film work.' I told him he had the look and the profile to star in the movies.

He then said to me, 'Acting? Acting's for fucking poofs!' and that was that. He then got offered to do a commercial for BT. He did it and made a decent wage out of it. He then done another commercial and then he ended up getting a part in *The Knock*.

Len's daughter Kelly and I ended up in *EastEnders* doing a bit of filming. There was this Indian woman who was vain as fuck on set. She was sort of putting Kelly down. So this Indian woman had been winding us up all day, and Kelly, who was usually quiet and very shy, turned to this woman and said, 'If you don't fuck off, I'll knock you spark out.' I could see that had come straight from her dad. I said to her on the way home, laughing, 'Where did that come from?' She then said, 'I don't know, she was doing my head in, though.' It must have taken a lot to have wound her up like that.

Me and Jamie also had a bit part in *The Bill*. We were playing inmates at Wandsworth Prison. I said to him, 'Isn't this spooky? Only a few months back, you were visiting your dad in here.' Six or seven nicks around London and we ended up there.

Lenny used to speak very highly of Richie Anderson and Arthur Thompson from up north. Lenny looked at Arthur like a dad figure himself. Lenny and Richie would always pop in and see Mitzy Walsh on the way up to Scotland. I remember Lenny telling me he had three fights in one day up in Scotland and he made a good bit of money.

When my cousin Bobby was boxing, Lenny would say, 'Bobby, you have got to look at that opponent over there as if he's just physically abused your missus and children.' That was just one side to Lenny that he used to use to wind himself up.

Another time, there was this bloke named Mickey who we used to call 'The Penguin'. He used to run this pub in Essex and he was a bit of a Krays fanatic. He would always ask me if I could ask Lenny if he could visit Ronnie Kray with us. Obviously, with me being a bit like Lenny and thinking of ways to make money, I said to Lenny, 'We could get something out of this, Len... he's got a nice few quid and he asked me again the other night. He's a nice bloke, he's always talking about them, so I've told him I'll see what I can do, but it will cost him a grand.' Lenny then said, 'Good boy, leave it with Uncle Len and I'll sort it out with Ronnie.'

So Lenny and I go round to see Ronnie. He walks in, immaculate as ever, in one of his many new suits. After a while, I says to him, 'Right, Ron, this is how it is, there's this bloke that runs a pub and he wants to come and meet you, so I've said to him I'll have to ask you and Lenny first, but I've told him it'ss going to be a grand if you say yes – you'll get 400 quid, Lenny has three and I get three as well. So what do you think about that then, Ron?'

He then leans back, thinking, and then leans forward and says, 'Yeah, that sounds good, but I've got one better than that... How about I have 500, Lenny has 500, and, if Lenny wants to give you something out of his, then it's up to him.'

Now, because I'd met Ronnie loads of times, I knew how to speak to him. I said to him, 'Come on, Ron, don't be like that, fucking hell, there's a nice day's wages for all of us...'

He came forward again, laughing, and said, 'Only joking, boy... that sounds good, I'll have four and Lenny and you have 300 each.'

So we arranged it for the following week. Now, the table was square like an old school table with four of you sitting at each end. And, because Broadmoor was a hospital, everyone had the same visiting rights. I'd gone there a few weeks earlier and Peter Sutcliffe was sitting a few yards from us in the same room.

Anyway, we introduce Mickey to Ronnie and Mickey then just sits there, not saying a word. About 20 minutes later, Ronnie still hasn't looked at him. All of a sudden, Mickey says, 'Excuse me, Mr Kray, can you tell me where the toilets are?' So Ronnie shows him the way to the toilets. Ronnie then says to me and Lenny, 'Watch this, I'll be back in a minute,' and he winks at us as he walks off to the toilet himself.

A couple of minutes later, Mickey comes back from the toilets and he's got piss all over his trousers. We couldn't really say too much then as Ronnie came back and winked and smiled at me and Lenny. We didn't give a fuck about whatever Ronnie said after that, as me and Lenny just wanted to get out of Broadmoor and get in the car and ask Mickey what had happened.

We got out about 20 minutes later and we asked Mickey what happened. He told us, 'Well, I'm in the toilet having a piss and Mr Kray said to me, "Obviously, I haven't said anything to you out there because I didn't want to show Jimmy and Lenny that I have taken a shine to you... you're a real nice boy, Mick, and I think you should come back and see me again on a regular basis...'

As this was going on, Mickey was so scared that he was pissing all over his own trousers. Ronnie then put his arm on Mick's shoulder and Mick carried on pissing on himself. By now, me and Lenny were curled up laughing as Mickey was telling us and Mickey said, 'I didn't realise I was pissing on myself as all I thought about at the time was that he was going to fuck me.'

Ronnie was a practical joker and liked doing things like that for a wind-up. We ended up making a good earner out of that because I must have taken another 60 or 70 people up to meet Ronnie; sometimes Lenny didn't come with me and I'd go with my uncle Albert, other times I'd go on my own.

Sometimes, I'd be around Len's and Reggie Kray would ring him four or five times a day. Lenny had a bellyful in the end and stopped talking to him. Then Reggie would ring him up a few weeks later and apologise. Reg would never phone up and ask how you are or how the family is, he always wanted something or he wanted Lenny to get people to go in and visit him.

Another day, the film stuntman Dave Lea came round to Len's house. Lenny then told me that Dave had passed his film script on to Sylvester Stallone. Lenny was telling me that Stallone said to Dave after reading Lenny's script for *The Guv'nor* that Lenny was the real Rocky Balboa. Craig Fairbrass, who was to play Lenny in the film, also used to say the same about Lenny. Craig had a little café up the Elephant and Castle and, some of the times I was up Lenny's in the morning, Craig used to phone him and say, 'Anything happening, Len?' Lenny was always on a high being told that it was going to happen, and this went on for years.

This one day, we were up on *The Krays* film set at the

pump house. It was like an old warehouse where they had assembled some of the sets. We had been doing some filming there and Kid Berg, the boxer, was there with us. He was a lovely old bloke and he would play hell with the girls on set. Lenny told me he had been a cracking world champion who had held the title for years. Also on the set that day was John McVicar, who was doing some writing backstage. Now, McVicar had upset a few people and Lenny ended up chasing him off the film set.

A couple of weeks later and I was with Lenny up the flat; we had only just done *The Krays* film. He was being interviewed by this bloke from the *East London Advertiser*. The bloke said to Lenny, 'Len, have you ever thought about doing a normal job?' Lenny then throws out a punch, as quick as lightning, laughing. Len used to do that a lot. The bloke nearly jumped out the window with fright. Lenny then says, 'Val, go and get that diamond ring I bought you a few months back.'

Val goes and gets it from her jewellery box, and Lenny says, 'See that, son, that came to a nice few quid.' He never said how much it cost.

One of Lenny's favourite words was 'scenario'. He'd put his hands out and he'd say, 'I'll give you a scenario, son. I can go out and have an unlicensed fight with someone and make ten grand, or I can go and work on the buses for a dozen years to make the same money. Now both of them are going to buy that diamond ring, but one of them will buy it in one night and the other will take a dozen years.' I think the reporter got the picture and said, 'I suppose I can see where you're coming from, Len.'

People used to ask, with all the fights Lenny had, what he

did with his money. What he did with it was spend it on his wife and kids, caravans and moving into a nicer home. You couldn't meet anyone who was more family-orientated than Lenny.

But one of the other things people don't know about Lenny was that he was a very generous person to people who he had grown up with, who had had nothing when they were kids, who still didn't have anything to this day. He used to drop round their houses and give them a few quid to see them all right. He also used to look after the families of his mates who had gone to jail.

Lenny used to do a lot of work for charity; he used to say to certain people, 'I'll do this to help this kid out, or I'll do that to give you a few quid, but make sure you don't tell anybody.' To me, that was bang on. That's how he was with me and I witnessed it with a few other people when I was in his company.

Lenny knew I had a good ear for people's accents and taking them off. He used to love me doing Bob Hoskins from *The Long Good Friday*. He'd phone me up and say, 'Son, come round, we are going down to Pinewood Studios.' We went down there a few times trying to get his film sorted. Lenny was putting a lot of money into the film but nothing was coming of it.

I was over in Lenny's house in Bexleyheath one day when Guy Ritchie and Matthew Vaughan came over there. Lenny said to Guy Ritchie, 'This is one of my relations – Jimmy. I want him to have a part in the movie [*Lock, Stock and Two Smoking Barrels*] as well.' I was then offered one of the parts of the Scousers in the film. I think Lenny got paid the same as Vinnie Jones. Vinnie donated all of his, I think, to a hospital in Watford where his wife had a life-saving heart operation. Lenny told me all the rest of the cast were given a smaller amount.

So I was all set for *Lock, Stock* and I was on the phone to Lenny one day and I just said to Lenny a wrong word again and that was it. Lenny then told Guy Ritchie that he didn't want me in the movie. I didn't ask him to get me back in because, when Lenny got it into his head, that was that.

We were talking again a few weeks later, but I wasn't going to be in the film, although he asked me a few times to go down and watch them filming. They completed the movie and they had a football match between the cast and crew. He asked me to come down and take part but I said no. I could not work out why he wanted me there as I wasn't in the film.

I was thens told that Lenny had cancer. I went to his first book signing in Dillons on Oxford Street. All his family was there to support him. He was advised not to go to the book signing, but because of the strength of the man and the size of his heart he turned up. I'd gone up there with my Albert and a few other people and just joined the queue the same as everybody else. The book author, Peter Gerrard, was signing all the books and Lenny was just autographing them. It got to my turn to get my book signed and I just whispered in his ear, 'I love you, Len,' and I gave him a kiss on the cheek and a hug.

Lenny always promised my mother from an early age that he would keep an eye on me. He kept his word that he would take me under his wing and make sure that I didn't go down the wrong path. Even up until now, my mother commends Lenny for what he did for me; probably, if it hadn't been for Lenny, I might be in prison now.

He used to say to me things like, 'You have been

scrapping again, son,' to which I'd reply, 'Yes', and he'd then say, 'Around them piss-pot areas again? Well, you know what to do – stop going to them places and start going to nice places and you won't get into scrapes any more.' That's the advice he gave me and it sounded good. The bottom line at the end of the day was, if there was any criticism or anybody who could advise somebody about being good or being bad, it was him. He had been there, seen it, done it and wore the T-shirt. He had all them fights, been a good guy, a bad guy, a fair guy and, most of all, a top family man.

He had done a lot of charity work which went unrecognised; some people liked him, some people didn't like him, and some people were jealous of him. He said to me once, 'Friends you can count on the one hand, Jimmy. I've got thousands of acquaintances, but the only friends I've got are my Val, Jamie and Kelly.'

I would like to think that he thought of me in that same light as them as well.

Another name I had first come across in *Lock, Stock and Two Smoking Barrels* was Tony McMahon. Tony had become friends with Lenny from a very early age and stayed friends with him right up until he had passed away. These days, Tony's a very successful businessman after taking Lenny's advice and investing in the property market. Tony still promotes around London and his Exposure night still packs out the clubs. I had a chat with Tony after Len's wife Val had given me his phone number. An interview was then set up and, after travelling for ages, I arrived at Tony's house.

Here's what he had to say about his life and what Lenny had meant to him.

TONY MCMAHON

I first met Lenny McLean when I was a young kid, about 16. I'd grown up with little education and, at that time, had no job; I wasn't really going anywhere in life. I was young and living on my own in Camden and would frequently go to the Camden Palace nightclub at weekends. I would go around the back and kick the doors in and charge people a few pounds to get in.

One occasion, Lenny caught me; we all feared him at the time, he was known as 'the Big Man'. We used to say to each other, 'Don't get caught by the Big Man.' Anyway, we started chatting and Lenny took a liking to me and, before I knew it, I was doing a bit of business with him.

I used to take all my pals down to the club and get the money off them before we got to the door. I'd go up to the front of the queue and say, 'Hi, Len, how are you? I've got some mates with me tonight.' I'd always have over 20 people with me. Lenny would reply, 'Come on then, all in, these are my guests.' No one would say anything to him. I would then meet with Lenny and give him half the money I had collected, which meant I had something for myself as well. That's basically how it all started; from then on, I become really good friends with Len.

By the time I was in my early twenties, I'd noticed the money you could make from the club scene. I said to Lenny, 'Len, I want to do the clubs.' He replied, 'Right, it's done for you.' Now, I hadn't done anything in my life to do with promotion. Lenny started things rolling and spoke with Dave Chippin, the manager of The Hippodrome club in Leicester Square, who then gave me a regular Friday night in the Gas Club. Lenny was the one who told me the date which I would be starting. I didn't want to let Lenny down, so I spoke to a lot of people and they helped me out and gave me a few tips.

My first night was in June 1996; I had about 400 people in there, the following week 200, and then 100. I was only young at the time and it was getting worse by the day. The following week, I really went for it and gave tickets out at half price and tried my best to promote the night well with good DJs, etc and, before I knew it, I was up to 700 a night. I never really looked back after that. I was now making good money from these parties and learning that successful events were all about promotion.

From day one when I got into the clubs, Lenny would come to every party right up until he passed away. Wherever the party was, Lenny would turn up to check on me and the night. He'd pull up in a car and say to the security, 'Get short stuff [short stuff was Lenny's nickname for people who weren't very big].' The security would then come in and find me.

An hour and two Diet Cokes later, Lenny would leave saying, in front of the security, 'Tony, any problems, give me a shout.' He would then drive off, leaving me to continue with my work. I'd get no problems because Lenny was behind me; his presence at the club was enough. I was still a young kid and making good money.

After a year of successful nights at the Gas Club with numbers increasing, I needed a larger venue. Before I knew it, Lenny had arranged for me to hold my parties in a bigger venue in Wandsworth and, soon after, I was attracting 2,000-plus people per promotion. My events were going from strength to strength and I will never forget the help I got from 'the Big Man'.

There was an incident in one of my parties where a few people had been thrown out. I hadn't told Lenny about it. A few months later, Lenny asked me about it. Lenny went mad that I hadn't told him. It turned out that the people who were thrown out were a bit naughty and were planning to come back and play hell there. Luckily for me, they found out Lenny was behind the party and left my night alone. That was the power and respect Len held on the door.

This one party I was doing, one of the security on the door was pinching the guest passes and selling them himself. I came across this and Lenny found out. He made all the security team stand in a row outside and he gave them a right bollocking. Lenny said to them, 'You pinch from him, then you are pinching from me...' He terrorised the lot of them. After that, they used to ask me for passes, and I began to feel more respect from the staff, they were respecting me through Lenny.

In Camden Palace one evening, there were these guys that I knew of. There must have been about ten of them and they were getting rowdier with each drink. Now, these guys were tough and had a bit of a reputation.

About four hours later, after copious amounts of alcohol, they were causing problems with the bar staff and other punters. Lenny appeared through the crowd and had a few words with one of them; the bloke threw a punch at Lenny and, before it connected, Lenny had already knocked him out. Within seconds, he's knocked out another two. The speed of him was amazing; the others noticed this and ran away.

Whenever there was an argument, no matter how many people were involved, Len would always get in there and solve it with his mouth or, if that failed, his fists. He gave them a chance and, if they didn't take it, the problem was solved... his way!

Another occasion I remember was at The Hippodrome one evening. Lenny was standing on the door with the management. Lenny said to them all, 'Right, now all of you move away from the door.' One of them said, 'Why, what you doing, Len?' He replied, 'For the next ten minutes, all the money that comes in is mine... these people are on Lenny's paying guest list.'

Everyone then moved from the door and Lenny would say, 'These are my guests... this is my guest...' and so on, even Chinese people he didn't know he would say were his guests. When the time was up and his pockets were heavy, he would then say, 'That's it, I'm off to eat my Chinese.' He'd then disappear into his room with his cousin John.

Later on in the night, he would walk just once round the club and say to the other doormen, 'Any problems, call me,' and with that he'd return to his room. Having Len working the door on your club prevented problems and everyone knew it. Who could argue with that?

It was around this time that Lenny advised me to buy my own house. I wasn't really interested as I was into flash cars and women, but Lenny kept on at me. He said, 'Tony, just buy it, you have got to buy it.' He drove me so mad in the end that I bought my first home. Looking back now, it's the best decision I ever made and I owe that decision, once again, to Lenny. The money I made from one house I invested into other property, and so on. Lenny had a vision for these things and he taught me a lot.

While this was going on, Lenny began getting into acting.

He had recently landed a part in *The Knock*. One morning, he rang me and said, 'Tony, come down, there's a move.' I said to him, 'What's the move?' He replied, 'I'm going to get you a part in *The Knock*.' I thought to myself, How can I get in there? I've never done any acting.

Regardless, he took me down to the studios and Lenny said to Paul Knight, the producer, 'Paul, do us a favour, put Tony in.' Paul replied, 'Yeah, no problem, it's done,' and that was that.

I had one line to learn – 'What's it to do with us, John?' Due to nerves, I went over the line in my head hundreds of times and eventually did the scene with Dennis Waterman. After filming, Lenny came over and started cuddling me, saying, 'That's it, son, you're in, you done blinding.' I then pointed at my hand where I had the one line written down, and we had a good laugh over that.

Even so, I knew he was proud of me no matter how small the part was. Another day, Lenny rang me up and told me to get ready as he was taking me for a part in some TV programme. He picked me up and revealed he wasn't really sure himself what part I was going for.

Lenny told the girl at reception that we had arrived. She couldn't find my name on the sheet but then Lenny explained we had the same agent and it was sorted. Lenny then disappeared for the audition and emerged after a short while. He then said to me, 'Quick, Tony, you have got to go in there and act like a car salesman.' All of a sudden, my name's being called. I go in and do the audition in the style Lenny had told me. It turned out that Lenny had told me the complete opposite style to what they wanted, and I realised this when the casting director asked me where my boxing shorts were. Ten minutes later and red-faced, I manage to escape from this boiling room to find Lenny in hysterics at my expense. I now knew it was his way of tricking me so he could get the part. I must have looked a complete idiot in there, and it's obvious what the outcome of that audition was. How embarrassing!

On another occasion, he phoned me up early one morning and said, 'Tony, come down, I'm putting you in *Lock, Stock*.' He always sprang things on me like this but that was what was so exciting.

I've gone down the studio where they were casting. I was supposed to be going for the part of the bloke hanging upside down having golf balls fired at him. I says to Len, 'Len, I don't fancy being hung upside down with my pants on having golf balls pelting towards me.' Lenny replies, 'Yeah, you are right, you can't have that,' so Lenny then says to Guy Ritchie, 'Guy, come on, give him a good bit.' Guy looks on his computer and finds the character of John in Dog's gang; he then prints the lines out and gives them to me. There must have been 25 lines… I'd only ever done one line in the past. Guy says, 'Have a look at it and tell me what you think.'

We left the studio and went to this restaurant for lunch. Now Lenny was good at reading situations and extremely streetwise. Before I even had a chance to look at the lines for the second time, he turned to me and said, 'Phone Guy now, tell him you love the part, you're over the moon with it. Then phone up our agent and tell him to contact Guy and sort your contract out.'

I felt Lenny was putting pressure on me; I'd only just had the lines in my possession. Even so, I did as the Big Man said and – bang! – it was sorted just like that. Lenny then says to me, 'Now that you've done that, do you feel better? And tell me what you were going to do.'

As I went to speak, Lenny said, 'No, stop, let me tell you what you were going to do… You would have took the lines home, you would have walked up and down with your missus for two weeks, you would have got the lines perfect in your head, you would then have rung Guy up and he would have said, "Sorry, Tony, I've already cast, filmed and released this feature, but don't worry, you'll be in the next one." That's what you would have done, isn't it?' What could I say – he was right!

We were on the set of *Lock, Stock* one day and one of the gangster cast members was 'giving it a little', so to speak. Lenny's walked by and this guy holds out his fist and says, 'Peace, Len,' in a cocky sort of way. Lenny, unimpressed, by his display, looks at him and says, 'Peace? Peace? If you walked down the bottom of your road and got lost, no one would know you… I'm known all over the world, now piss off!' Embarrassed, the bloke puts his hand down and says, 'I must have caught him on a bad day,' as Lenny walked off. Lenny couldn't have it with 'plastic gangsters', which was his expression.

There'd be times in *Lock, Stock* when Lenny would help rewrite the scripts. Lenny would say, 'No, but that's not right,' and he'd change the lines. He'd do his part and often chuck three or four other words in at the end. Everyone was happy with his ideas.

After *Lock, Stock* had finished filming, Lenny, Guy Ritchie, Matthew Vaughan and I met up for a bite to eat. The four of us were discussing Guy's new film *Snatch*. Lenny and I introduced Guy and Matthew to some of our friends down

Hatton Garden. We spent hours together talking about diamonds and other issues regarding the film and began getting a real taste for it. Guy says to Lenny, 'You're in it... you are going to be in *Snatch*,' but Lenny replies, 'Listen, don't worry too much about me, but promise me Tony's in it, that's all I ask for.'

Sadly, it was this time that my dearest friend passed away, which was followed by the release of *Lock, Stock and Two Smoking Barrels*. Determined to do Lenny proud, I kept in contact with Guy right up until casting, but never got that part in *Snatch*. I was quite upset about it. How right was the Big Man... no contract, no part!

I loved listening to Lenny's stories. He was telling me once how he had gone with his mate Graham to collect a debt at this property. They were having problems collecting the money so Lenny says to Graham, 'Go and dig a grave... we are going to put this guy in it.'

Graham starts digging and the bloke who owed the money goes back inside the house with Lenny and tries to sort out this mess that he is in. He assures Lenny that he'll have the money there in two hours. So they wait. Two hours later, the money turns up and everything was sorted. Lenny leaves the house and, all of a sudden, he remembers about Graham. He goes round the back of the house and finds Graham in this hole about six foot down and he's still digging. You can imagine what Graham said to Lenny.

I received a phone call from Val one day and I remember her words – 'Look, Tony, Lenny's not well.' Val explained what was wrong and I was left with that feeling of disbelief. That night, I had a party and, for the first time, Lenny didn't pass by; I knew this was serious. The following day, I drove to the hospital with Val. I couldn't believe he was ill; he'd been jogging round the park only days before. Obviously, I knew by now he had cancer but, to me, he looked like he had nothing wrong with him. There, in front of me, was the Lenny I had grown to love, acting as if there wasn't a problem in the world. He'd never mentioned to me that he was unwell but, I suppose, that was another way of protecting the people he cared about the most.

I spent nearly every day with him after that. I'd pick him up and take him here and there, spending our days like we used to. It was a great sadness to me when Lenny passed away as he had been like a father to me. He took me under his wing and pushed me in all the right directions, developing me to be one of the biggest club promoters in the UK. He entered me into the acting world, which sent me to places I'd only ever of dreamed of. He did so much for me, my experiences with Len were endless. I miss him deeply.

Another close friend of Lenny's from a very young age was John Huntley. John was a former Page 7 male model and had been close to Lenny all through his life. John also had the task of reading a speech at Lenny's funeral. Yet again, Val had passed John's number to me and we had a good chat over the phone. Lenny clearly meant a great deal to him.

JOHN HUNTLEY

The first time I heard of the name Lenny McLean was when I went to his first fight with Roy Shaw. Shaw at the time had an awesome reputation and Lenny was a lot younger and just starting out. Lenny, even at that age, wasn't afraid of anybody. I don't think Lenny had taken the fight seriously, being so young. Lenny basically just ran out of steam and the ref stopped it after a few rounds. Lenny's trainers then told him that he had to start going to a proper gym and work on his stamina, and that's what he did. He joined Freddie Hill's gym in 1978.

I was training on the bags in there when he came in looking for Freddie, and he had a good look around and then asked me where Freddie was. As soon as I met him, I felt his presence. He looked awesome as he walked around the gym. He then hit this speedball which had been up years with a big hook, and it went flying across the gym.

Freddie then turned up and Lenny explained to him that he needed his help in getting fit. Lenny then started training like a professional fighter; he'd do his road work, bag work and started sparring with people like Tony Sibson and the Finnegan brothers.

As soon as Lenny had warmed up and was ready for sparring, they used to put me in first with him. They used to call me 'Warm-up Man'. Freddie would then have Lenny slipping my punches rather than just standing there and taking them. So, for the first couple of rounds, I'd be firing jabs out at Lenny. After a while, Lenny got quite good at it. Anyway, by the time the second fight had come with Shaw, it was all over. I don't think Roy Shaw was ever the same after that.

Lenny was such a personality, once you have been in his company you realised what he was like. I took a liking to him right away, he was a real laugh to be around. People hear about this fearsome reputation, but, in actual fact, he was fantastic company. If Lenny didn't turn up one day in the gym, there would be no atmosphere there. He was just a real funny, likeable sort of guy.

The fights Lenny did lose in the ring, though, were to good ex-professional boxers, but, on the cobbles or bare-knuckle, he was awesome, no one could touch him; he was so fast and powerful, there was no way he could lose. I remember when he had a straightener with Cliff Fields on the cobbles and Lenny just destroyed him, but, in their previous fight in the ring, Cliff had won.

I was front row for the fight and Lenny destroyed him – only the ropes were keeping Cliffy up. Lenny took it to him from the first bell and Cliffy didn't throw a punch back. Cliffy was in a right state, he was split open and blood was gushing out of his forehead; if it had been a pro fight, it would have been stopped. The heads were still going in and I think Lenny just ran out of steam again after hitting Cliffy so much.

Cliffy then threw a combination and, out of pure exhaustion, Lenny went down and was counted out.

Lenny gave me a call one day and asked me whether I'd be interested in opening this new pub he had just taken over called The Guv'ner's. I was in all the newspapers at the time, as I had just been voted Page 7 model of the year. So Lenny thought it would be good publicity to get me involved. So me and my girlfriend at the time, Dee Wells, and another good mate of Lenny's, Mick Theo, opened the pub up and it appeared in a few newspapers.

A couple of years later, I was round Lenny's house the day he was going to fight Bradshaw. Lenny didn't have a care in the world and said to us, 'I suppose I better go.' So I said, 'I'll come with you now, Len.' He replies, 'No, I'll be all right, John, it's not going to take long.' I think he knew it was going to kick off afterwards and he didn't want me there. He then says to me and Val, 'Do you want something from the

Chinese later?' I say, 'Don't worry about the Chinese… start thinking about the fight.' Lenny replies, 'Don't worry about the fight, that will take me five minutes. Do you want some chicken fried rice?' Honestly, he was so cool and didn't have one bit of worry in him and, within a couple of hours, he was back with the food.

He was also very popular; you only had to walk down the street with him for about half-a-mile and 100 people would ask how he was.

Lenny wasn't a bad guy, he was a nice bloke; I never knew Lenny to hurt anybody unless they had it coming. A lot of people wanted to be around Lenny, not because of his reputation, but he was just good company.

He was always in a rush in life, though. If someone wanted to do something the following week, he'd say, 'Well, why can't we do it tomorrow?'

I don't think I ever saw Lenny upset or in a temper. Every time I went round to see him, we just had a laugh and a joke. I don't think he really liked the violent side. He was much happier being around nice people and having a laugh and a joke. I don't think Lenny liked working the doors; it was only when he was in that environment people would see the other side to him, but I never did.

He'd had a hard life and, just when things were coming right for him, he became ill. I usually popped round Lenny's at least once a week for a chat. I went round there one day and there were a few members of his family there. I went in to see him and asked him was everything all right, and he replied, 'Not really, John… I've just been told I've got cancer.' I was speechless.

I tried going to see him as much as I could until he passed

away. Val then asked me if I would give a speech at the funeral. I was honoured to do this, but also very nervous. There were loads of people there but everything went well. There's no doubt in my mind, if Lenny was around now and he'd had the publicity Vinnie Jones had got from *Lock, Stock*, then he would be in America now. They would have loved Lenny out there, he was the real thing. He was a character and had a way of entertaining everyone.

Lenny was so proud of his family; he loved Val and his kids to bits, his family meant his whole world to him. He was a one-off, I will never forget him. I miss him and it was an honour to have known him and become his closest mate.

3
Gloved Up

Even from a young age, Lenny had started fighting – he had to, really. After suffering years of abuse from a bastard of a stepfather, he had to learn to defend himself. Throughout his teens into his early twenties, Lenny would be fighting day in, day out. Lenny was still bouncing in clubs and pubs and fighting most nights. He was also picking up good cash with his bare-knuckle fights. Word then got to Lenny that there was a fighter named Harry 'The Buck' Starbuck, who was a right handful, who'd had a few fights and was unbeaten. Lenny made a challenge to Eddie Richardson who was backing Starbuck, but Richardson turned down the offer. Lenny continued to train and work the doors.

By now it was 1975, and the unlicensed scene was just blooming. The show to get the ball rolling was set up by a bloke named Joey Pyle who had organised a fight between Roy Shaw and Donny 'The Bull' Adams. Adams, at the time, was apparently named 'King of the Gypsies' – he had fought 48 times and was unbeaten, but exactly whom he had beaten remains a mystery to this day. The fight had everyone talking all over London and Shaw didn't let anybody down by smashing the gypsy to pieces in seconds. The unlicensed scene had finally taken off and people were coming from all over to fight on Pyle's shows. Pyle had now partnered up with Alex Steene, who was helping to promote the shows.

A couple of weeks before the Shaw v Adams fight, Lenny had seen a poster advertising the bout in a pub in Hoxton called The Green Man. While drinking with a few of his mates, Lenny started mouthing off about the fighters in the poster. Now, the barman, who had just taken over the pub, goes and sticks his nose in, and he and Lenny start having words. After a heated exchange, Lenny says to the bloke, 'Make sure you tell that Shaw I'll fight him anywhere.'

After a while, the bloke goes to see Roy Shaw and tells him he has a problem with McLean. Shaw goes to the pub straight away to sort it out, but Lenny wasn't there. Rumours start to fly about Shaw's appearance in the pub and, pretty soon, the whole of London was buzzing with excitement that these two hard men were about to meet. People were warning Shaw of Lenny's reputation, as Lenny, by now, had beaten a lot of London's hardest men.

Lenny had then asked an acquaintance to ask Joey Pyle to sort the fight out with Shaw. But, at the time, Joey had never heard of McLean and had lined Shaw up with a few other fights. It was only a few weeks later, when a very young promoter and his partner turned up and had a meeting with Joey, that he took them seriously. Joey thought Lenny wasn't ready for the big time quite yet, but the promoter had promised arses on seats.

The fight was arranged on a 'winner takes all' basis. Lenny now thought he would go and check out what Shaw looked like. Roy was fighting a big, tall boxer named Terry Hollingsworth, who was an ABA champion at a club in Croydon called Cinatras. Lenny had booked some ringside seats and had gone with his then manager.

Shaw had taken Hollingsworth apart in the first round in under a minute with body punches, and finally stopped him with a hook to the chin. Lenny, finally, had the chance to get in the ring and hype the fight and challenge Shaw to a winner-takes-all fight for three grand. Roy accepted immediately and the fight was now set.

Even after watching Shaw's demolition of Hollingsworth, Lenny still thought he could beat him easily. Lenny was used to going at people and putting them away in seconds with his bare fists. Up until thens, Lenny had never lost a fight and would win most in under a minute; it had never crossed his mind fighting past a minute, but Shaw knew how to use the ring and save his breath until the later rounds – something Lenny had no experience of.

The fight was set for Monday, 23 May 1977, a ten-rounder in the same nightclub, Cinatras. The papers had even picked up on the fight and Lenny was telling them in his usual confident, cocky manner that he was going to take Roy's head off. Roy had different plans for the fight, though.

So the night arrived and the place was packed to the rafters. Lenny had made his way to the club with his cousin Johnny Wall, who was going to be his corner man, and a few others. The six-fight under-card got under way, and the crowd was buzzing by the time the main event was upon them. Also on the bill this night was Ron Redrup, Lewis Bentley, Steve

Richards, Eddie Garner, Peter Cain, Brian Hudson, Joe Lazarus, Mickey May and Patsy Gutteridge.

McLean was still confident he was going to take Shaw easily. Before the bout was set to start, Lenny had been given a pair of gloves by Joey Pyle which kept opening. It wasn't so much the size of the gloves, it was the size of Lenny's hands. Now, with the fight minutes away, there wasn't much Lenny could do. He couldn't pull out, as it would have looked like he was bottling it.

Lenny's music then started playing and he and Johnny Wall ran down to the ring. Lenny was shadow boxing in the ring while talking to Johnny. Roy Shaw's music then started blaring out, and the crowd started cheering. The crowd, by now, are going crazy as Shaw makes his way into the ring. A gap opens up like there's a rhino coming through.

Lenny's still talking to Johnny and shadow boxing as Shaw gets into the ring. Shaw's entrance would have scared most normal men half to death, but Lenny wasn't one to be intimidated so easily. Ex-boxer turned stuntman Nosher Powell introduced both men to the crowd. The atmosphere, by now, was amazing, you could cut it with a knife. After months of waiting, the fight was finally about to begin.

The bell goes and both men go straight to the middle of the ring, trying to take each other's head off. Lenny then starts to showboat and Roy hits him with a cracking body shot. Lenny's still laughing and shouting remarks out to the crowd. Shaw is now going to work on Lenny's body flat out. Lenny tries his best to jab at Shaw, but Shaw keeps getting under it and keeps working to the body.

The pace of the fight was non-stop in the first round. Lenny's attitude had now changed a little, he could see he was in for a fight unlike any other. Lenny had looked zapped going back to his corner. Shaw was still looking good and very confident.

The bell went for the second round and Shaw was straight into Lenny, pushing him into a corner. Lenny tried his best to get out, but Shaw knew how to use his weight and kept Lenny on the ropes. Shaw had now started to go to the head and chin, as well as the body. Lenny looked drained and could hardly throw a punch. He still had a bit of energy to keep winding Shaw up, though. The bell then went for the end of the round and, by now, both men were on their last legs. Shaw had worn himself out by throwing so many punches.

Again, though, Shaw had gathered some energy in between rounds and went straight at Lenny again in Round Three. Shaw cornered Lenny again, and hit him straight on the chin with an uppercut; Shaw had taken many a man out before him with this punch, but yet again, Lenny didn't budge. By now, Lenny was bleeding and his legs were no longer with him. He'd throw a punch back here and there, but with no power. Shaw then caught Lenny with a couple of combinations, rocking him back on to the ropes. Lenny, although sensing defeat, still found time to smile at Shaw and call him on. A final outburst of punches from Shaw again saw Lenny landing up against the ropes. Shaw then landed a big right hand straight into Lenny's face and the referee finally stepped in to stop the fight. Shaw's hand was raised in victory.

This was the first fight Lenny had ever lost. Lenny was gutted as the Shaw camp celebrated. Lenny had to go home without a penny – the loser got nothing. Lenny then told Joey Pyle to sort out a rematch as soon as he could.

Lenny went home that night absolutely gutted – he knew

he wasn't fit and he had underestimated Shaw. The defeat had finally woken Lenny up to the boxing ring and he knew he had to start training properly. Under the guidance of Freddie Hill and the professional boxer Kevin Finnegan, and the likes of other unlicensed boxers such as Steve 'Columbo' Richards, Lenny became a changed man. He was now starting to look like a boxer. Training every day and regular runs around Victoria Park was what was needed to pull off a win against the still unbeaten Shaw. Lenny had also told his cousin Bobby Warren to go and sort a rematch out with Joey Pyle and Alex Steene, who were Shaw's promoters.

It was at the Alexandra Palace on 25 August 1977, where Roy Shaw had just beaten the American Ron Stander, that Lenny got in the ring and made the challenge. Wearing a black suit and looking immaculate, he jumped between the ropes and, within seconds, was congratulating Roy and shaking his hand; he then challenged Shaw to a rematch. Roy was now on the verge of retiring and had told a few newspapers that Stander had been his last fight. Lenny carried on challenging Shaw and, in the end, Shaw agreed to a rematch. This was the fight every unlicensed fan in London at the time wanted to see.

Lenny had now upped his training for the return; he wanted Shaw's title. He wanted to become the Guv'nor. Roy Shaw, however, hadn't taken the rematch seriously – perhaps he felt he could handle Lenny the same way he had in their first fight. Shaw hadn't upped his training and even admitted himself he had become lazy; he didn't need the money and he really didn't need the fight, he had nothing to prove. He had beaten Lenny once, but he still took the fight knowing Lenny had come on in leaps and bounds.

A lot of people at the time thought Lenny was just too big and strong for him, but Shaw was still unbeaten and he still had it at the back of his mind that he had beaten Lenny once. People started betting all over London with a lot of the money going on Shaw to take the fight again after the performance he had given in the first contest.

Finally, the rematch was set for 10 April 1978 at Cinatra's nightclub in Croydon. The night had been organised by E Hamid in aid of The Freddie Mills Boys Club for Handicapped Children. Joe Pyle and Alex Steene had been flying the tickets out and over 2,000 people had turned up to watch the event.

The under-card had kicked off at 8.00pm with such fighters as Steve 'Columbo' Richards, Patsy Gutteridge, Danny Chippendale and various others. The atmosphere was building up throughout the night. Lenny's music then starts playing and he makes his way down to the ring. Dressed in his white gown, Lenny looked really calm and ready to fight. Shaw's music then starts and he runs down to the ring being led by Alex Steene. As Shaw's about to enter the ring, he stumbles over twice. He then gets into the ring and starts running around, punching his hand in the air. Then there's a bit of a ceremony in the ring with plaques being presented to other people.

Roy gets asked by a cameraman, 'Why do they call you The Mean Machine?' to which Roy replies, 'Because I'm mean.' Lenny takes off his gown and starts doing muscle poses at the audience. The ring is then cleared and Nosher Powell announces both men to the crowd. The bell goes and Lenny takes the centre of the ring while Shaw moves around him. Lenny keeps Shaw off with some fast, sharp jabs. Shaw starts throwing big hooks, trying to take Lenny's head off. Lenny back-pedals and counters Shaw with jabs. Shaw starts throwing straight punches to Lenny's body, but Lenny has himself tucked up. Shaw then goes at Lenny and throws a double left hook, but Lenny beats him to the punch and hits Shaw with a fast, solid right hook, followed by a combination of punches.

Shaw goes flying back on to the ropes and Lenny hits him with another onslaught of punches, dropping Shaw to the floor. Lenny then drops to his knees on top of Shaw and starts smashing him in the face with his right hand. The referee finally pulls Lenny off Shaw. Lenny tries stamping on Shaw but misses as he's pulled off.

A couple of corner men jump in the ring to try and calm Lenny down. Shaw gets up and wobbles back to his corner, looking dazed but with his hands still up. Joe Carrington's in the ring going nuts at Lenny. The ring is filling up again with officials and corner men trying to calm Lenny down. The ring then clears and both boxers go at each other again. Lenny then hits a dazed Shaw with a combination of punches again. Shaw keeps coming forward taking everything. Lenny then catches Shaw with another three right hooks to the back of the head, dropping him again. The referee jumps in and pushes Lenny off.

A couple of officials are holding Lenny back again as he's trying to get at Shaw. Shaw gets up again; Lenny pushes the officials and the referee out of the way and goes at Shaw again. Shaw starts throwing a few punches back, but Lenny holds his head down as he hooks him. The referee then steps in to finish the round. Lenny stands up in his corner sucking air in. Joe Pyle looks on a bit shocked that Shaw's been knocked down and at what he's just witnessed.

A half-naked ring girl enters the ring to show the crowd the sign to start Round Two. Both men go at each other again. Shaw comes out with a jab that seems to shake Lenny a little bit. Shaw tries pushing Lenny on to the ropes and hits him with a few body shots. Lenny pushes him off and hits him with a few hooks. By now, both men are getting tired. Shaw keeps coming forward, but the zap has now been taken out of him from that first big right hook. Lenny keeps Shaw on the end of his jab. Shaw then comes forward again and walks straight on to a full left hook, followed by a big right hook and another two solid punches straight on the chin. Shaw goes flying backwards in between the second and third rope and lands on the timekeeper's table.

Lenny looks on as a couple of people in the front row catch him. Lenny then starts jumping up and down celebrating. Joe Carrington and a few others get Shaw up to his corner and try and calm him down. Shaw still wanted to fight and didn't know what had happened, as Nosher Powell announced the winner. Lenny and his camp continue celebrating their victory.

A couple of months after the fight, Shaw goes on TV and blames his loss on an overdose of ginseng liquid. Lenny, who was also on the programme, responds with, 'He's talking about, he took this, and he took that. I don't care what he took, the only thing he took was a right-hander, and he ended up in the second row.'

After winning the rematch, Lenny was buzzing. A fight was then set up at the Rainbow Theatre in Finsbury Park with a doorman named Solli Francis. Francis had recently got stabbed and wasn't right going into the fight, but Lenny showed no mercy and won easily, stopping Solli in the first round. A challenge was then made from an ex-pro boxer named Cliff Fields from Dunstable. Fields had won the ABA championship when he'd been in the Navy; he then turned pro and won the Southern Area title, and he had also fought Richard Dunn for the British Heavyweight title.

Fields, who had earned the nickname 'Iron Man', was a mountain of a man who had left the pro game because he used to cut easily. Cliff then starts shouting loads of abuse at Lenny. Now, I don't know if Lenny had known about Cliff's past record, but, being Lenny, he accepted the fight straight away.

In the meantime, the final decider in the Shaw v McLean saga was lined up for 11 September 1978 at the Rainbow Theatre in Finsbury Park. Posters were put up everywhere advertising the fight as 'The Close Encounter for a Third Time for the Unofficial Heavyweight Championship of Great Britain'. Lenny was now advertised as 'Lennie "Boy" McLean, The Coolest Daddy of Them All'. Ringside tickets had been selling for £12.50 and the fight was in aid of Children's Muscular Dystrophy and Autistic Children. It was said that there was over £100,000 placed on side-bets.

Another sell-out show with over 3,000 spectators rammed into the building for the final deciding battle, and who was going to be the referee, none other than the man Lenny was to fight next, Cliffy Fields. Cliff was to referee the bout and then take on the winner himself.

The fight was scheduled for ten three-minute rounds, but Lenny had different things in mind for Shaw. The under-card had again kicked off at 8.00pm, featuring such fighters as Steve 'Columbo' Richards, little Danny Chippendale, Tommy Adams, Micky May and a few others. Both men had trained like hell for this deciding fight to settle, once and for all, who was to become the Guv'nor.

Roy Shaw was pacing up and down in his changing room hyping himself up, while Lenny was just sitting down looking relaxed as if nothing was happening. Camera crews were sticking their noses in for the slightest opportunity to film both men before they came to the ring. Both men then said a few words for the camera. A confident Shaw looked at one cameraman and says, 'Put that on tape – McLean's a poof.'

Shaw and his entourage then get the nod and they make their way down the stairs to the back area. Shaw's music starts blaring from the loudspeaker and Shaw makes his way to the ring looking really confident.

He enters the ring with his hand punching the air to Gary Glitter's 'Leader of the Pack' anthem. Shaw, with his knee heavily bandaged from an injury, continues to circle the ring.

Cliff Fields looks on from the corner of the ring waiting for Lenny to enter. Lenny's music then starts playing and the crowd goes nuts. Lenny starts running down the aisle punching the air. He is led into the ring, followed by Bobby Warren. Lenny enters the ring and starts showboating to the crowd. The ring is packed with officials, cameramen and all the corner men. After a couple of minutes, both men are announced to standing ovations. The ring starts to clear and the bell rings for the start of Round One.

Both men go at each other flat out and both throw a left hook at the same time. Shaw keeps coming forward throwing hooks at Lenny. Lenny starts back-pedalling and throws hooks and jabs back at Shaw. Both men, by now, are throwing knock-out punches and just soaking the shots up. Lenny, having the size over Shaw, starts holding Shaw's head down while throwing some little uppercuts at him. Shaw keeps going to the body as Lenny holds him down. But Lenny has Shaw tucked in really close, so Shaw can't get much power into his punches. The referee continues to let Lenny hold Shaw's head down. Shaw then manages to get Lenny up against the ropes while both men exchange punches. Fields finally steps in to break both men up, and tells them to continue boxing.

Shaw throws a big straight right, missing Lenny completely. As he misses, Lenny catches Shaw with a sharp right hook, snapping Shaw's neck round. Most men would have been put away with that punch, but Shaw was a breed apart. Shaw stumbles forward, a bit dazed, and now Lenny can see an opening and starts bombarding Shaw with hooks and punches from all sorts of angles. Shaw tries his best to hold on to Lenny, to regain some of his senses, but Lenny's punches are too powerful and Shaw can't keep him off. Lenny, by now, is catching Shaw with every punch he throws. After another onslaught of unanswered punches, Shaw starts to go, and Lenny then finishes him with three solid right hooks. Fields steps in and pushes Lenny away as Shaw hits the floor. Lenny's corner men are now sensing a win, and are going nuts, yelling Lenny on. Lenny's trying to get at Shaw but Fields keeps pushing him back.

Next thing you know, Shaw's back up on his feet – the crowd can't believe what they are seeing. The referee, Fields, for some strange reason, gives Shaw just a three count and asks him, 'Do you want to continue?' The fight should have been stopped by now as Shaw was unsteady on his feet and could hardly stand, but Shaw nods at Fields and the fight continues. Lenny goes straight back at Shaw, hitting him with a solid jab. Shaw goes flying back and Lenny starts throwing big hooks again, nearly all of them landing right on the button. Shaw still refuses to go down again. Lenny then goes for one last onslaught, catching Shaw with a couple of big right hooks. After spinning Shaw's head, Lenny catches Shaw with one final punch to the side of the head, dropping him to the floor. Fields rushes in and pushes Lenny off Shaw in case he was going to do anything stupid. Lenny then starts celebrating and showboating around the ring.

Lenny's corner man helps a few others to lift Shaw off the floor. Lenny starts shouting at the crowd, 'I'm the Guv'nor...' By now, Shaw's corner man, Joe Carrington, is trying to calm him down as he doesn't know what's happened. Lenny then starts shouting again, 'Who's the Guv'nor?' as the crowd are now chanting Lenny's name. Fields looks on calmly, knowing he has to face Lenny next in a few months' time. Lenny continues to carry on showboating as Shaw leaves the ring. The McLean camp are over the moon as Lenny finally leaves the ring. Lenny had finally become the Guv'nor.

The challenges now started coming from everywhere. Lenny, who was now 27 years old, had loved every minute of his victory. The McLean camp had made Lenny open to all challengers, even offering John L Gardner, who was the new BBB Champion, a bout for which he would have received £20,000 win, lose or draw, but nothing ever came of it. Then Lenny bit off a bit more than he could chew as he had agreed to fight the ex-pro boxer Cliffy Fields at the Rainbow Theatre in Finsbury Park.

A lot of Lenny's relatives and close friends advised Lenny not to fight Cliffy, but Lenny loved a challenge and the fight was set for 4 December 1978. It was in aid of Children's Muscular Dystrophy and Autistic Children. The under-card had again kicked off with fighters like Johnny McDade, Stevie Elwood, Johnny Ricky, Terry Scrutton, Ralph Harris, Seymour

Elwood, Tommy Adams, Bobby Goldsmith, David Young and Alfie Smith. Lenny weighed in on the night at around 15 stone 5 pounds. Fields weighed in a lot heavier. A couple of days earlier, Lenny had come down with the 'flu and couldn't get rid of it. It was too late to pull out at this stage, so Lenny went ahead with the fight.

On the night, the music starts blaring and Lenny enters the ring to 'Daddy Cool' by The Darts. Fields then enters the ring to 'Jungle Rocker' by Hank Marzell. The referee was another ex-boxer named Danny Fontalio.

Lenny goes at Fields from the opening bell and gives his all, trying to take him out. The experienced Fields soaks everything up and, by this time, Lenny has punched himself out; Fields then begins to open up. A combination of punches ends up putting McLean on the floor and Fields claiming a victory. A lot of the people in the crowd couldn't believe that Lenny had lost to Fields. Before leaving the changing room that night, Lenny went and congratulated Fields.

Lenny and his camp then started doing a bit of business with Joey Pyle and Alex Steene. Lenny got offered a fight with a bloke by the name of Paul Sykes from Wakefield. Now, Sykes was a good, strong boxer who had spent some time inside. So Lenny and his camp went to check out Sykes fighting in a bout at Wembley Arena. Sykes lost the bout and, before you knew it, a deal had been set up for a fight on 29 November 1979 at the Rainbow Theatre in Finsbury Park.

Posters were put up everywhere and tickets started selling like hot cakes and everyone started calling it the 'Bout of the Century'. Lenny started training really hard, as he knew he was going to be in for one hell of a fight. Both boxers were almost exactly the same height and weight and age.

With the fight nearly upon them, Paul Sykes ended up going out drinking and fighting with a few bouncers. How seriously Sykes was taking the fight nobody knows, as you'd never see a boxer out a couple of days before a fight. Perhaps this was just an excuse, as he wasn't ready for the fight, but Sykes told Alex Steene and Joey Pyle the fight was off, as he sustained a serious cut fighting bouncers in a nightclub.

Joe Pyle and his partner Brian Emmet then set up a fight between Lenny and 'Psycho' Dave Spellen. Posters were put up everywhere advertising it as 'The Fight That's a Must'. With not long to go, Spellen pulled out with a broken hand and Lenny wasn't very happy.

So in stepped another boxer named Johnny Waldron at the last minute. The fight was at The Cat's Whiskers in Streatham. Lenny had got over confident in the fight, stuck his chin out and said, 'Come on, put it here.' Johnny hit him and, a few punches later, Lenny was knocked down. Cliff Fields had now entered the ring and was making challenges as Lenny was coming round. Lenny then started losing it and rushed at Fields and whoever else was in the ring, throwing punches.

A fight was set up with Portsmouth hard man Kevin Paddock. Paddock had come from a family of fighters. Lenny had gone at Paddock like a bull but Paddock was a very good defensive fighter. Paddock tucked himself up well and took all that Lenny hit him with. Lenny ended up punching himself out and Paddock started jabbing his head off and taking the fight on points – it was a rather quiet affair by Lenny's standards. Lenny thought he had done just enough to win the fight, and got a bit of a shock when the referee raised Paddock's arm. A rematch was lined up, but never came off.

Lenny's comeback fight after the loss to Paddock was set up

with the experienced and hard-hitting Johnny Clarke from Streatham. Reg Chapman Promotions had put a six-fight bill on at the Mayfair Rooms in Tottenham. Also on the bill were boxers such as Steve Conway, Terry Johnson, Terry Scrutton, Patsy Russell, Donny Carter, Paul McCormack, Speed Mack, John Dane, Lenny's cousin Johnny Wall and the unlicensed fighter Roy York. Roy went on to referee the McLean v Bradshaw fight a couple of years later, and Roy's younger brother, 'Man Mountain' Dave York, would also end up fighting Lenny. Lenny's fight was set for ten three-minute rounds. Both men weighed nearly 16 stone on the night of the fight and the referee was Donny Adams.

It was another sold-out show, rammed to the rafters. Clarke had entered the ring in a red robe to Status Quo's 'Rocking All Over the World'. He started shadow boxing in the middle of the ring. Lenny's music then came blaring through the loudspeaker and Lenny came running down through the crowd in a white robe with his hood up.

Unlicensed fighter Steve Columbo led Lenny into the ring. A fan appeared out of nowhere and jumped in Lenny's way, nearly blocking his path. Lenny just ignored him, concentrating on the fight ahead of him. Lenny got into the ring and went straight at Clarke, trying to intimidate him. The MC for the night stepped in and pushed Lenny back. Lenny ripped his robe off and threw it. The place by now is buzzing and the atmosphere is electric. Lenny then starts walking around the ring, punching his gloves, psyching himself up. Lenny tries going at Clarke again and Columbo jumps in Lenny's way and pushes him back. Lenny starts doing full-frontal muscle poses and tries to go at Clarke again. Yet again, Columbo gets in the way. By now, Lenny is really playing up to the crowd with muscle poses. The MC announces Lenny and he walks to the middle of the ring with his hands in the air. Clarke is then announced to the crowd, who are still cheering Lenny.

Both men go at each other from the bell, and Clarke starts jabbing and moving around as Lenny walks forward through his punches. Lenny moves back and forth, dodging Clarke's punches. Both men start throwing big hooks as well as combinations of punches at each other. Lenny keeps coming forward, chasing Clarke, until Clarke holds on to him. Lenny then goes flying forward with big hooks and finally drops Clarke to the canvas with a right hook to the body. Donny Adams pulls Lenny off as he smashes Clarke on the floor. Clarke shoots back up off the floor in seconds. The crowd are now yelling Lenny on. Both men exchange big hooks until the bell goes for the end of the round. Clarke walks back to his corner with his hands held high, trying to wind Lenny up.

The bell goes for Round Two and both men go at each other flat out for a while. Lenny then backs into the ropes as Clarke starts throwing big hooks. Clarke now has Lenny in the corner and both men start throwing big hooks and uppercuts. Lenny's ducking and weaving, and spots an opening; he then throws a peach of a right uppercut, catching Clarke straight on the chin. Clarke hits the floor like he's been shot with a gun and ends up sprawled across the canvas. Lenny steps over him as the referee starts counting to ten. Lenny starts taking his gum shield out as he heads back to his corner, knowing that Clarke didn't have a chance of getting back up.

Clarke's corner men run in and take his gum shield out as Lenny's celebrating in the ring. Lenny's son and his friend run into the ring and start hugging Lenny. Lenny then starts celebrating and posing for the crowd. Another boxer enters the ring in a robe and starts hugging Lenny. By now, Clarke's corner men start lifting him off the floor and Lenny goes over and hugs him. Lenny then continues to celebrate as his music starts blaring again.

Also along the way, Lenny fought Ron Redrup. Redrup was by now past his best and was a lot smaller than Lenny. Redrup had over 60 fights and hadn't lost many; he was also a former ABA champion. Lenny entered the ring as confident as ever with his blue-and-yellow shorts. A camera crew were also there and Lenny played up to the cameras, showboating and winding them up. Lenny went at Redrup from the bell like a bull in a china shop. Redrup couldn't handle the big hooks and uppercuts from Lenny and he held on for his life throughout the fight. The fight was stopped after a few rounds with Redrup being cut open.

Lenny then turned up at the Ilford Palais where Roy Shaw was fighting Lou 'Wild Thing' Yates. The venue was crammed yet again. Shaw had taken Yates apart and stopped him in the third round. As Shaw's celebrating, the challenges start to appear. Kevin Paddock gets in the ring and Shaw accepts the challenge. Lenny then starts going down through the crowd, pushing people and chucking chairs out of his way. He enters the ring and everyone surrounds him as he's shouting abuse at Shaw.

Why Lenny wanted another go at Shaw, I don't know, as he had already beaten him twice by then. Perhaps he was just staying in the spotlight. Lenny then got out of the ring and a lot of people were booing him as he made his way out of the building. Shaw went in various magazines saying that, once he'd taken care of Paddock in his next fight, then he would take care of McLean. Yet again, why that fight didn't come off, I don't know, as Shaw retired in his next bout against Paddock.

In what was to be Roy Shaw's last fight, on 24 November 1981 at the Ilford Palais, he fought an eight-round bout against Kevin Paddock. The referee was ex-pro boxer Jimmy Tippet. Lenny watched as Paddock took everything Shaw had to give him. Roy had won the fight very easily, taking every round. Before the celebrating had begun, Lenny, dressed in a brown suede jacket, climbed through the ropes and was one of the first to congratulate Roy with a hug. This was a fighter's respect and Roy returned the gesture. Lou Yates was then called into the ring and a challenge was set up between him and McLean. Lenny shook Yates's hand and then turned to walk off, but, before he left the ring, he gave the crowd a quick show of shadow boxing. Lenny grabbed the microphone and said to the crowd, 'I'm going to knock him out in two rounds.' Roy was then left to carry on celebrating his win with the music blaring. Roy never fought again, for some reason, and Lenny's fight with Yates never came off either.

Roy and Lenny continued meeting at various boxing shows with both men wanting to get it on again. Roy went on *The Garry Bushell Show* years later and said that he had thrown the second fight. Roy said to Garry, 'Who's going to back McLean? I'd already done him easy once in three rounds, no one's going to put their money on him. So I put my purse money on him and I went over.'

Whether this was true or just an excuse, only Roy could answer. I personally don't think that someone with Roy's reputation, and being undefeated, would have thrown a fight, especially to someone he was supposed to have hated so much.

In the same show, Shaw challenged Lenny to another fight yet again. Garry then told the viewers that he had phoned Lenny and told him that Shaw had made a challenge to him again and Lenny had said, 'Can you point it out to your viewers that I beat Roy in 18 seconds last time, and that I am ready for a rematch.'

Unfortunately, the fight nearly all of London would have paid twice to see never came off.

Rumours were also circulating that Lenny was going to fight a couple of northern hard men. A fight was supposed to have been set up with Lee Duffy, but never came off; a fight was also being lined up with Viv Graham, but rumours have it that Graham had seen a video of Lenny fighting and didn't want to know.

Then, on 15 April 1986, Lenny was involved in one of the most talked-about moments in unlicensed boxing. A bloke named Reggie Parker, who had boxed unlicensed himself in the past, had staged an unlicensed show at the Yorkshire Grey pub in Eltham. Posters were put up everywhere advertising it as 'The Street Fight of the Year'. The cameras were filming for documentaries and Lenny was to fight a bloke named Bryan Bradshaw, nicknamed the 'Mad Gypsy', at the top of the bill.

Lenny was topping the three-bout show, as well as other boxers like Gary Heart, Del Boy Paul and Rocky Kelly. Lenny arrived at the pub in a red jumper and black leather jacket, telling the cameramen that he was going to knock Bradshaw out and that he was going to smash his head in. People like Harry Starbuck were turning up to watch. Lenny then told the door staff to give him a good search just to wind him up for a laugh. Roy Shaw turned up but Lenny told the door staff that he didn't want him there and they refused him entrance. Shaw stayed outside, not looking very happy for a while in his Land Rover.

Bradshaw, a scrap dealer who only had about six fights and was unbeaten, entered the ring first. The place was now buzzing with excitement as 500 fight fans paying up to £15 a ticket yelled and screamed as Lenny entered the ring.

Lenny walks around the ring and you could see in his eyes that he was on a mission. Lenny walks up to Bradshaw and squats down and starts growling at him with the veins popping out of his neck. Lenny walks off looking like he's about to explode at any minute.

Both men are called to the centre of the ring by ex-unlicensed fighter, now turned referee, Roy York. York starts telling them a few rules and then tells them to shake hands. Bradshaw, not being put off by any of Lenny's growling earlier, sticks a headbutt into Lenny as Lenny's looking at the floor. Lenny goes flying back; he then touches his head with his glove to see if he's bleeding. Reg Parker rings the bell to start the fight. Lenny walks back to Bradshaw, cool as a cucumber, nodding to himself that Bradshaw is going to have it. As Bradshaw comes out of his corner, Lenny catches him with a full-on right hook to the side of the head. Before Lenny can follow it with another punch, Bradshaw has hit the deck. Lenny, by now in a raging temper, stamps right on Bradshaw's head. He then goes down and hits him with a right hook to the face, smashing Bradshaw's head to the canvas once again.

The referee looks on, wondering what to do. Lenny, by now, has lost it completely and is in a full-on rage and is going to be hard to stop. The referee finally tries to make his way in to pull Lenny off. One of Bradshaw's corner men now enters the ring, too. Lenny then lifts Bradshaw's head up off the floor with his left hand and starts smashing right hooks into his face.

By now, Lenny's own corner man, Nick Netley, has got into the ring as well. Lenny has another rage and pushes them all off, and kicks Bradshaw full in the face, finally knocking him out cold. The referee and the other corner men then grab around Lenny and pull him back. Bradshaw's body now lies there motionless as Lenny shrugs everybody off him and goes at him again.

The crowd are looking on gobsmacked at what they are witnessing; another two stamps and a kick to the face before Nick Netley finally goes down low and bundles Lenny to the ropes. Another of Lenny's other corner men, and even Reg Parker, run into the ring and jump on Lenny, finally calming the madman down.

Bradshaw's corner man puts Bradshaw on to his side and the referee helps to pull his tongue out. Lenny continues to celebrate and leaves the ring with Bradshaw still being taken care of.

After Lenny and his entourage had left the building, the cameramen caught up with Bradshaw, but he refused to comment. The fight was big news, appearing all over TV programmes, including the *News at Ten*, supposedly to show the dangers of unlicensed boxing.

But that couple of seconds of film brought Lenny into the spotlight and people have not stopped talking about it since. Lenny continued to tick over in training and a lot of questions were asked about that fight. Word was getting round to those who didn't know that Lenny was an absolute maniac.

Lenny continued to work on the doors and did some debt collecting in the days as well, although he was thinking about calling it a day and concentrating on a TV career. Then he got a chance to top the bill again fighting a bloke named David York from Tottenham who had earned the nickname 'Man Mountain York'. York was 24 years of age and about 23 stone with the height of a basketball player. Dave's brother, Roy York, had been the referee in Len's last fight against Bradshaw and was in Dave's corner for this fight.

Posters were put about everywhere with York saying, 'Lenny has had his day.' McLean followed this with: 'May God have mercy on his soul.' Lenny's good mate Kenny Mac had organised the show and the date was set for 7 September 1986 at Woodford Town Football Club in Essex. The show was in aid of the Lord's Taverners Coaches for Handicapped Children. The day kicked off at about one o'clock with the first bout and the weather was excellent. The day had gone really well and the crowd were now buzzing with anticipation for the main event.

York enters first and stands in his corner awaiting Lenny. Lenny then comes through the crowd and Lenny's corner man holds the ropes open for him to enter the ring. Lenny, looking like he's on a mission, has skin-tight white trousers on, looking like a fighter from the old days. Lenny strolls across the ring looking confident, as he gives the six-foot-seven York a stare. Lenny lifts his hands to the crowd as if he has won the fight already. He starts loosening up and starts shadow boxing, as the big giant of a man watches, not looking one bit intimidated.

The referee then calls both men to the middle of the ring and, before they can touch gloves, the bell has gone for the start of the round. Lenny takes the centre of the ring, as the bigger York moves around him. Lenny starts bobbing and weaving and then throws a big left hook. York pushes him off, but Lenny's back on him in a flash. York, now trapped in a corner, catches Lenny with a big one-two combination, and then he pushes Lenny away like he's a little boy. But Lenny only knows one way to fight and that's to come forward.

Lenny catches York with a big left hook again, and York moves quickly out of the corner and catches Lenny with a straight right to the face. York continues to throw punches but Lenny just walks through them. Lenny then backs York into a corner and slams about six body punches into him. York replies with a few hooks back at Lenny.

The crowd are by now at fever pitch as both men are giving their all. Lenny continues to chop away at the big man, who starts to cover up. Another straight right, followed by a couple of big left hooks on the button, and York looks like he's about to drop. The ropes hold him up as he fights back bravely. Lenny starts throwing uppercuts and body shots at York, but the big man's huge frame soaks them all up.

York, knowing he can't take much more of this onslaught, grabs around Lenny's neck and holds him down but Lenny manages to get his head out of the hold and he headbutts York straight in the face. York carries on holding Lenny and slams a head into Lenny himself. Lenny slams another back and by now it's like a game of tennis.

Both men are starting to tire. York then gets a second wind from somewhere and backs Lenny into a corner with a combination of punches. Both men start to wrestle and then York slams another head into Lenny. Both men keep exchanging combinations of hooks. Lenny slams another head into York as York leans on him. Lenny throws a sharp right hook landing on York's jaw, dropping him to his knees. As York's on his knees, Lenny drops down and smashes him in the stomach. York's now looking up at Lenny as Lenny's still trying to hit him.

A few corner men jump into the ring and raise Lenny's hand; for some strange reason, the fight is over. York wasn't offered a chance to get back up and fight, not that he probably wanted to. Perhaps his towel had been thrown in. Lenny then apologises to the referee for hitting York while he was on the floor. Lenny calms down a little and starts raising his arms up to the crowd signalling his win. York starts to get up off the floor looking a bit gutted, and sits down in his corner. Lenny makes a quick exit from the ring and disappears into the crowd.

I don't know if he knew this himself, or if all his fans had known this at the time, but this was to be Lenny's last time in the squared ring – and what a fight it was.

Lenny's reputation is unrivalled in the unlicensed scene, and there were many who wanted to express their admiration for what Lenny managed to achieve.

STEVE 'COLUMBO' RICHARDS

I liked the big man Lenny a lot, we got on really well. A giant of a man, we used to train together, sparring, etc. I remember Lenny coming to the gym after losing to Roy Shaw. I give him a right bollocking for losing and we trained really hard for the next fight together, sparring and pads, etc. I also fought on the same night Lenny went on to beat Shaw in their rematch.

CLIFF FIELDS

The first time I heard of the name Lenny McLean was when I was back living in Dunstable. I was drinking in the Eight Bells pub when the manager said to me, 'They got this bloke in London knocking everybody out and I'll give you £1,000 to fight him.' I was skint at the time and £1,000 was a lot of money back then, so I accepted the challenge.

In the meantime, I had been approached and asked to referee a re-match between Lenny and Roy Shaw, and then take on the winner. I accepted and refereed Lenny McLean and Roy Shaw in their third fight at the Rainbow Theatre.

I then went on to beat the winner of that fight – Lenny – on 4 December 1978 at the Rainbow Theatre. After the fight, I went back to the changing room and my brother Roger was there to congratulate me. Lenny comes in the changing room and says, 'Well done, fair dos, you fucking beat me,' and we shook hands. Lenny adds, 'I'll get you next time though…'

Lenny then asked me to come up and see him one night. So I took up his offer, went round his flat and met his wife. She was a lovely lady. His kids took a liking to me as well. I became good friends with Lenny, he even gave me two of his suits, fitted me perfect; he was a good man.

Lenny used to make me laugh a lot, he was a great friend of mine. The last time I seen Lenny was when I stayed at his house for a weekend back in 1981. I never heard much from him after that. He was good to me and good with me. I only witnessed a gent.

My old manager Johnny Stevens told me the news about Lenny just after he had passed away. John was the landlord of the Eight Bells pub, the pub I was in when I first heard the name Lenny McLean. Whenever he was in my company, he

The big man, psyched up and ready for action.

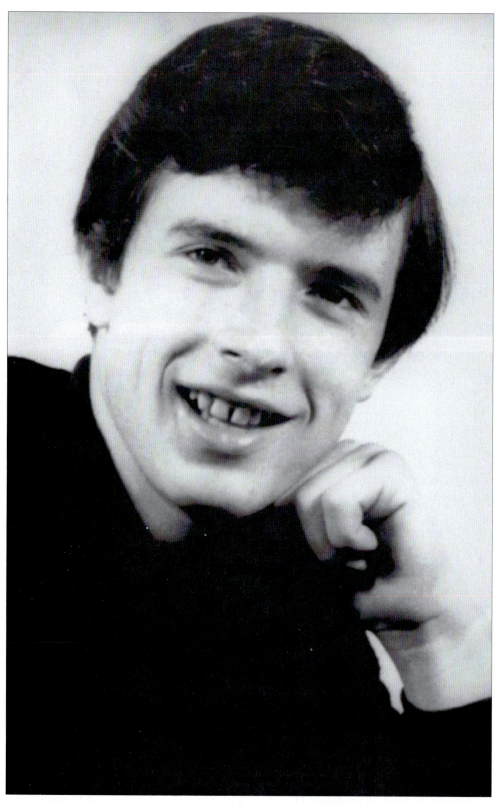

Alfie Hayes, who was best mates with Lenny from a young age.

BOXING

Sponsored by
GOLA SPORTS LIMITED
London Road, Bozeat,
nr. Wellingborough, Northants. NN9 7JS.

at the **RAINBOW THEATRE**
FINSBURY PARK, LONDON
on
Thursday 29th November 1979

Lennie
'Boy'
McLean
Hoxton

Tshaka
Islington

v

v

Paul Sykes
Wakefield

Doors Open
7.00pm

Programmes advertising
two of Lenny's bouts.

BOXING

at the
RAINBOW THEATRE
FINSBURY PARK, LONDON
on
Monday 4th December 1978

IN AID OF CHILDRENS MUSCULAR
DYSTROPHY & AUTISTIC CHILDREN

Lenny 'Boy' McLean
PLUS SUPPORTING BOUTS

Cliff Fields

Doors Open
7.00pm

Boxing Commences
8.00pm

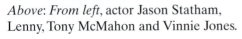

Above: *From left*, actor Jason Statham, Lenny, Tony McMahon and Vinnie Jones.

Below: Tony Dubens, who met Lenny while working on the doors.

Below right: Lenny with stunt man Dave Lea, with whom he wanted to work on *The Guv'nor* film.

Above: Len with Alfie Hayes at his pub, the Guv'ners.

Below: With Alfie and his sister Rose.

Above: Robbie Butler, who learned a lot from Lenny.

Below: Scott Mytton, enjoying a night at the Guv'ners.

was a gentleman. That's how I knew him, that's how I'll remember him.

Unlicensed fight promoter and boxing trainer Alan Mortlock met Lenny at a very young age. Alan also has his own autobiography out called *Meeting the Guv'nor*. I caught up with Alan on the phone and I explained to him that he had beaten me to it for the title for this book! We then had a good laugh about it and he explained to me what that title had meant in his book and that I should go out and get it. Alan still runs his own unlicensed shows around the UK and has his own website at www.ibaboxing.com. He is another member of the fight game on whom Lenny made a massive impression.

ALAN MORTLOCK

I had heard of the name Lenny McLean from a very young age. I have always been involved in the fight game and I started off by doing martial arts. I was then doing my own kickboxing shows. It was only later on in life that I got involved in the unlicensed fight game. I was first introduced to Lenny around the early Eighties.

I was training one day with my mate from South London. We had been for a run around Greenwich Park, and we had gone back to a gym in Greenwich called Slim Jim's. As me and my mate got back in the gym, they were weighing Lenny on these scales and he looked massive. He had a fight coming up in the next few weeks and he looked ripped and was full of muscles. He must have been at least 20 stone. Lenny then went and done a few rounds on this big leather bag. Someone asked my mate would he hold the bag for Lenny while Lenny let a few big hits go into it. My mate accepted and we just watched Lenny smashing this bag. The next thing you know, Lenny's hit it with a cracking shot and the bag's come straight off the rafters, hitting the floor, and taking my mate with it. I'm sure my mate had the imprint of the bag on him. We all burst out laughing as Lenny looked on.

We all finished training and went for a shower. After that, about ten of us went into this tea area and we had a good chat. I remember it like it was yesterday and that memory of Lenny has always stuck at the back of my mind.

MIKE CLAYDEN

First of all, I must say that, apart from Anthony Thomas, I must be the only person in this book who hasn't met Lenny McLean, but in a strange way I feel I have.

Why? Well, back in the late Seventies I used to train in martial arts at a sports centre called The Old Gaol in Abingdon in Oxfordshire.

There, I met the bare-knuckle fighter Paddy Monaghan and had the privilege of watching him train with unlicensed boxers like the late Dave Pierce.

Back then, I had no idea that Paddy was actually fighting alongside Lenny McLean in illegal bare-knuckle bouts around the UK. This was all kept very quiet, away from the police and general public alike.

So, fast forward to 2005, and I find myself sitting with Anthony and Lenny's childhood friend Alfie Hayes in a pie and mash shop in Hoxton in the East End of London. Anthony had invited me to accompany him to an interview he was doing with Alfie for this book. Anthony and I had formed a friendship while exchanging emails and phone calls in regard to his website which is, of course, dedicated to Lenny McLean.

Anthony knew that I was seriously interested in the Guv'nor ever since I had read Lenny's autobiography, and seen his appearances in *The Knock*. I was bowled over by Lenny's huge screen presence and charisma, while the tales of his fighting exploits featured in his book thrilled and shocked me in equal measure.

That day I spent in the good company of Anthony and Alfie will remain with me for a very long time, I can tell you. Alfie gave a cracking interview to Anthony and a great deal of his precious time to us that day. He also very kindly took us on a guided tour around Hoxton and Bethnal Green, pointing out many places where he and Lenny had been together.

Alfie kept us laughing all day long with his East End sense of humour and little take-offs of Len's phrases and expressions.

His admiration for Lenny was very clear, and you could see he was enjoying rolling back the years as we all stood together outside Godwin House.

Later, Alfie took us into Bethnal Green and Valance Road where the home of the Krays had once stood. Finally, our tour came to an end and Alfie said his goodbyes as he dropped us off at Bethnal Green Station. Anthony and I made our way back home both happy with the interview and tour he had given.

It was with immense sadness that I learned from Anthony that Alfie had passed away a few months later. I found Alfie to be a great character and a true East Ender in every sense of the word. Rest in peace, Alfie, you made this Lenny McLean fan a very happy one.

Like Anthony, when word gets round that you are a fan, all

kinds of people start to come out of the woodwork and that's when Lady Luck plays her part.

For years, I had heard rumours of a Lenny McLean video that featured rare footage of Lenny sparring and training at Kenny Mac's car lot. I made it known that I was interested in getting hold of this video, knowing that the chances were very slim of hearing anything positive. Then, one morning, I came down the stairs to find on the doormat a brown Jiffy bag postmarked 'London'. Inside was an unlabelled video cassette with a note which read, 'From a friend… enjoy.'

Bloody porno, I thought, as I slid the cassette into the video recorder and waited, intrigued at what it was all about.

Suddenly, there was a bearded Lenny McLean looking absolutely huge in a dressing room surrounded by his entourage. This, I knew, was something special – a big lad in a white T-shirt egging on Lenny with, 'He's shitting himself out there, Lenny… bash his fuckin' brains out.' Lenny then says who he wants to go in front of him as he is led out.

As big Lenny moves into the corridor, he can hardly get through the changing-room door because his sheer size fills it. I realised then that what I was watching was the build-up to Lenny's fight with 'Man Mountain York' at Woodford football ground. Ever the showman, the Guv'nor growls that his record is not playing and won't go on 'til it is. The video then cuts to colour footage of Lenny fighting York, actually shot at ringside. Until then, all I had seen was some grainy black-and-white video shot a long way from the actual fight itself, but here you felt as if you were part of the action. Lenny slams into York with body punches and uppercuts and, later, his notorious headbutts.

Soon the fight is over with Lenny landing a blow to York's

abdomen that bends him double as he topples over on to the floor. Lenny tries again to hit the prone York, but is stopped by the ref.

The camera cuts again to the dressing room as a victorious Lenny leans heavily on an aide and talks about the fight to everyone in the room.

The video fuzzed over for a few seconds and then there was footage of Len's fight with John Clarke held at the Rainbow Theatre. But, again, there was a surprise in store, for I had only ever seen an edited version of the two-rounder before. Here, it was in its full glory as the Guv'nor battered Clarke around the ring until finishing him off in the second with an astonishing uppercut which knocked Clarke spark out.

Just when I thought I had seen it all, the video fuzzed over again and then cleared to reveal Lenny McLean standing with his trainer Kenny Mac in his car lot in Kingsland Road, London.

Bloody hell! I thought. 'I've hit the jackpot. It was the footage I had heard rumours about for years.

It was around 1982, when Lenny McLean was training with his cousin Johnny Wall, also a very good boxer, for an upcoming fight with Johnny Waldron. Wall was to be Len's sparring partner and, as the video footage unfolded before my eyes, it showed a sparring match that was extraordinary. Between runs round Victoria Park and pounding the heavy bags in Kenny's barn, the sparring amounts to about 15 rounds. Kenny's yard consists of a 'boxing ring' with ropes tied to four tall gas bottles on each corner. The lorries parked at the front of the forecourt are positioned to hide the spectacle going behind them from the main road. To the left of the ring is Kenny's office and to the right is a large corrugated barn in which the punching bags hang. Around the 'ring' sit a few spectators and corner men.

Lenny McLean is wearing a maroon, short-sleeved Lonsdale sweatshirt and tracksuit bottoms. His cousin Johnny Wall is wearing similar attire and a red headguard. Kenny Mac is struggling to get Len's massive hands into his boxing gloves, while Johnny stands to his right having Vaseline applied to his face.

John is a tall man, roughly the same height as Len, but a lot slimmer and not as muscular. His hair is long and fashionably permed for the era. Once the two men are ready, Kenny kicks the gas bottle – ding! – and the sparring starts.

At first, both men appear to take it nice and casual and, then, in Round Two, things start to warm up. Both Lenny and Johnny begin firing some good head shots off and Johnny shows some nifty footwork, but Lenny is not wearing a headguard and receives a cut above his left eye. Although he is aware of it, the sparring goes on 'til Kenny calls time. 'Let's have a look at that eye, Len,' says Kenny, and Lenny strolls over to him so he can take a look.

Third round and still Lenny is not wearing the headguard. Johnny unleashes several terrific blows to Len's face but the big fella doesn't even flinch and seems to soak it up. Lenny then slams some of the hardest body shots I have ever seen into the right side of Johnny's abdomen, knocking him around the ring as he does so. You can clearly hear the whoosh of air being banged out of Johnny's lungs by these huge, powerful blows. Suddenly, Johnny shouts, 'Your eye, your eye!' and the fight is stopped.

The cut above Len's eye has begun to bleed, so, after a quick clean-up, Kenny fetches Len a black headguard.

Round Four kicks off, but Lenny finds the headgear is slipping off and complains to Kenny that he can't see, so the fight is stopped again to tighten the straps up. By now, four boys of about 12 years old have wandered into the yard. The red-haired boy is Lenny's son, and he's with his mates.

'All right, Dad,' he says. 'Yeah, hello, son,' Lenny replies as he gets ready for the fifth round of sparring. This time, the headgear stays on and the two men really begin to go at it, exchanging furious punches, and all the time Lenny keeps on coming forward, head down but never flinching.

The seventh round is similar to the sixth, only Lenny has taken the decision not to wear the guard as it pisses him off. At the end of the round, Johnny walks over to the cameraman with Kenny, while Lenny gargles some water.

Kenny asks, 'What do you think of Lenny, John?' and he replies, 'He's a fucking hard bastard!' and nods gravely to himself.

It's clear from this remark that he means it, as he can't believe that Lenny seems to be able to soak up so much punishment and still keep on coming. While Len's son and his mates fool about, everyone agrees to a tea break and they go into Kenny's office.

Lenny fools about with a pair of glasses while putting on a posh accent making everyone laugh. Lenny sits behind a desk and looks up at the camera. 'Have you got that camera on me?' 'Yeah,' says the cameraman laughing to himself, 'I've had it on you all the time.'

Much lively banter is passed around the room and then Kenny announces that Lenny and Johnny are going over to Victoria Park for a run and some exercise. We are then treated to a shot of Lenny and Johnny running around the perimeter of Victoria Park together. Kenny is following them on a bicycle, pedalling like mad to keep up. The cameraman is shooting in front of them from an open-top car as Len and Johnny come running beside the car. Someone says that Lenny looks like the Bionic Man and calls out to him, asking how he feels. 'Feel good, but didn't sleep 'til late last night thinking about the fight. Tell you what… I'll take him out in two,' he shouts back as he speeds on past the car.

Later, the two men exercise together while Kenny urges them on. Press-ups, sit-ups and stretches are the order of the day. Kenny Mac might have been portrayed in the past as a cheeky chappie, but, make no mistake, he's a hard taskmaster who wants the best out of them, and pushes the two to work harder.

The tape cuts again to Kenny's yard and this time Lenny appears to have changed into a black T-shirt and white shorts and is wearing a red headguard. Johnny Wall is also kitted out in similar attire.

Ding! Kenny kicks the gas bottle and shouts, 'Away you go,' and they start another fearsome round of sparring. Halfway through the round, Lenny smashes an uppercut into Johnny's jaw, lifting him off his feet and knocking his headgear off at the same time. Lenny bangs in another uppercut for good measure. 'Whoa, whoa,' cries Kenny. 'Slow down, Len, for fuck's sake.' If the rounds were consecutive, we would now be at Round Eleven and, out of the two of them, Johnny is looking tired.

Lenny belts John with a good punch, knocking his mouthguard out, and the fight is stopped for a few minutes.

The gloves come off and the two men saunter into the barn and start punching the heavy bags for a while. It's here you really appreciate the power behind Lenny's punches, as every time the bag is hit it swings up almost horizontal with the ceiling.

All the time, Kenny is timing the workout on his watch until he calls time and the two go back to the last rounds of sparring for the day.

This time, Johnny really tries his best to knock Lenny's head off, but the man is immovable and, at one point, drops his arms and lets Johnny hit him with three good ones directly to his head.

Lenny laughs wickedly, sensing Johnny's frustration in not being able to put him down. The fighting finally halts in what amounts to an amazing 15 rounds of solid, hard sparring between two very tough men.

The tape fuzzed over again and that was the end of it. I sat back and thought about what I had just seen. I still could not believe my eyes and still had no idea where the video had come from. Perhaps one day I will.

Lenny never won that fight with Johnny Waldron, despite training so hard for it. Technically, Waldron knew his ring craft and knew how Lenny operated as a boxer and, in doing so, had the upper hand.

Personally, this doesn't take anything away from Lenny McLean, as most people agree that Lenny was first and foremost a street fighter and a bare-knuckle boxer.

On the cobbles and with no gloves, Lenny was unstoppable but, in the ring, restricted by gloves and the Queensbury Rules, he sometimes failed against some very experienced boxers. His title – the Guv'nor – was earned because he fought anyone and everything life threw at him, and that's why he took that title with him to the grave.

4
Respect

If there was one thing Lenny achieved more than anything else, it was respect. It takes a lot to earn respect and it doesn't just happen overnight. But from a very young age, Lenny was well respected. Associating himself with different people from all sorts of circles, Lenny began gaining the respect of everyone, young and old. I travelled thousands of miles and met a few well-respected people to hear what they had to say.

The first person that I travelled to meet was Dave Courtney. After reading a few stories about Lenny in Dave's book *Stop the Ride, I Want to Get Off*, I managed to get hold of his mobile number and give him a ring. I told him about the website and that I was looking for a few stories for the book I was doing.

Dave started telling me about Lenny and himself. I then received an invitation to go up to his place and have a chat with him. So me, my brother Steve and my mate Julian left at four in the morning and arrived outside Courtney's house by breakfast. Courtney took us for breakfast in his Jag and started telling us a few stories about Lenny and places he used to go.

I met Courtney a few times after that and he always spoke very highly of Lenny. Then, after spending the weekend with Stellakis Stylianou doing interviews for this book, Stilks took me to Dave's house and he agreed to do a one-on-one interview with me. Dave looked well and had pulled himself back from the brink of death after a horrific car smash. He was his normal, jolly self. We went into his living room and Dave spilled the beans about his time with Lenny.

DAVE COURTNEY

I first heard about Lenny when I was a young fella working as a dustman. He was sort of the hero of the 'Jack the Lads' around that era. I personally believe there will never be another Lenny McLean. Apart from the prize fighting that he done, he actually became famous as a battling doorman. Everything's changed now, but years ago a place like the Camden Palace only had six doormen working there – two working outside, two working inside upstairs, and two working inside downstairs, and it held 2,000 people.

These days, I think they have about 24 men working there and they all have walkie-talkies. In them days, doormen were close and he'd save your life if you were in trouble. You didn't have walkie-talkies, you'd just shout, 'Lenny, help me, help me,' and you fought for your life and hoped the big fucker would run. He didn't really have to throw punches; he could just run into a crowd and knock five or six over. You had to be a tasty bastard to actually get through the night; if you lost a fight, the guv'nor of the club would sack you and get a better fighter in.

You'll probably never see another Lenny McLean these days, as they would get arrested after the first fight.

Now, fighting is the same as any contact sport in the world; you can only be good at it if you do it a lot. Lenny, he would have four or five fights a night. I've known him to go to work with a broken hand, actually strapping his hand up and carrying on fighting as normal. He used to be a fucking awesome sight. I actually saw him throw a normal-sized man through the air. I don't know how you would judge that in a gym, but I actually seen him grab a man by the bollocks with one hand and grab his face with the other and actually throw him through the air at head height. How could you fight a bloke like that? What would a punch do? Lenny in full flight with adrenalin pumping would be hard to stop; you could be the best boxer in the world but, if he just runs at you, there's nothing you could do.

Personally, I think the weight and height difference with Lenny and Roy Shaw was what made Lenny win the fights, but I think, if Lenny had been the same size as Shaw, Roy would have won as a boxer. But, as a doorman, there was no one in the world – and I've been surrounded by fighting doormen all my life – who could have lived with the man in that era, when doormen were doormen.

Lenny was always impeccably dressed on the door and a very funny man. I first saw him when I bought a ticket to see him box years ago. I was a nightclub man myself and he was the talk of the town. I used to do a little bit of boxing myself and it was Lenny who actually made me realise that I should retire; I like very much to be the best at whatever I do, or at least up there with them. But when you actually look at people like Lenny McLean, Roy Shaw and Columbo, you do realise that you're never going to be like that, so I thought to myself I'd better knock that on the head.

I had a 30-second encounter with Lenny while sparring at the Thomas a'Becket gym in the Old Kent Road. I put my hands up and he hit the gloves so hard that my own gloves knocked me out. There were no hard feelings – it's a game. He knew that I would have done it to him, even though I didn't stand a fucking chance. He'd eat people like me four or five times a day.

Whereas many people get the fear element before a fight, it was the complete opposite with Lenny; he grew with the big event, he knew he was going to destroy his opponents and, in the clubs, he knew there was no little firm in that club that could beat him if they were 50-handed. He generally believed that, and nine times out of ten he was right.

The first time I ever talked to him was over in a car lot in East London. He was training there, smashing cars up. He was very loud and was trying to pull car doors off, he was sweating and his veins were popping out of his T-shirt.

I remember one night down the Camden Palace we were having a little bit of trouble with the ICF. In them days, it was totally different to today; these days, people are more chilled out and are on pills, but, in them days, fights would start over nothing.

It's gone off and I saw Lenny standing there like a Christmas tree with people all hanging off his arms and some around his neck. Next thing you know, he's chucking them everywhere and screaming at them; it was an awesome sight.

As well as the Camden Palace, I worked with him in another club in Camden near the market. I also worked in The Hippodrome with him as well for a while. Lenny was aware of the sunbed incident that I had, which they used in *Lock, Stock and Two Smoking Barrels*. I wouldn't actually say Lenny was a villain; he was a tasty bastard and a fucking good fighter. God gives everyone one gift and he was one tasty bastard.

I once made a documentary called *The Bermondsey Boy* and asked Lenny if he wanted a part in it. I was working with him at the time and it was an ideal chance to plug the film on his life he was hoping to make. It was at this time he went to jail for a while and a lot of people were saying Lenny wasn't too happy with the documentary. I don't think Lenny was too bothered with it, as we carried on doing jobs together after it.

The first time he met my ex-missus Jen, he lifted her up in the air outside the door of The Hippodrome. I saw Lenny go over the top a few times when he didn't need to, but who am I to judge, because there's some things that you go half-hearted into and someone could pull a knife or something. So, if he wanted to go full on every time, then that's his rules, but it usually only took one punch.

I saw Lenny train a few times; he was not the most technically good boxer I've seen, but you could see the ferociousness in every single shot. He would try and knock you out with his jab. He had a very unusual programme, to say the least; he had an aura around him in the ring, outside the ring and definitely in training, and thank fuck he had the same aura when we were debt collecting. I'd be standing beside him, explaining to people what they owed and that, and they just couldn't take their eyes off Lenny. Now, he didn't have to give them a hard-nut look like Vinnie Jones tries to do with his eyebrows; Lenny just looked that way and, even if they didn't owe the money, they usually paid us – he was absolutely fantastic to go with.

I seen him pick this one person up off the floor by his throat once when we were debt collecting. Lenny says to him, 'Listen to him, he's trying to be nice, now I don't want to do what I do.' Len's exact words then were, 'You either pay Dave now, or you will pay after I smash you round the fucking room... so listen to the man.'

He handled his debt-collecting jobs very professionally. One time, this geezer took one look at Lenny and started shouting, 'Call the police!' Lenny went, 'Order a fucking ambulance while you're at it!' The geezer fainted on the spot and we just wet ourselves laughing.

On another debt-collection job, we were outnumbered in a car scrapyard but Lenny decked a couple of geezers straight off, then he said, 'That evens things up a bit.'

I was pretty good with my tongue; I'm not the best fighter in the world by a long shot, but I employ the best fighters. I had Lenny's number and I rung him a few times when I had trouble and he came with me; instead of ringing up an army of people, I had Lenny stand beside me and it was all sorted out nicely.

Lenny never considered himself the bad guy; these people had owed the money for something or another.

In most cases, people would call the police but, when I went collecting with Lenny, this never happened, as the last thing anyone would want was to have that big fucker after you. I seen him pop a few car windows in temper with the side of his fist and not even cut himself.

I once saw Lenny have a bare-knuckle fight in a horse box in Epsom. Lenny went in and, 30 seconds later, he was back out.

I once boxed on the same bill as Lenny, fighting this bloke named Buster something who worked at Luton car plant. I usually sold a lot of tickets as I was a doorman.

I seen Lenny in a temper a few times but he was very good at pretending he'd lost his temper when he hadn't, so it was a good move. You'd look at him and think he's a loose cannon, but it would usually defuse the situation.

Now, Lenny McLean in his own right was a fucking awesome sight, but Lenny McLean with the hump was something else. I was in a few fights with Lenny while we were in The Hippodrome. Once a month, you'd get all the home teams playing home, so you'd get thousands of northerners staying down in London on the Saturday night. We had our work cut out those nights.

This one night, I was running away from the police from this other club. Lenny had clocked me running towards him with the police following. As I passed him, he jumped in front of the police with his arms waving everywhere and stopped them in his tracks asking what was wrong; by now, I was long gone and thanked Lenny later for his help.

While working at the Palace, Lenny used to cut the tips off bag gloves and would wear them with his suit – if that isn't coming dressed for action I don't know what is. Lenny once gave me a knuckle duster and said, 'It's no good to me, Dave, I can't get my fucking fingers in it... the only way I could use that is to throw it at some fucker.'

The last time I saw Lenny alive was when he was filming *Lock, Stock and Two Smoking Barrels*. I then found out the day he died and sent my condolences up to his house. I went to the funeral, which was well put together and very respectable.

Bernie Davies from the Welsh Valleys found his way up to London in the early 1990s to make some money. Becoming good mates with Dave Courtney, he then earned the nickname of Agent Number 10. Since then, Bernie has earned the respect of the London people and has even appeared in a few books, such as Kate Kray's *The Art of Violence* and Jocelyn Bain Hogg's *The Firm*. He has also been in numerous newspaper and magazine articles. I met Bernie over a cup of tea and he recalled some of his meetings with Lenny McLean.

BERNIE DAVIES

Back in the early Nineties, I was in correspondence with Reggie Kray. I had started writing to him and had built up a good friendship with him. I had always been fascinated with the Krays, even from a very young age. I was visiting Reggie quite often in Maidstone Prison and I was doing a bit of business between him and his other two brothers, Ronnie and Charlie. I then went to this pub opposite the prison one day and I started talking to Dave Courtney who was also visiting Reggie. Now, I had met Courtney before that, when he was down in Wales bringing food parcels down to the miners' strike in the winter of 1984. At the time, I didn't know him personally, but I just clocked this flash Cockney who was smoking a cigar, as he had stood out a bit.

Later that day, after visiting Reggie, I went back into London with Dave Courtney and spent the night out drinking with him; we kind of clicked and have been best mates ever since then.

I ended up doing a lot of work for Courtney throughout the years and got involved in the London scene. I was also writing to Ronnie, and Charlie came down a few times to stay with me.

Throughout the years, the name Lenny McLean had always been in the background – the Main Man, the Guvnor, etc. – that was the vibe up there in that group or circle. He was known as the top man on the cobbles. I'd heard about all his famous fights like Roy Shaw and a few others. I then got involved in a few bare-knuckle fights myself around 1993.

I'd been banned from fighting amateur a long time ago. A good friend of mine, who was an unlicensed promoter, was organising a few of these bare-knuckle shows. I was training and sparring with Joe Pyle Jnr at the time; it wasn't your usual paying show to the public. All the main faces were there. There were four of us fighting on the bill in this big industrial estate.

I'll always remember that day; it was a cold winter's day, and it was in this big garage with roller-shutter doors with a chain and a pulley. In the middle of the shutters you had this little door which you had to bend down and squeeze through to get in. There were a few gypsies in there who were going to fight.

I was fighting this Eastern European bloke, so a few fighters and I were getting ready, psyching ourselves up, and I was about to have my fight. There were about 30 people there watching, including Joey Jnr and Tony Lambrianou and a few others. There must have been ten seconds to go before my fight when there's this big bang on the shutter doors. No one was sure what was happening, everyone thought it was a raid. Before the boys could open the shutters, you could hear two strong Cockney voices shouting, 'Open these fucking shutters… open these fucking shutters now.' So one of the boys shouts to them, 'Bend down and come in through the small door.'

The voice replied, 'I'm not going through that fucking door… I'm not getting oil on my fucking suit… open these fucking roller-shutters.'

So everything was stopped to let these two people in. The roller-shutters come up, and I remember looking at the light when the shutters went up and it was like an eclipse of the sun.

It was Lenny McLean and Dave Courtney. Courtney didn't want to get oil on his Armani suit by squeezing through that little door, and I don't think Lenny would have fitted through it. The man looked fucking awesome and about 22 stone.

The shutters come back down and everything settled down again. I started to psych myself up again ready for my fight when, all of a sudden, Lenny's mobile phone goes off. You could hear Lenny saying, 'Yeah… yeah… where? Fucking hell, I'll be there now.' Next thing you know, it all had to stop again for the roller-shutter doors to open to let Lenny out.

As he was going, Dave ran over to me and said, 'Make sure you fucking win this.' I said to Dave, 'I haven't come here to lose.' Dave says, 'You better fucking win this, because Lenny's put a fucking bet on you, so make sure you win this.'

I'd had a few fights for Joey Jnr in the past and I think he had told Lenny what I was capable of. I don't know if Lenny was going to fight that day or just watch, as sometimes he was the kind of guy to take something, spur of the moment.

Talk about being under pressure, though. Two weeks earlier, I'd been in almost the same situation. I hate it when it's personal with money; if there's a purse on a fight and someone wins or loses, then it's down to the bookie and the punters. But, when people are putting their personal money (side-bets) on, it puts added pressure on you.

This bloke named Jeff Fenaroli had organised a Lurcher and Terrier Dog Show in Aberaman in Wales. These blokes had come from Gloucestershire and they were all big lumpers and wanted to have a crack. They wanted to arm wrestle first, so a hat was taken around and everyone's money was on me to beat their wrestler. There was murders there and a mass brawl erupted. It landed up later with shotguns being stuck through letterboxes in people's houses, all over a fucking arm-wrestling match I had in a pub. So you don't need the pressure of people saying they have got money on you because I've seen what happens when it gets personal.

Going back to the fight, though, I'll never forget those words Courtney said, 'Make sure you win this fucking fight, as Lenny has put some money on you.' Anyway, the fight actually got under way in the end.

I didn't see Lenny again until about a year-and-a-half later in 1995. I'd been doing security with Dave Courtney for Ronnie Kray's funeral and about 40 of us had moved on from The Blind Beggar in the night, around the corner to The Guv'ner's pub. As soon as I went in there, I was amazed – all the walls were black and there were photos of the Krays and other boxers.

I was looking at some photos and then got hit with a big thud on the back of my shoulder, and a voice goes, 'Hello, Bernie, all right there?' He had still recognised me from that previous fight I had. He shook my hand. His hands were like shovels; I haven't got small hands myself, but they felt like twice the size of mine. He said, 'I'm glad you done well in that fight and I didn't lose my money… Come and meet a few people I know.'

I went and met them and had a few drinks and that and got on really well. I had a good old chat with Lenny for a while before he carried on mingling.

I met him a few times over the years after that. I saw him train once on a heavy punchbag and the bloke just had awesome power and really gave his all. You never knew with Lenny, he'd turn up at some events and, if there was someone there that would be mad enough to have a crack at him, he'd take the big fucking jacket off and have it on, there and then. Most of us would prepare for it and be there with a tracksuit and gumshield. He did a lot spur of the moment. He'd say in a growling voice, 'C'mon, let's fucking have it.'

I went with Dave Courtney and Lenny on a couple of debt-collecting jobs. Seeing Lenny in a temper growling with his veins bursting through the neck of his shirt was a sight to see.

I hadn't seen Lenny for a while and then I received a phone call from Dave Courtney saying that he had passed away. I must say, I've seen both sides of Lenny. I've seen him happy and in a good mood and then I've seen him in a temper, but all the memories I have of Lenny are good. That's the way I'll always remember him.

RESPECT

JAN LAMB – THE ANGEL OF THE UNDERWORLD

I met Lenny some years back, and he came across as a lovely gentleman, a big 'gentle giant'. He was a caring and kind man who would have done anything for his family. He bought a lovely house out Staplehurst way, if I remember correctly; they were all looked after very well by him. Lenny came across as a fierce man with some people, but I think you have to be like that if you want to get by in this world.

People were frightened of him because of his size but, at the same time, people loved him. They knew he was only really frightening when he was fighting.

All right, there were times out of fighting, but he stood up for what was right and I don't see anything wrong with that. There are lots of people out there who knew him and liked him but are afraid to say so in case they get slagged off for it. To me, they're not up to much if they can't speak their own minds for worrying about what others will say to them.

Lenny was always laughing and joking about, and that's how it should be, there's no harm in that. If Joe Bloggs down the road can laugh and joke, then why couldn't Lenny? Now the 'gentle giant' is fighting in the ring from above… God bless you, Lenny.

I first met Tony Lambrianou at Charles Bronson's wedding reception at Dave Courtney's pub a few years ago. I had a little chat with him and I explained that I run a website about Lenny McLean. He spoke very highly of Lenny on that day. I then had the chance to catch up with him at an unlicensed boxing show in the Hammersmith Palais. I told him I was now writing a book about Lenny McLean and he remembered me from before. As we chatted, he spoke very highly of Lenny again. I could see it was the wrong time to be pestering him, as there were a few people waiting to have his autograph, so I arranged to speak with him the next time I would see him. I never had the chance to catch up with Tony again, as he sadly passed away a few months later. I was struck, though, even in the short time we spoke, by what Tony had to say about Lenny.

TONY LAMBRIANOU

Lenny was a really hard bloke, probably the hardest man I've ever known. He could be really violent. I first met him one night when I went up to the Camden Palace; he looked after us all night. He was also a character and a gentleman around ladies. He was also a very polite man. I went to his funeral to pay my respects to him. It's a shame Lenny wasn't here tonight, because he would have loved all this.

After reading about Charlie Bronson's challenge to fight Lenny McLean in the 1980s, I thought I'd write to him and see what was his version of events was. Charlie had also spoken very highly of Lenny in his book *Legends*, so I asked him whether he'd be interested in contributing to this book, and he replied straight away.

CHARLES BRONSON

Lenny McLean… I can really only say good about the guy.

It was Paul Edmunds and Davey Hunt, both Canning Town chaps, who approached Lenny McLean to fight me – winner takes all. Lenny did not take the challenge up.

Why? My only real reason I can give is: (1) he was at this time flush; (2) he was doing TV work and top jobs; (3) (this is the one I believe) he had lost his hunger.

RESPECT

I met Lenny the once in The Hippodrome. We had a nice drink and a chat. Lenny was a big man, powerful, but fighters run out of gas when their mind is not 100 per cent into it. He knew I was just out of jail, he knew I was fresh and hungry.

Why did he need it? He didn't. Lenny, to me, was a great man and he achieved so much in his life, but I'd have loved that battle. Why? 'Cos I was fucking skint. It was a big pay day for me, for him it was peanuts, and for me it was my life, my dream come true. Once he'd made up his mind, I just went my own way.

Weeks later, I was nicked on an armed blag and the rest is history.

I only ever met Lenny the once but that was enough to have a lasting memory. He must have had the biggest fists on the planet.

I personally admired the guy. He had a nice way of life and knew how to conduct himself in any situation, whether in violence or just being polite. He was a proper family man.

He was a very sincere man.

He said what he meant.

And meant what he said.

And that, for me, says it all.

Respect.

I caught up with gangland legend Mad Frankie Fraser on one of his famous gangland tours. Mad Frank had various books out and appeared on many documentaries and was even having a film made of his life. It was while I was in The Blind Beggar near the end of the tour that I managed to get Frank on his own for a few minutes and he recalled some memories about Lenny.

FRANKIE FRASER

I'd heard of the name Lenny McLean for years and then I got hold of a video of a few of his fights; he bashed this one bloke right up, made a right mess of him. I think he was fighting some gypsy on there.

I think the first time I ever met him was at a benefit show at the Law Society's Hall in Chancery Lane. They had this night to help out this boxing timekeeper who'd had a stroke. Charlie Richardson was also there and we had a cracking night. He was doing a bit of minding at the time. We used to see each other quite a bit after that at dos and things.

One good story someone told me about Lenny was when he was locked up inside. This young bloke was put in a cell with him and Lenny told him that there was to be no farting in the cell. The kid just nodded at Lenny because he was scared and thought Lenny was for real. Lenny then farts twice and says to the bloke, 'They are for both of us.'

I also knew Lenny's uncle, Bobby Warren, years ago, after we spent some time inside together, another nice man.

The only thing I had against Lenny was that he was taller then me.

Lenny was a good bloke, he was a nice man and I liked him... I can't speak highly enough of him.

One of Lenny's good friends throughout his life was Flanagan, Britain's first ever Page 3 girl in 1972. Flanagan had been in Lenny's life right up until the end. I had a nice chat on the phone with her and she sent me a nice photo and some thoughts about Lenny.

RESPECT

FLANAGAN

It's been six years now since I lost my old friend Lenny McLean and, every time someone tells me this or that man is the hardest man they have met, it brings back Lenny so vividly. To have a fight in the street for 15 minutes or to be a bully verbally to men or women doesn't make you a hard man. I am one of the few people living that knows all the 'hard men' in Britain. Lenny McLean was the hardest man I've ever met.

I first met him when he was about 20 years of age when he'd been asked to do some minding. He was a huge man with a marvellous body, a rugged face and beautiful hands. I was then about 28 years old and had become Violet Kray's hairdresser, so I was in the Krays' house every week.

Around this time, I had heard of a gang of thugs around the Kingsland Road area who were terrorising women, so I went and had a word with Lenny and told him about it. The next night, Lenny walked past this club and just stood at the door.

After a while, the four thugs turned up and looked surprised when they saw Lenny standing there. Me and a girlfriend, who I was out with that night, were sat in my Mini by the side of the kerb near the club. There was then a bit of a commotion and Lenny's hit one on the jaw; he's then picked up the tallest one and smashed him against the wall. Then he grabbed hold of the other two and banged their heads together. There was blood everywhere, people who were passing were screaming one of them then ran to a phone box calling, 'Police, police!'

I offered to drive Lenny anywhere to get him away from there, but he said to me, 'Everyone's seen me, so we'll wait for them.' Two policemen arrived and Lenny said to them,

'Just cleaning the rubbish off the streets, officers.' Lenny then told them he had two lady witnesses and that the gang of thugs were going to attack them just as he had walked by. The policemen looked at the guy with a broken jaw and smiled; he had obviously recognised him and knew of the bloke's past record. We gave our stories and I drove Lenny home. From then on, he was our Sir Galahad.

The next night, I was around Violet's house and I told Ronnie and Reggie about the incident; even they were impressed, although Ronnie did say, 'Lenny should have shot the bastards.'

I went to a few of Lenny's fights, including two with Roy Shaw. I also sat in the Old Bailey when a 'not guilty' was read out. Lenny looked around at his beloved wife Val and then burst out singing, 'Always look on the bright side of life…' The judge couldn't believe it, but we could. The big man with the even bigger heart was free.

Women loved Lenny because they knew, if they were ever hurt or abused, he would defend them. He admired very few people and, one day, about six months before he had died, I asked him, 'Lenny, of all the people you have met – you know, royalty, film stars, gangsters, the Mafia, the Twins – who do you most admire?' His reply was two words – Mother Teresa – and he meant it.

Then, on Tuesday, 28 July 1998, his book author Peter Gerrard and me stood at Liverpool Street Station in a bookshop waiting for him to sign his book. There were hundreds of people waiting for him. Peter then went to the phone and was told he had passed away, just as his book was to become a bestseller. Me and Peter signed his books for him and told all the people buying the book stories about him.

RESPECT

I'm still telling stories, Lenny. The gangsters are all gone now, Lenny, but they all had respect for you.

East End gangster Danny Woolard was jailed for his part in the infamous Snowhill Robbery. Danny's first book *We Dared* hit the shops last year. Danny is now concentrating on writing his second book, *Nothing to Prove*. I caught up with Danny in a café, and he was happy to tell me about Lenny McLean.

DANNY WOOLARD

The first time I seen Lenny McLean was when Roy Shaw was fighting… I think it was in Cinatra's in London. Lenny jumped in and challenged Roy to a 20-grand side-bet. Anyway, the fight was called on and, after a few rounds, Lenny stood in the corner and quit, he wouldn't fight; he wasn't knocked down, he wasn't hurt, he just quit. Lenny then got Kevin Finnegan and a couple of others to train him really hard. I'm sure Lenny must have had his gloves doctored as he hit Roy once, and no one can knock Roy Shaw out with one punch, no one in the world, because he can take a punch. Lenny then gets out of the ring and rips his gloves off as he's still celebrating.

They then had a third fight and it more or less was the same scenario, a few punches and the fight was over. My mate, who had a bit of a run-in with Lenny a few years earlier in a pub in Hoxton, challenged Lenny to an unlicensed fight but it never came off. My old partner who I used to do a few shows with, named Terry Butwell, used to go to Freddie Hill's gym and spar with Lenny quite a lot; I think he trains Lenny's son Jamie now.

KATE KRAY

On the front cover of Lenny McLean's book *The Guv'nor*, he says about himself, 'I look what I am, a hard bastard!' And make no mistake, he was just that. He was everything anyone expected a gangster, a tough guy or a fighter to be; he epitomised them all. Lenny was old school, a man with old-fashioned values who rose to the occasion in his fine suit and silk tie embroidered with a certain dignity.

But Lenny was also a family man. His wife Val and his children Jamie and Kelly came before anything or anybody. That was evident the first time I met him. The other thing I didn't expect was his warmth. On our first brief meeting, he grabbed my hand and shook it like he really was genuinely pleased to see me. A big man with a big heart. God bless Lenny!

Born in Sunderland, George Craig had gone down the wrong path early and had ended up in jail for various offences. On coming out of jail, George decided to change his life around. He then poured all his time and energy into building up what must be one of the most successful charities in the north of England, the Lazarus Foundation.

George's exploits throughout the years can be read in his brilliant book *Mud Sticks*.

I travelled up north and spent the day with George, who had witnessed Lenny in action in the 1980s.

GEORGE CRAIG

The first time I had heard of the name Lenny McLean was in the early Eighties when this bloke was chucking his name around. I had to go down to London from Sunderland to collect some money and sort a debt out. A bloke owed someone up my way 40 grand and they were trying to frighten him off with Lenny's name.

Anyway, I made my way to Mile End. I had a pal down in London who ran a clothes shop and he took us down to Roman Road.

We then went to the The Green Man pub and my mate introduced me to Lenny, and I explained the situation to him. I said to Lenny, 'The kid's owed 40 grand and he wants it fucking paid.' I explained to Lenny what it was all about.

Lenny said to me that he would sort it out and the bloke would pay the debt. But he wanted a drink out of it, so Lenny came away with a few grand out of it and we were all happy.

The first impression I got of him is that he was like a cross between a Neanderthal man and Attila the Hun. He really was a brute, he was just a fucking beast. I thought to myself when I met him, I hope we can sort this out man to man without any trouble or I'll have to shoot this fucker, as he looked an animal.

The next time I saw Lenny was when he was up in Glasgow with a pal of mine, the late Arthur Thompson. Lenny and Arthur had been doing a bit of wheeling and dealing together. Lenny used to collect some money for Arthur, which really tells you how respected Lenny was, a London man collecting money in Scotland. Arthur was basically running Glasgow at the time. Lenny then agreed to a fight, and Arthur went and set a bout up for him in a club near Arthur's house. The fight was at the back of the club in the backyard. Lenny had these six-ounce gloves on which were really worn out. Why they bothered wearing them I don't know; they may as well have gone bare-knuckle. Lenny was fighting this bloke from Aberdeen, a really big bloke who was about six foot two. Lenny had gone at him and really fucked him up, and then Lenny knocked him out in the second round and he was out cold for quite a while.

It reminded me of the scene in *Rocky* when Stallone is hitting the slab of beef until his hands are bleeding. Lenny was just a fucking powerhouse. He was an animal, and he had sheer raw aggression.

Lenny then had another fight, but it was bare-knuckle this time. He was fighting this bloke who worked on the oil rigs; the bloke was a right handful but Lenny done him. Now I had seen Lenny fight in his last fight, so I knew what he was capable of, so I bet on him to win and I made a nice few grand out of it. The fight didn't last long and Lenny knocked him out cold yet again. Lenny also had the ability, at the snap of his finger, to turn into an animal; some people need to work themselves up, but he could knock it off and on.

This kid once went missing and had gone down to London. Lenny put a few feelers out and tried finding him. Arthur respected Lenny a lot and, when Lenny went to jail, Arthur stayed in touch with him.

Lenny continued to go up to Scotland doing work for Arthur. When Lenny was up in Scotland, he would always be on the phone to his wife and be asking how the kids were; he was a family man and would always head back straight away so he could be with his wife. He was a family-orientated man. If I say he had a weakness, it would be his family. Lenny was well respected by a lot of people up our way. I only met Lenny a few times, but I got on well with him, he was a real nice bloke and a proper gentleman.

RESPECT

I first came across Essex-born Ian a few years ago after seeing him in an episode on the TV programme *Godfathers* about the Mafia in the UK. A mate of mine gave me his number and we started corresponding regularly and Ian's life started to open up in front of me. His life story was unlike any other person's I had ever heard of, or read about. Ian had been charged with Mafia crimes, named as an enforcer for one of the most violent Mafia families in Sicily, and was on Interpol's top list of international criminals.

After years of corresponding, I finally met up with him and persuaded him to let me write his own biography. In between writing his book, we took time out, and he remembered meeting the great Lenny McLean.

IAN HEWS

I'd bumped into Lenny on more than one occasion, a giant of a man with a fearsome reputation for his fighting exploits in and out of the ring, a man who would fight anyone if the price was right.

The first time I saw Lenny McLean was in Hoxton Market in the East End of London. It was just before he fought Roy Shaw for the first time and his name meant nothing at all to me; I had never heard of him, and I don't think too many others had either, but in Hoxton it was a different matter. To the locals, he was unbeatable and McLean had a big reputation as a fighter to be feared.

A friend of mine had this massage parlour at the back of the market and it was doing good business, then a couple of the local villains turned up and started to demand a few quid because they had the hump and could see how well it was doing. He gave me a call and asked if I would go up there and tell these arseholes off. Some of the girls were so scared they were refusing to work and he wasn't happy and neither were they.

The market was a busy little place and everyone seemed to know everyone else's business. If a stranger appeared on the scene, it soon went around, and I made no secret that it was me who was looking after the massage parlour from now on, so piss-heads and trouble-makers were not welcome and I wanted everyone to know it.

One morning, I'm sitting in the market café having my breakfast, when a short, stocky bloke walked in. I didn't notice him at first but suddenly he starts shouting at the staff. The café was empty and I'm sitting right at the back, waiting for my breakfast. As I looked over, he sits down at a table by the front door. He then starts ordering food and the staff were still running around in panic trying to keep him happy. The staff in the café knew who I was and they obviously knew who he was, so I'm thinking this is a set-up and they know it's just about to go off. Probably their worst nightmare and mine as well, because I was wondering how many of his pals were going to barge in at any second. One of the staff then starts pouring him out a cup of tea and he suddenly goes mental; he grabs the bloke by the throat and slings him across the café into a couple of empty tables. He picks up a chair and throws it at the counter, smashing all the plates and glasses. The next minute, he calmly sits down as if nothing has happened and tells them to bring him another breakfast.

By now I'd had enough. I call the boss over in a loud voice and tell him to get my fucking food first as I'm still hungry and this prick can wait.

By now, the noise of the plates being broken had echoed down to the market and a crowd of people were gathering outside to see what was going on. The bloke must have been about 16 stone, he was a big lump and he was looking for trouble. He wasn't one of the local piss-heads or idiots, he was being paid to cause trouble or to do someone and he didn't give a fuck and everyone knew it.

He then looks over at me and says, 'What's your fucking problem?' I now knew it was going to go off there and then, but I didn't fancy it in the café, especially as I was about 11 stone and he was built like an American wrestler. I wanted to get him outside where I had a better chance, so I quickly point to the door and say, 'Fuck you, you prick, let's take it outside.'

We both started heading towards the door and the street outside; as I approached the door, I could see another big bloke outside looking through the window and bouncing up and down as if he wanted to go ten rounds with Mike Tyson. That man I now know was Lenny McLean.

The walk from the back of the café to the street only took a couple of seconds but, in that time, a million things were going through my mind – this was not like a boxing ring, there was no referee, no rules and I had no intention of losing. If I had to rip his eyes out to win, then I would have done it, but by now my biggest worry was seeing Lenny outside frothing at the mouth.

He was still jumping up and down and was obviously getting ready to lump someone and I wasn't sure who that was, me or the other bloke, but, as the door opened, McLean's fist smashed straight into his face, lifting him right off the ground. He was out before he even hit the ground.

McLean was screaming like a fucking banshee and he was loving it, like most winners do. Maybe it was an old score that had to be settled or just McLean protecting one of his interests. I didn't have a clue and I wasn't about to ask. I stepped over the loser who was still in the doorway completely out of it. McLean looked at me and nodded his head; he walked off down towards the market, still celebrating his one-punch knockout, knowing everyone had seen it, including me.

A couple of months later, a fight was set up between Lenny and Roy Shaw. I was gutted as I couldn't make it as I was locked up at the time. A couple of my mates went to the fight and brought me a full match report a couple of days later. I heard Lenny had joined a proper training camp and he went on to beat Shaw twice. I knew what Lenny could do after witnessing his power and speed that day in Hoxton.

Why they never had a fourth fight, I don't know, it would have sold out anywhere.

Lenny McLean was a hard man and one of the best at his trade. You can't take anything away from Lenny, he came back after that first loss and beat Shaw twice; he did something that no other fighter has ever been able to do and that's why he deserved the title as the Guv'nor. It was his moment in time and he went for it, he done it.

Another name I had heard of as soon as I started doing the website was the legendary Joey Pyle. Joe had started the unlicensed fighting scene back in the 1970s and had appeared in various books. Then, in 2003, he finally released his own biography entitled *Notorious*. I had met Joe a few times over the years and he always spoke very highly of Lenny. A mate of mine then gave me Joe's number and, when I spoke to him, he agreed to do an interview.

A mate of mine named Bernard offered to drive me to London and we eventually arrived in Joe's home town. When Joe turned up, he was immaculate as ever. He suggested doing the interview in his car, a gleaming Jag, and, as we climbed in, he commented that I looked like a young Lenny.

JOE PYLE

I first heard of Lenny McLean when I was promoting Roy Shaw. There were little stories going round about this local tough kid from Hoxton. Roy Shaw was the Guv'nor and, obviously, we had a lot of challenges around that time. People wanted to get on the firm and fight Roy because it was a pay day, but they all got knocked out first round. I mean, if you look at it that way, anyone today would jump in the ring with the world champion to get a pay day and fall over in the first round. You had to earn the respect to get in that position, and sell a few tickets.

Anyway, Roy had a few fights and defeated everybody. Then someone that knew Lenny Boy came to see me and said that his boy Lenny would fight Roy. So I said, 'Well, I don't know, how many tickets can you sell?' I thought, if he could sell a load of tickets, we could get it on. He said, 'I can sell half of what you got,' so I said, 'All right, then, we'll have a "winner take all" basis.'

So the fight was all set up and we put it on at Cinatra's in Croydon. Roy had a good reputation and a good following and, when he fought Lenny, it brought Lenny into the limelight, and Lenny admitted that. Lenny had a lot of drawing power as well, but not as much as Roy, as the opponents weren't there.

I met Lenny when I went in the changing room to give him his gloves. It was funny as he had such big hands and couldn't get the gloves on, and so he always blamed me for his loss. Lenny said to me, 'I can't close my hands,' so I said to him, 'Well, they are the same size as Roy's... take your bandages off.' You couldn't give him a bigger pair of gloves if you tried. Lenny was still complaining before the fight started, but there was still nothing I could do.

Anyway the referee had stopped it in the fourth round after McLean had taken a lot of punishment. Lenny even admitted that Shaw was the better man on that night.

After that, there was another fight which Roy didn't do any training for, he did nothing, and Lenny beat him. But, by then, Lenny had learned how to box.

Then there was the next fight, and Lenny's people wanted to put the fight on themselves. They said, 'We want to promote it,' and, as they had beaten Roy, they could call the shots. So I said, 'All right, but we have it on a "winner takes all" basis again.'

With that, Lenny beat Roy again. Roy said he took a load of stuff. When I was in the dressing room, he did not look himself. If you look at the videos, he looks different to how he normally looks. He looked half asleep, he had no go in him; even when he ran into the ring he looked like a dead horse getting in there, and he just went in there and got knocked out and it was all over.

Lenny then became the Guv'nor and he held it with respect and he was respected. I then got nicked, and I'll give full respect to Len, he came round to see my wife while I was in the nick, and he gave her £500. I was passed by the police as a Cat AA prisoner and he always visited me, so I had a lot of time for Lenny.

In the early Eighties, me and my other partner Brian Emmet were promoting a fight between Lenny and Dave 'Psycho' Spelling, but Spelling pulled out with a broken hand. So in stepped another boxer named Johnny Waldron. The fight was at The Cat's Whiskers in Streatham. When I put it on with Johnny, he was supposed to go over, he was supposed to go down. But Johnny wouldn't go down. McLean then came out and put his chin out and got caught, and down he went. Lenny was really gutted and went straight back to the gym and wanted a return. I also remember Lenny knocking out Johnny Clarke at the Rainbow Theatre.

But Lenny was a game fucker on the cobbles as well; I'd be more frightened of him on the cobbles than in the ring. Standing out there he was a big strong fucker, and could do more outside than he could in the ring. He was totally different when it came to a real fight.

I seen Lenny train a bit, he was a good trainer, and he trained up at Freddie Hill's gym. He was sparring with Chrissie and Kevin Finnegan. That's where he learned how to box. When I saw him start off, he didn't have a lot of idea, then suddenly he learned a lot. He came on a bundle from sparring up there all the time.

Like I said, I'd be more frightened of him out there than in the ring. Put him out on the street and he was a dangerous bastard, he was a fucking danger; he'd rip your head off, a big strong man and a wicked bastard as well. He was a good man to have on your side. I respected him.

Last but not least is the well-respected Charlie Richardson. I'd spent some time in Charlie's company and he had always spoken very highly of Lenny. A very successful businessman these days, Charlie took time out of his very busy schedule to offer some insights into the impression Lenny made on him.

CHARLIE RICHARDSON

I first heard of the name Lenny McLean and the reputation he had while I was in prison. He then came to visit me one day with Alex Steene and Joe Pyle. We got on very well and he then started visiting me regular.

Lenny brought a couple of his fights in on video. Most of the other inmates and I must have watched them every day for a week. When I came out of jail, Lenny often used to come around the office.

We went to various boxing shows all the time. This one night there was a charity dinner for the Ex-Boxers Association and I spent the night in the company of Lenny, Frankie Fraser, Alex Steene and other famous boxers.

When Lenny was in Brixton on remand for that murder charge, there was a young kid in there called Mark Thomburrow who I knew and Lenny really looked after him like a father. He was good like that.

When Lenny came out, him and his wife visited the boy; I thought that was very kind of him. When Lenny was ill, I used to go and visit him with Johnny Nash. Johnny used to visit Lenny nearly every day when Lenny was ill at his home. I remember going over to the East End a couple of times when Lenny had The Guv'ner's pub; it was quite successful and he ran it well.

RESPECT

When my kid used to go up to the West End to the nightclubs, I had no worries because I knew Lenny was on the door up there working. He'd make sure they would be in the VIP lounge and he'd really look after them with free drinks and champagne, he always made a fuss of them. You never had any worries when they were up there, which was wonderful.

I then heard Lenny had sadly passed away from a good friend of mine John Huntley. I went to the funeral to pay my final respects to him and his family.

It was a shame Lenny had passed away so young, as he was just breaking into acting and the movies and didn't get the recognition he deserved.

Everybody got on well with Lenny and he wasn't a bully; if he could do someone a good turn, then he would.

Lenny was a good man. He was a nice fella, a very respectable family man. I had a lot of time for Lenny, and so did everybody else who knew him.

5

Stir Crazy

There's no denying that Lenny's stretch in prison was one of the worst parts of his life. Being up on a murder charge with the possibility of never getting out can't be good for anyone. The thought of never being with his family again and getting on with the things he did in everyday life would be enough to turn any sane man mad.

I had heard various rumours throughout the years that Lenny had been this and that in jail but, at the end of the day, that's all they were – rumours. I had this funny scene in my head, a bit like the film *Stir Crazy* when Richard Pryor and Gene Wilder are crying on the floor of their cell while this huge, bald bloke enters. How could you ever imagine sharing a cell with the big man? One wrong word and you would be history.

Anyway, I was contacted by a mate of Lenny's who had been on remand with him in Brixton Prison. Finally, I would get to the bottom of it. We spoke on the phone and he invited me to go and stay with him for the day. He was another character right out of the McLean fold.

So I packed my bags and headed off on another five-hour journey. No sooner had I arrived than the kettle was straight on. I could see right away he had a story to tell. His long-time mate Tommy, who had also been in Brixton with him and Lenny, was there, too.

I unpacked my tape recorder as the kettle was boiling for Round Two. By now, the bloke was taking Lenny off to a tee as he was telling me stories. For the next two hours, I was enthralled by the many stories as he was reliving them over and over again.

PAUL MORRIS

I first came across Lenny in Brixton Prison and we hit it off straight away. I was in there on remand for murder, awaiting a trial, and he was in for the same as me. What had happened, just to give you a bit of a background, was something like this – there was this bloke who was living in these flats a couple of doors away from my sister on the same landing. Now this bloke was a horrible man who used to wind everyone up and abuse his girlfriend. The stuff he used to do to her just wasn't right for any human being to suffer. I'd had a run-in with him a few times on the balcony.

So this one night, Tommy and myself had been drinking and we thought we would go in and see him and try to put the frighteners on him. Tommy had been on drugs at the time as well and didn't really know what he was doing. As we have gone into the bloke's flat, Tommy spotted one of the bloke's guns in the cupboard by the front door. Tommy's grabbed it and shot one into the wall to scare the bloke and then they have started wrestling with this gun. I've joined in and tried getting it off the both of them. Tommy's then let one off accidentally and the bloke's gone down on the floor.

We both panicked and we left the place, but I later got caught by the police. Tommy then went and handed himself in and told them that I didn't do it, but no one would believe him. The police tried saying that I had done it, even though Tommy admitted doing it. The only part of the case that I was found guilty for was for being in possession of a firearm without a certificate, because I had got rid of the weapon. Tommy was found guilty of manslaughter with provocation, which meant that he had been provoked to fire the gun. I ended up getting four years and Tommy got ten years.

I felt suicidal in prison knowing that everyone thought it was me. I felt like the front of a car window that had been hit with a hammer and smashed into thousands of little pieces. I nearly ended it all this one night and then I thought of Tommy who was beside me in my cell – after all, he would have to be the one to find me. From then on, I started to pull myself together, and piece the window back together, just like a jigsaw.

Anyway, while Tommy and I were on remand in Brixton Prison, we came across this bloke named Lenny McLean. To be honest, I'd never heard of him. I done a bit of boxing when I was younger, but I was always interested in pro boxing, so I'd never really heard much about the unlicensed game until I heard the stories from Lenny.

The first time I saw him was on the landing in Brixton and I thought to myself, Look at the size of that bloke. A few whispers were going around that that's big Lenny McLean, he's the Guv'nor, street fighter, etc. It was then I started getting interested in him. This was around 1990. The screws gave Lenny a cleaner's job, as this would give him a chance to get out of his cell a bit more often.

The first time I ever met Lenny was when I went into his cell. Being the number-one cleaner I had to let the boys know what job they done. I was pretty good with all the boys and Lenny said to me, 'Hello, son, don't go giving me any fucking dodgy jobs.' I replied, 'Lenny, I'm one of your own, my name is Paul, and I'm in charge of this little mob here, I'll sort you out a nice little number, Len.' He replied, 'Good boy, good boy.'

You couldn't get an easier job inside and he would just kick all the dirty clothes into one corner and say to one of the boys, 'Go on, son, do us a favour and I'll give you a big fat roll-up. Pick that dirty washing up for me, my old back's playing up.' From that very first meeting, we just clicked and became good mates.

I was then sharing a cell with Tommy at the time and Lenny was right opposite us.

Lenny was sharing a cell with this Dutch bloke. I don't think Lenny liked him that much. Lenny used to light matches up for his roll-ups and then throw them at the bloke. The bloke came up to me one day and said in his Dutch accent, 'You have got to try and tell Lenny not to throw matches at me. He's trying to burn me.' The bloke ended up getting moved after a few months.

This one day I said to Lenny, 'Do you want a smoke of this joint?' Lenny said, 'I've never smoked that shit before.' I said to him, 'Relax, Len, take it with you and have it later. Don't smoke it all at once, have a few puffs and then out it in the ashtray.' He said, 'All right, son… are you sure it won't hurt?' I replied, 'I wouldn't dare hurt you, Len.'

Anyway, the next morning he's come out of his cell and he

looked like a ghost. I've said to him, 'Lenny, how did you get on with that?' He replied, 'How did I get on with that? I fucking shit myself twice and fell out of bed once.' We had a good laugh about it. I can certainly say that was the last time Lenny ever touched a joint.

This screw comes past Lenny's cell one morning and bangs on his door and shouts, 'Morning, McLean.' Lenny's come out of his cell in his pants and shouted, 'Who the fuck just called me McLean?' This little screw just stopped dead and Lenny's gone right in his face and says to him, 'My name's Lenny and not McLean. I'm not in fucking school.' Len then goes back in his cell as the screw looks like he's about to faint.

Another time, this bloke was in the showers and he came out with a towel on. The prison guards went nuts on him as you are supposed to be fully dressed while coming out of the showers. Lenny comes out a few minutes later and not one screw would look at him, everyone put their head down. That's how frightened of him they were.

I was having a shower one day and Lenny was showing me the buckshot marks where he had been shot in the arse; not a pretty sight, I can tell you.

Lenny also used to help me serve the food up. It was only then I started to realise how popular he was. He used to come to the kitchens with us and collect the food. We would then go back and put it on all the hot plates. We would be feeding about 250 people. I guarantee about 200 of them would ask how he was; it used to get him down at times. Most of them would ask, 'All right, Len?' He would reply, 'How the fuck am I all right? I'm in a fucking poxy prison, not a five-star hotel.' He also hated the word 'sweet'. He'd say to people, 'What's fucking sweet about this piss-hole?'

He'd ask all the inmates, 'What are you in here for, son?' On their reply, he'd call them a fucking mug, shaking his head as if he was really gutted for them.

We had this prison officer who we used to call 'Clarence the Cross-eyed Lion' because he had a lazy eye. One day, the prison officer says to me, 'Paul, some of the staff have noticed that Lenny isn't doing too much.' So I replied, 'So what do you want me to do about it?' He says, 'Well, have a word with him; you're in charge.'

So I go and see Lenny and I say to him, 'Len, I've just been pulled by the screws, mate... they have been asking me about your job, and they noticed that you have not been doing your work.' Lenny then says, 'Pulled? Who's pulled you? What the fuck have you done wrong? Who's pulled you?' So I told him the prison officer's name and he's gone out on that landing and starts screaming the bloke's surname. The officer comes down and Lenny's given it to him verbally and the bloke's turned white. The officer then comes on to me and says, 'Paul, what did you tell Lenny for?' I said to him, 'Because you fucking told me to.' He walked off, still looking like he had seen a ghost.

There was also this other prison officer who was talking to Lenny about a fight he had with about seven men one night and he was knocking them everywhere. I was looking at him and thinking there was more meat on a butcher's pencil. Lenny's made this quick move and puts his arm around the back of this bloke's head. Lenny says to him, 'What happens if you get this close then?' By now, Lenny's looking in this guy's eyes about a foot away from his face. The officer says, 'Well, I'll nut him then, won't I?' Lenny then pulls him in and does a snap with his teeth right by his nose.

He had been so close I was waiting for Lenny to spit his nose out. The bloke then turned white again as Lenny let him go, laughing.

I remember Lenny telling me one day that he had broken his best friend's jaw over some prostitute. Lenny and his mate were on a drinking session one day and Lenny's mate had got involved with this little prostitute. They were both well pissed at the time and Lenny says to his mate, 'Come on, we have got to make a move.' This prostitute says, 'Don't tell him what to do.' Lenny replies, 'Shut your fucking trap, you, I'm talking to my pal.' Lenny's mate says to him, 'Don't talk to her like that, Len.'

That upset Lenny and Lenny's gone at him and smashed the bloke's face to pieces. The bloke ended up in hospital with police around him. Lenny's mate told the police to fuck off when he came round. Lenny told me, from that day on, he hadn't touched a drop of alcohol.

Because I was the number-one cleaner, I was trusted to clean the principal officer's room that was in charge of the wing. Once I was cleaning in there, I'd pick the phone up and make it look like I was dusting it and then I would hit nine which would get me an outside line. I would then ring Val's house number.

Sometimes when I used to phone Val, I'd go back to Len's cell and he'd ask me, 'Did she say she loved me, Paul?' and, as I was about to answer, he'd say, 'Don't tell me, Paul, let me do a roll-up first.' He was like a big lovable, cuddly bear at times. I lost count of the times I phoned Val for him.

Lenny always wanted to know what the solicitor said. I'd read his case over and over again with him. He used to do a lot of people's heads in with that case, although he meant well. I knew his case backwards in the end because I heard it so often.

We were talking about boxing this once and I said to Lenny, 'How do you go about selling tickets for your fights then, Len?' He replied, 'Well, I have a photo of my face like this [squelches face up] and from then onwards people want to come and see me fight.' We'd talk a lot about his fights. He mentioned that the one in America was his hardest.

To know Lenny for ten months inside is like, I suppose, five years on the outside. Me, Len and Tommy helped each other so much inside and we got ourselves through it. Lenny was very choosy, he told me many times, 'You're under my wing, son. I can't believe you phone my wife every night. There are six screws outside that office. How you do it, I don't know.'

I didn't see Lenny train much in prison, but then you used to do a lot of the training in your cells on your own, like bench-pressing your bed or press-ups or sit-ups.

The Welshman Gary Taylor who went on to become the World's Strongest Man used to be in charge of the training in the gym. Lenny used to say to him, 'Mr Taylor, I'm going to get you into movies.'

I measured Lenny's fist one day and it made two of mine put together. His hands were huge, like sledgehammers.

Lenny used to love his roll-ups. He used to give the screws money and they would bring him five or six pouches of tobacco. He'd have this massive tobacco pouch. He used to have about four ounces of tobacco in a two-ounce pouch.

Towards the end of his sentence in Brixton, Lenny was finding it very hard. He knew he was innocent and it was just killing him that he couldn't be with his wife and kids.

The prison officers just couldn't handle him and his attitude and they started drugging him up. He was in a hell of a mess. I saw him this one day and he was like a zombie. To see a big man like Lenny like that made me ill. I'd scream down at him from the balcony, 'Lenny, get off them drugs, mate...' He'd just look up and didn't even know who I was. They then caught Lenny with the mobile phone, and they ended up moving him to Belmarsh.

He had his trial and they then moved him to Wandsworth to finish his sentence off. When he was in Wandsworth, Lenny was in B Wing and we were in D Wing. We would still see him a lot as we had to pass him to get to the kitchens. Lenny used to say to some of the inmates, 'Come here, son, you look like you need fattening up, have Lenny's bit.' Lenny then got released from Wandsworth.

Lenny kept to his word and visited me and Tommy quite a few times on a joint visit. He used to say to the screws, 'Guv'nor, look after these two, they are my cousins.' This one day, he had this tray and he had overloaded it with sweets, they were falling off it as he walked up to us. He then gave us a photo of himself from *The Knock* programme he was about to star in.

Lenny was telling us when he came to see us that one of his friends had just refurbished a pub in the East End and he was looking for a name for it. Lenny had so much respect for Tommy that he called the pub after Tommy's nickname. Lenny then brought the photos in to show us the next time he visited.

Lenny then got me a day's parole while I was in Wandsworth. Lenny was owed a favour from this security firm. So I got a letter from this firm who were based in London and they had arranged an interview for a job for me. Anyway, one of the screws didn't believe me that the letter was real and he phoned the firm up. There was nothing he could do then as the bloke on the other end told him it was true and that they wanted me for an interview.

So Lenny picks me up from the prison around eight in the morning and my missus is in the car with him. We had a big cuddle and then he drove me up to Victoria. He then stops the car and puts about 80 quid in my hand, and says, 'See that hotel over there, now get in there and get your nuts squeezed and have a good day and don't be late back.' I replied, 'What about the job interview, Len?' He replies, 'Fuck the job interview... I've got you out for the day.'

That was an absolute classic by Lenny which I'll never forget.

Another time, I failed to return from home leave. I'd lost my partner during this murder trial due to pressure, so she ran away. I eventually caught up with her and we went and stayed in Birmingham. I phoned Lenny because he said, if I was ever in trouble, to give him a ring. So I phoned him up and he said, 'Where are you, son?' I replied, 'Birmingham, Len.' He said to me, 'Good boy, you are out of the way. Now do yourself a favour and get back down here and Lenny's going to look after you.'

So that's exactly what I done; I came back to East London and Lenny found me a little house in Canary Wharf with these born-again Christians. Because they were born-again Christians they tried telling me and my missus that we couldn't have sex. I'd say to them, 'What are you on about? I've got two kids.' They would reply, 'But you are not married.' They would come in the bedroom throwing holy water all over the place. I thought to myself, What's Len done to me? He's fitted me up.

Lenny took me to the barber's for a haircut, and he suited me up. He then found me a job up the West End ticket flying for the nightclubs.

I was finally recaptured and sent back to Wandsworth where I lost all my remission for going on the run, but I didn't mind now as I had patched things up with my missus.

I escaped from this other prison one night in the early hours of the morning. I got to my missus's mother's house and I was only in there for half-an-hour and the police turned up. I was still in prison clothes. I was so gutted. I was only out half-an-hour and it took me four hours to get there.

My missus was visiting me one day and the governor from Wandsworth, who was the most decent man in the service, came in and said, 'Can I ask your missus some questions?' He then asked her if it was her fault that I kept escaping from prisons. She told him, 'Yes,' and he then told me to put an application in for home leave. He took a personal liking to me and I didn't let that man down.

He let me out a few times after that on home leave. He was a very fair man and a true gentleman. He then told me that, if I behaved myself for the next six months, I would get my remission back and, fair play to him, he stood by his word.

Not long after I finally got released, I went up to Cairo Jack's with Lenny and we were sitting there and he said to me, 'They are giving me £100 a night here… I come at eight and I go home at eleven.' All Lenny was doing was just sitting there, but that was enough most of the time. Then this bloke goes up to the bar and he starts complaining about the food. I said to Lenny, 'Have you seen that bloke over there playing hell with the bar staff?' Lenny says to me so calmly, 'As long as he doesn't touch her, son, then he's all right, but, if he does, I'll paralyse the fucker.'

Another time, there was this bunch of rowdy youngsters and they were playing up. Lenny goes over to them and says, 'Now listen you fucking lot, look at you, you're nine stone sopping wet, you have got about eight pints of lager in you and you think you can fight the world. Now fuck off out or I'll fucking kill the lot of you.' And before you knew it, they were gone.

I don't think he had to hit anyone, as just his presence scared most of them. That reminds me of one of Lenny's favourite sayings: 'Oh, remember to apologise when you wake up.'

I remember being around Lenny's house and he had a phone call from this bloke who was telling him that someone had pinched his newspaper patch. Lenny said to him, 'Leave it to me.' Lenny then phoned this bloke up and said, 'Do you know who this is? This is big Lenny... now do yourself a favour. Get off that fucking patch or I'm going to come round and wring your neck. And the other thing is, I want £500 in the post by Monday morning for my woman.'

Within ten minutes, Lenny's mate had rung and thanked him as the bloke had given him his patch back. Lenny had done that all over the phone; just his voice would scare people.

I once went training with Lenny when I was on the run. We went to this car breaker's yard and Lenny got stuck into this car. He was like the incredible hulk trying to rip the doors and the bonnet off. He must have been on this car for over two hours and it was a hell of a mess. It was quite a funny sight to see.

I went to the gym with him a few times and he used to move and punch continuously for at least an hour around this bag and he'd be dripping with sweat.

I had many letters from Lenny when I was in prison. He'd always finish them with, 'Your pal and friend always… ' I had one postcard from Spain saying that it was good to be home with his lovely wife and family. I also had letters saying he was going to look after me when I got out. He told me in one letter to tell Tommy to tell people inside that he was Lenny's cousin and that would give him some respect.

In another letter, Lenny said to me, 'I have met a lot of people in my life, Paul. I can truly say from my heart you're one of the best. You are a man's man and truly I won't forget you or our friendship in them bad times while we were on remand. Me, you and Tom gave each other support in the bad times… you are truly the old school and a good man. There will be a job for you when you come home. Once again, your friend, I will never forget you, Paul, my pal, your friend always, Lenny McLean.'

Another time he told me, 'Be strong now, you've got your whole life in front of you. You have got a lovely wife and two beautiful children. You have got to put this prison sentence behind you and get on with your life. Paul, you will never get over the remand of murder, which will be with you for the rest of your days. I know because I still think of that time. The sentence is nothing, the murder charge has fucked my head up, but you've got to carry on with your life. When you come home, your whole world is your wife and children, look after them. As I said to you in Brixton, when you made them phone calls, I never forget a favour. Keep strong. Your pal and friend always, Lenny McLean.'

I lost touch with Lenny around 1992 as he was just getting into the TV world. I found out from a mate in Fulham a few years later that Lenny had got cancer and I just couldn't believe it. I was gobsmacked.

I told Lenny the truth that I didn't kill the bloke, and he'd agreed with me. Thinking about it now, I don't know if Lenny fully believed me. I felt a bit wounded by that because I felt that Lenny had come like the rest of them and didn't believe the truth.

I've always respected Val for the way she is and the way she looked after her man in all those years of prison. Lenny arranged it with his Val to meet my partner and they would come up together and visit us. I used to see nothing but love and respect from Lenny to his family.

Lenny just wanted to get on with his time inside. He wasn't a bully in any way; some people used to get on his nerves. A lot of the screws used to ask for his autograph. He was well respected even though he was inside. The prison officers feared him; not one prison officer would have a go at him, they had to go in six-handed; he was just too strong to stop.

I think if you pissed him off then he could be your world's worst nightmare but, from what I seen of him, he'd do anything to help you. I never saw Lenny fighting in jail but then he didn't really have to. As far as Lenny was concerned, all he had to do was growl. The way he could talk to people would scare the life out of them.

Lenny had pure respect from all the inmates, and he could also be very funny at times, and he could take off Jimmy Cagney to a tee.

Lenny was the most confident man I have ever met; I

always felt safe and comfortable in his presence. He had a powerful personality, good sense of humour, and he was really funny. I had total respect for the man.

I wish he was here today. He was 100 per cent original, he really was. I loved him dearly in my own way. Your pal, and friend always, Paul Morris.

6
Role Model

Before Lenny had reached film stardom in *Lock, Stock and Two Smoking Barrels*, he had appeared in many TV documentaries and programmes. Even from as early as the late 1970s, people had started taking an interest and Lenny had appeared in the documentary called *The Guv'nor*. Here is a taster of Lenny's involvement in some of those programmes.

TONIGHT SHOW

(Interviewer asks Lenny about a recent gang fight he was in.)

Lenny: I knocked about six out, pulled the sticks out and went to work, and the rest of them all run.

Interviewer: What do you mean by, 'you pulled the sticks out'?

Lenny: Well, you know, when you get a firm come after you about 15-handed, you've got to, you know, you got to use a stick. I used to have a stick on the door and I used to use that, you know, because when people look for trouble, when they come in looking for trouble, you know, and they're determined, you got to hurt them... you know. But that was my job on the door, but anyway that's neither here or there now, I'm into this fighting game.

Interviewer: What happened to the 15 people?

Lenny: Well, I don't know, I'm not worried about them, long as I wasn't hurt, you know.

Interviewer: But you were at the time.

Lenny: Yeah, but only my hands, my hands from where I went into them. No marks on there, though *(touching his face)*. Is it?

Interviewer: And you knocked some of them out?

Lenny: About six or seven and the rest of them run, the rest of them run because they were cowards.

(Interviewer then accuses Lenny of sounding like a bully.)

Lenny: No, you're joking – gentleman, not a bully, gentleman. You got to fight to get anywhere; if you don't fight then you're just one of the crowd and one of the crowd don't get nothing. I started off, I was a kid fighting, and I was the best when I was a kid and I want to be the best now, that's why I do these fights.

Interviewer: So what sort of fights were you involved in when you were a kid?

Lenny: Street fights, and I'm just carrying on now, you know, just fighting 'cause I like fighting.

Interviewer: But when you say you had to fight to survive...

Lenny: Well, you had to fight in the East End, didn't

you? If you don't fight in the East End, you end up
with the elbow, you get nothing, you know, you got
to survive in the East End, and, uh, be the best
fighter. Be the Guv'nor. You know, I just picked up a
paper one day and, uh, it was that Shawy in the
paper saying he was the Guv'nor… he's the best
fighter in London… and I knew I could beat him. I
knew I could beat him, so a few friends and I got
together, stuck a few quid up and challenged him.
*(Interviewer starts talking about Lenny's second fight with
Roy Shaw.)*
Lenny: I got in there nice and strong and fit and
knocked him out in 50 seconds. I hit him so hard
he wound up in the second row.
Interviewer: He said he had taken some…
Lenny: All he took was a right-hander and wound up
in the second row, and he's rucking about he took
this and he took that… I don't care what he took.
Monday night I will do the same again.
Interviewer: Why's it so important to beat him in this
particular fight?
Lenny: Well, I've got a bee in my bonnet about him.
It's a bit of a grudge fight. You know, he reckons he
can beat me… there's no way he can beat me,
there's no way. He's not strong enough, I'll knock
him out.

Television and newspaper critic-turned-author Garry Bushell
had a chance to catch up with Lenny a few years ago while he
was doing interviews for his television programme *Bushell on
the Box*. Garry has vivid memories of Lenny.

GARRY BUSHELL

I first met Lenny McLean in the Eighties when he lived in East London. I'd known of him by reputation for many years and was chuffed to discover that he had a mind as lively as those formidable fists.

When Lenny recalled his legendary street fights, there was always a twinkle in his eyes as he was reliving them. I met him again and interviewed him for the Sun newspaper in the early Nineties. A few years later, in 1996, he came on my show. Lenny was making a big impact as a villain in LWT's *The Knock*. The acting came easy to him, he lived the part, and the batterings he'd endured hadn't deadened his brain.

Lenny McLean could have stepped right out of the pages of a book. He was a big man, but not much wider than a truck, and he had this serious physical presence. When Lenny walked into a room, you knew it. Things usually went quiet.

When Lenny walked into my bar to film his appearance on my ITV show *Bushell on the Box*, the producer turned so white he was almost see-through. It was like he had just sat up in the bath and spotted a piranha circling his scrotum. The mere look of McLean was enough to intimidate the crew. My sound man, Neil, a karate black belt, admitted afterwards that he had spent the whole interview wondering whether he could have dropped the big man if Lenny had thrown a strop. His conclusion was, 'Not an effing chance!'

But, naturally, Lenny was a perfect gent. He respected my home, he was pleasant and polite, an entertaining guest, and he gave his time freely to the local tearaways who had rallied in my back garden. McLean had long been a legend to working-class Londoners who considered him the Rocky Marciano of the unlicensed boxing world and, after the show, he found himself mobbed by a small army of spotty teenagers. Lenny's big bulldog face broke into an enormous grin. But he didn't bask in the glory and entertain them with gory tales of who he'd up-ended on the cobbles. The message he gave those kids was quite different. 'Shit up 'ere...' he boomed, poking a giant finger at his nose, '... nut don't like it.' Over and over again, 'Shit up 'ere, nut don't like it...' In other words, cocaine mucks up your brain. I'd venture his little talk was a damn sight more effective than any lame government 'Just Say No' poster campaign.

Roy Shaw once swore blind that Lenny had only beaten him because he had taken the ginseng vitamin drink. When asked about Roy Shaw's claim, Lenny had replied, 'Yes, it could have been the ginseng that he took... on the other hand, though, it could have been the big right-hander he took that put him in the third row.'

While we were filming the show, Lenny showed me his remarkable hand speed quite a few times. We had a good laugh recording the interview and comedy sketches and got on really well. Lenny McLean was as much a gent as he was a giant. He was also a very funny bloke. It was a pleasure to have known him.

BUSHELL ON THE BOX

Garry: Lenny, Lenny McLean, for years the most awesome man in Britain, 20,000 street fights, broken limbs, shot... what made you decide to become an actor?

Lenny: It started hurting me, Garry... seriously, Garry, I've been minding the roughest, toughest pubs in town – Brixton, East London – I've been shot twice, stabbed. I must have had 20,000 bar-room brawls, I've broke my hands 15 times. I've got pins in my hands, but what actually turned me, Garry, was when I was nicked for that murder, which I never done, and it was proven at the Old Bailey. I used to lay in the cell and think to myself, I'm in here, I'm looking at a life sentence for nothing, so I thought to myself, you know, if I ever got out of this, I promised myself I'd go down a different road.

And when you see them prats on the TV, all acting tough… guys who are as silly as a box of flies… I thought I'd get into the acting game, as I am the real thing, and Bruce Willis, who I found to be a lovely man, absolute gentleman, down to earth, he told me jokes, a good guy. That film's out next year, and I have got myself five episodes of *The Knock*. I would like to thank Paul Knight, who's a lovely man, because, when I went up for the casting, the casting director said, because I was always there behind the scenes afterwards, the casting director said, 'We don't want him. He's a proper tough guy, we want an actor.' So Paul Knight said, 'No, this guy, we'll give him a chance, he's got an agent, he's got an Equity card, we'll give him a chance,' and I'd just like to thank him, lovely man.

Garry: We have just seen last Sunday, the episode went out when you are overpowered by some of these Customs officers, and I though this must have been the best bit of acting you have ever done in your life because for you to be…

Lenny: It was a hard bit of acting because it's the first

Len with his beloved Val.

On the doors.

Above: Mick Theo and Lenny take a break.

Below: The author with bouncers Stilks and Don Austin.

Lenny touched the lives of so many people…

Above: With Helen Keating, Charlie Kray and Maureen Flanagan.

Below left: With Alex Steene, who helped to promote the fights, and Jimmy Andrews.

Below right: With old friend Dave Courtney.

Above: Lenny in action against Ron Redrup.

Below: A sad day – the great man's funeral. Here's just one of the many floral tributes to the Guv'nor.

time I've ever been on the floor… no, let me tell you what happened. When we done the scene, I couldn't go over, and they were trying to get me down saying, 'Come on, Lenny, come on, Lenny,' and I said, 'No,' and they went, 'Cut.' The director came over and said, 'Lenny, you got to go over.' I said, 'All right then… how do you do it?' and he said, 'Put your legs in and your knees and you fall.' So I said I'll do that.

So I went over and he said, 'Thanks for going over, Lenny,' and I said, 'I don't mind, it's a film, but it would never happen in real life,' and we had a laugh. There was some lovely people there.

Garry: Len, your real life is like a movie script, it reads like one, and your biography is coming out very soon.

Lenny: My biography was done by a guy named Peter Gerrard, a fantastic writer. The biography's coming out… what they are trying to do is bring it out the same time as the movie, because we actually have finance now after 11 years. The film was going to be called *The Guv'nor* but, because it don't relate in America, they have changed it to *Total Respect*, because in America 'the Guv'nor' means you're up for Presidency but, over here, it means the toughest man in town.

Garry: Who are they going to get who'll be convincing playing you?

Lenny: I don't know. They are looking at a couple of possibles… what about Tom Cruise? Nah, I'm only joking, I don't really know, I'll leave that up to them. All I am on this is the adviser on the set, but as long as they find a good actor. But remember, this film don't need a star, the film will make the actor a star, its like another *Rocky* film but with bare knuckles, and it's a true story, so I think it's going to do well.

Garry: What advice would you give to the bloke who plays you?

Lenny: I'll talk to him, won't I? I'll just say be tough, be good, be fair and be fast.

ARENA

(Lenny is being interviewed by Paul Lynch.)

Lenny: Show me your hands… not bad, not as bad as mine but don't forget I'm a lot older. I mean, I've had bare-knuckle fights for money, I've had unlicensed fights for money and, as you say, in the Seventies and the Eighties, I was the absolute Guv'nor on the cobbles. No one in England could beat me.

Now I'm retired because I had a bit of trouble a couple of years ago, so now I'm using this *(points to his brain)* and I'm doing a lot of poetry. But let me give you a bit of advice – always keep yourself fit, always be strong, and train hard, even though bare-knuckle fighting don't normally last more than two minutes. Always keep yourself fit and strong and remember, as you fight, you start getting a reputation and there will always be mugs out there looking for a rep, so always be on your guard and always keep strong. If you are strong you'll always be in front of the other guy, always remember that.

Keep strong and fit and hate, from there *(pointing to his head)* to your ankle, hate so much.

Say we are having a fight; before the fight, I think I hate him, I hate him. Why do I hate him? He's just interfered with my wife, he's interfered with my kids and I take his head right off, take his head right off, smash everything because of hate.

I left school and I started fighting in clubs and pubs, and they went, 'Lenny's the toughest guy…' Lenny's this, Lenny's that, and I thought, I like this. I like the idea of this, and then some businesspeople put some money together and I was fighting bare-knuckle and bashing everyone up, and getting a few quid.

Paul: And getting a few belts yourself?

Lenny: No, not street fighting, never, I'm too quick and too aggressive. I've never lost a fight on the cobbles… you take one or two but, when you're cranky and you're having a tear-up, these don't hurt *(punches himself in face)* because you're too busy going to work yourself to worry about little bits of pain.

Say we are having a fight *(Lenny then shows Paul what he would do, he throws a couple of punches and then a headbutt, and then goes to bite his ear off)*, put you out of the game, that's how I would do it.

Listen, you're about 14 years younger than me, get your few quid, and put it into something, because it's hardly the greatest game in the world [bare-knuckle fighting] but it's an easy few quid, because I'm not taking the piss but you're what I call 'in the game', brand spanking new. You know, I've been in it so long, I've been minding clubs and fighting all my life. All my life I've been fighting. Come on, there's got to be a better life than that; I want to know what's in that bowl, because all I keep seeing is people going to the bowl and getting the cream. I don't get no cream, all I get is the agg, so now I want some cream. I'm entitled to it, so now I want what I'm entitled to. I'm 45 nearly and I want some cream, I think I'm entitled to it, don't you?

Son, there's my hand, there's my heart... be the strongest and the toughest in the game, because it's a hard game. All right, boy, I love yah.

BERMONDSEY BOY OUT-TAKES

(In 1992, Dave Courtney made a TV documentary called Bermondsey Boy. *Dave asked Lenny if he wanted a part in it. While filming this, the cameras kept rolling and Dave and Lenny did a very rare interview in one of Lenny's mates' yards in London. This interview appears courtesy of Dave Courtney.)*

Lenny: Dave's a very good friend of mine and a character, a well-known character in East London, always ducking and diving, always busy.
Interviewer: Why are you the hardest man in Britain?
Lenny: Because I am. I've been fighting everybody, all-comers. I've never ducked anyone, and they are now doing a £10 million movie about my life, and I am the hardest man in Britain, without a doubt. But I've retired now, and I'm going on to better

things… they are doing my life story and I hope I get a lot of money out of it and I can retire.

Lenny: (Asked about his bare-knuckle fights) I used to go to Derby Day fighting gypsies. It was around '75 and '77. Funny enough, in this place where we are sitting now *(Kenny Mac's car yard)*. There used to be a big hut out there and I used to fight bare-knuckle. I'd just fight anyone who wanted to have a fight for money.

People call me an animal, but I don't think you're an animal fighting another big, powerful guy for a few quid; you are not interfering with anyone, the public, you are leaving them alone. You are just fighting people who want to fight.

And from there we went on to the unlicensed fighting, where the public would come and watch, but then you would have to wear gloves because the police would nick you. So I used to fight top of the bill on the unlicensed shows and that's where I got to know Dave, because he used to fight on the same bills.

The last fight I had was at Woodford – he was six foot seven and 24 stone. I was sitting in the dressing room, and that's where I met Dave. He came in and his nose was bleeding and he was shouting. I then said to him, 'What's the matter with you?' and he said, 'I can't understand this, I've just had a fight with a geezer. I've nutted him and kicked him in the knackers and I've got disqualified, Len. What's it all about?' I said, 'I don't know, but, if he disqualifies me, I'll kill him stone dead.'

See, we are characters... I mean, I don't care what people say about us, we are characters. You know Dave does a lot of film work and I'm getting into the film world, but we do what we have to do for a few quid.

Interviewer: When did you start fighting?

Lenny: Well, I started fighting, I think, I was about two months old... someone had nicked my bottle. Nah, my father died when I was four and what happened was, my mum was beautiful, 26, with five kids. My stepfather then slipped in and married my mum. He wanted my mum, but he didn't want the booby prize which was the kids. So he broke my jaw when I was five, he put me in hospital... broke my leg when I was about eleven... he was just a horrible bully.

Then, all of a sudden, I looked around one day, I must have been about 17, I looked at my stepfather and I thought, I'll fucking give him who's the Guv'nor, and then he fucked off – I have not seen him since. I knew I said I wouldn't hit him, he must be about 63 years old now, but I'll tell him where he went wrong.

Interviewer: What did you get up to other than the fights?

Lenny: Well, you know, ducking and diving, doing a bit of debt collecting, minding a few people, minding a few clubs. Do what I have to do to make a living. I was saying to Dave the other day, Dave said he was in a bit of trouble with this and that. Dave said, 'Len, when's it going to end?' and I said,

'Dave, you got to understand, I think you do understand because you're old enough now, we are born in East London, but other people say they are born in East London, but if they want to work the system they wind up potless and skint.'

In East London, you got to kick or be kicked, and I wasn't prepared to be kicked. So I became the toughest guy. Dave does his ducking and diving and whatever he's got to do, a bit of debt collecting, because we have to, to get a living, because you know, we are not prepared to go the system way. The system way you'll end up with nothing. You read it in the paper every day – Mrs So and So, 86, died of pneumonia, freezing cold, trying to put two bob in the electric. The system is no good.

Dave: We get more opportunity than anyone else, because who we are supposed to be, like Lenny, who you are. You get offers all the time, it's not like we run round looking for it, people approach you all the time to do things. It ends up your way of life, whether you want it or not.

Lenny: Nine times out of ten, we don't want it, Dave, do we? We don't want it. I mean, funnily enough, I'm sitting here talking to you now and I had to meet earlier with you people because I have got a meet at two o'clock. I'm going down London Airport because somebody owes someone £150,000 and they are not going to pay. So I'm going to talk to these people and I'm going to get the money for them.

Interviewer: How are you going to do that then?

Dave: (*Laughing*) They'll pay.

Lenny: Well, we'll talk to them first and then if they don't pay up, well, they usually pay funnily enough. The thing is, when my film goes, we'll get out a few quid and it will be nice to say I'm not interested, but we do our thing to make a living.

(Dave is asked if he's seen Lenny fighting, and which one was the most colourful.)

Dave: Yeah, a lot, they are all colourful fights. There isn't one better than the other. The poor man's a lunatic, you should feel sorry for him really. He can't help what he does. He's a half-man, half-bear, I think.

Lenny: Thank you very much, Dave, I mean, that's a compliment coming from another East Ender. You know, if it came from someone in St John's Wood, I think he would be taking the piss, because he don't know our way of life. But Dave was born under the same stone as me.

Interviewer: Tell us about a couple of your fights.

Lenny: I had a bare-knuckle fight, not an unlicensed one. Funnily enough, we had it in here; there's a guy peeping round the corner there, he promoted it. It was anything goes, but what happened was, I slung the first right hand and I caught him high on the forehead and broke my hand. I then hit him with a left hook and he went over. Remember, it's an all-in fight.

So I'm lying on top of him but I can't hit him any more. I've broke this hand and I've broke this thumb, so I bent over and I took a liberty I suppose. I bit half his ear off, his bottom lip and I bit his throat, but I won the prize. He went to hospital and, when he came out, he thought I went too strong. So he got a gun.

Well, a pal of mine borrowed my car at the time. I said to him, now, be a bit slippery as there's someone flying about with a gun. My mate then said to me, 'I'm only going round the corner.'

My mate ended up having his leg blown off from the knee. They thought it was me. Then a meet was called and he had to behave himself, because I'm afraid someone would have died. We ended up shaking hands after that.

I've had some terrible fights, but that's the way it is, that's the way it goes, innit?'

Interviewer: Do you enjoy it?

Lenny: Not so much enjoy it… whatever I do, I do it for money. So I suppose, really, in the old days, people like us would be called gunslingers… whatever we do, we do it for money. But if I had degrees in this and that, I'd then be doing other things, but I was born in the East End, where you have got to shape up and knock them out to get a few quid – end of.

Dave: Everybody's gifted at something, it's just this man can have a row and that's it, you understand what I mean. He's the best fighter there is, the best, and that's his gift, so, whether he wanted it or not, that's what he's best at. You don't turn into a fighter – you are born one. You know, and that's what he is… he's helped me out a couple of times.

Lenny: It's in there *(pointing at his heart)*, it comes

from in there. It don't come from being shown or being taught, it's in there. As Dave said, he had a couple of bits of trouble and he's phoned me up. I'll give the kid a lot of credit, he's a lot younger than me, he's game. That's what it's all about, and he would die with you.

Interviewer: If you could have planned your career out again, would you do it differently?

Lenny: I wouldn't change my life. The thing is, I wouldn't let people use me so much. You know, in my earlier days, someone would phone me up in trouble and I would be straight there. What I should have done was, instead of going and having murders and tear-ups for nothing, I should have said, 'Hold up, that's got to come to so and so.' It was only when I got a bit older that I started saying, 'That will cost you so and so…'

You know, when I'm debt collecting, I want the money up front and I get it… I won't do nothing for nothing.

Interviewer: What training do you do?

Lenny: I do weights, a bit of bag work. I always keep my hand in there, have a little spar about.

Dave: That's if he can find a sparring partner. He comes down the gym sometimes, there's all these chaps, young fit boys, all the pros and the unlicensed boys, little waist and big chests, and they really think they are the business. Lenny comes in with his fucking kit on and he stands there and says, 'Well, who's going to spar with me then?' You can see everyone looking away thinking, Fuck that!

178

Lenny: Me and Dave train two or three times a week up the club. I said to Dave, 'You got to keep well because all these up-and-coming youngsters keep fancying the job.' As the years go on, they look at you, and they fancy the job, so what you do is you train mentally… instead of being 41, you're 31. I mean, that's the way I do it.

Dave: There isn't a lot of hard men round now, it's just these young kids around 17 or 18, they are not frightened of anyone; you have got to have your wits about you.

Lenny: See, the young ones today, they got no respect. The trouble is they are putting shit up their nose, shit in their veins and they really don't give a monkey's who you are. They don't know if they are coming or going or what day it is. They are dangerous, because they got no respect.

You read in the papers all these old girls and boys getting mugged, or you see on the news the other night some young girl getting stabbed in the mouth. Let's be fair, people who do that are off their nuts, and they are all drugged up, they do it for tuppence. They don't care, because they are out of their nuts.

When we was younger, I mean, if you see an old girl walking, I'd say to my pals, 'Oh, its Mrs So and So, can I help you with your bags?' and it's no cobblers, anyone our age will tell you, we'd help Mrs So and So to her door and, if we got tuppence, we'd be well pleased. That's the way we were brought up, but kids today, they put it up their nose and in their veins and they don't care.

Dave: Because we work the clubs, you see it all the time, you know what drugs can do, so it helps us out not to take it, we have got the edge over them because we are straight.

Lenny: If I'm on a door of a club, I don't give... well, I might give them a half-inch, I tell them once and that's it, then I'll take their heads right off, because these young kids, you show them kindness, and they will take kindness for a weakness. Nice people, now you can show nice people kindness and they will go when you walk away, 'Isn't he a nice guy?' You show a mug or these young kids kindness, they then think, He doesn't seem that strong, does he?

I mean, the other week down the club, someone's glassed someone. I didn't say to the kid, 'Why did you glass him?' I took his head right off, because what right did he have to stick a glass in someone's face? Anyway, I knocked the guy out and, when he was unconscious, I said to the one who got glassed, 'Why did he glass you?' and the bloke replied, 'Well, because I am going out with this girl he used to go out with three years ago,' and that's stupid, and he got a scar right down his face.

Interviewer: Do you demand respect?

Lenny: What I meant earlier was, the youngsters show no respect to yourself, they got no respect to the old people. They show me respect... why are they showing me respect? They show me respect because they are frightened of me, because, if they can't show me respect, I will unload them *(shows his fists to the cameras)* and I ain't a bully. A bully is someone who picks and chooses anyone. I'll fight the world, that's the difference. I'll fight King Kong. And, as my friend said, I have got nothing to prove. They are doing a £10 million movie about me. I've done all my proving years ago, but with the youngsters today, it's like my mate said, 'If they ain't got a knife on them, they feel naked.'

Interviewer: Have you ever lost a fight?

Lenny: Never, on the cobbles. I'm telling you, I've never lost a fight on the cobbles, because like I said earlier, it comes from in there *(points to his heart)* there's so much hate in there when I fight, and it hurts me. There's so much hate inside me, because I don't dig anybody out, I have got my reputation.

They are making a film about me. I'm 41, when this comes out I'll be 42, so I have got no reason to dig anybody out. But people come to me pissed and half fancy the job… well, I take their heads right off… why should they dig me out? I suppose, really, it's like years ago, the old gunslinging days, they want your reputation. I train four or five times a week now and, you know, if they want my reputation, they have got to die for it. And if they fancy the job, afterwards they will think they have been to hell and back.

Interviewer: Do you ever lose your temper?

Lenny: Now, I always try and be very polite. Truthfully, believe it or not, always try and be polite. My pal said to me a long time ago, and Dave also said this to me, people say, 'Len, you bring a lot on yourself. I've seen you when you talk to people, you talk very nice, but, if there's trouble in the club, you go, "Now excuse me, now listen, you must not do that." You do that psychology, Len, you're trying to draw them in, because a couple of times you said the same and they have gone, "Well, who are you?" and you have gone in and broke their jaw… well, another time, you have gone in and growled at them, and they don't want to know.'

Well, there's two ways you could do it, depends what I'm like on the day. Sometimes, I go in and talk nice and they say something, and I have taken their head off. Another time I growl at them and they say nothing. So I suppose there's something really at the back of my mind.

Dave: When you're confident of your own abilities you can afford to be polite first, as you know you're not going to lose.

Lenny: We try and nip it in the bud; it's a terrible thing when you're dealing with drunks, kids or drug addicts, it's very hard. They can't see reason, and I give them a little tiny bit, and then I won't give them anything else, then – bang – I unload them.

Listen to this, I had a pal about four years ago, you know the guy I'm talking about, Dave – Bernie – he used to mind a club over in Brixton. I worked with the guy, not a bad guy, but another job came up and people asked me to go somewhere else for more money. So I went somewhere else.

Anyway, this guy was working on the door about four or five weeks later after I left and he got hold of a skinny kid, must have weighed about eight stone, and he's pushed the skinny kid out into the club. Anyway, when he went home that night, he parks his car in the garage, he turns round and the bloke's standing there with a gun... he's put two bullets in his head and one in his cheekbone, blew his head right off.

When they got hold of the mug the next day and nicked him, all the drugs had worn off. They said to him, 'Why did you do it?' He said, 'I can't remember... I was out of my nut.'

But it's no excuse, Bernie's six foot under. What it is, it tars the good kids, they all get tarred with the same brush; I suppose there's good kids out there. It's a crazy world.

Interviewer: Tell us about your most colourful fights.

Lenny: Well, I've had some good fights; I've had a lot of good fights. I mean, I fought the hardest man in London for a lot of money. I fought the hardest man in Scotland; I fought all round – East London, South London, I fought anyone who wanted a fight.

Dave: Your most publicised fight was against Shaw, though, I think, wasn't it?

Lenny: Yeah, Roy was the most publicised fight, but I've retired now. I'm on to other things. I'm getting into this film world, because, you know, Dave's an actor now, every time you see him he's been in a film.

Interviewer: Give us an example of your most colourful fight.

Lenny: I'll give you an example. I was minding a club one day and I had a fight with a little estate firm... you remember them, Kenny? They were 18-handed. I put nine in hospital and the other nine run away. They banged me up in the nick and they said, 'Lenny, we can't nick you, we have got to send it to the DPP, come back in three weeks.'

So I went back in three weeks and, in other words, the DPP said there's no way we can nick one man fighting against 18. It will be laughed out of court.

Anyway, I was on the door a fortnight after that, and a rat, I still don't know his name today, got off a motorbike with a crash helmet on, crept up to the door with a double-barrel shot gun and shot me in the back. I had about 3,000 stitches. He shot me up the arse, and he blew half my arse off. So what I done, it done my nut, I couldn't run all that fast. I chased him, he got on his motorbike and went up the road and slipped away.

Another time, I come home from minding a club. I've pulled up in the car and, as I got out of the car, a car drove past me and they shot me in the back as well, but I've always said these people who shoot people in the back, I think they are cowards. The thing is, I like a man to come up and say, 'Lenny, I've got the hump with you, come on, let's have a fight,' then I'll have all the respect in the world for them. And then, after the fight, I'll go up the hospital and take them a present, because I respect them. But all these cowards who shoot people in the back, I've got no time for them, because my little baby could shoot someone in the back, just aim and pull the trigger.

Dave: If you live this way, you put yourself on offer,

you target yourself for people to do that; you're waiting for someone to have a pop at you.

Lenny: 'Course you are, we're all the same, Dave, it's not the point; you're waiting for someone to have a pop at you. They are going to come. It's like I said before, the old cowboy days, you get the young gunslinger who wants to get a reputation.

Interviewer: Is that right, you have got the same barrister?

Lenny: Yeah, Ralph Haeems, he's the best. He's the absolute Guv'nor in that game, and he's the top man. Funnily enough, my friend, he's in court tomorrow, but, if there's any justice in this world, he'll walk out of there because it was a misunderstanding and I think he's innocent. I mean, I would say that, but what I've heard through the grapevine is another dozen people feel the same and, if there's justice in the world, he'll walk out of there tomorrow, please God.

But our way of life, you know, put it this way, I wouldn't recommend it to anybody. My son and my daughter, my son's 19 and my daughter's 18, and they go to work and I love them. And you know, they are not my way of life, they take after my wife, and they are very polite and nice. Don't get me wrong, I'm very polite and nice, but they are not my way of life. They have been brought up to be lovely, beautiful children.

It's like Dave – he wouldn't want his kids to be flying about the West End and be doing what he does. You don't want your family to be doing it.

185

Dave: What happens is, because you have done it, and you have lived that life and you know the pitfalls, your kids will have a better upbringing. But someone that goes to primary, because you know the pitfalls and you can keep them away from it, so they are getting good tuition from indoors, if you understand what I mean.

Lenny: You can take the most educated person in the world, a top professor or top doctor, and take them to a pub or club and ask them how do they feel and they would say, 'It's quite nice in here.' They haven't got a clue. You know why? It's because they aren't streetwise. We can walk into a club or pub and we'll know there will be murders in there in a minute. How do we know? We can smell it, the atmosphere... is that right, Dave? It's what you call street sense. It's the atmosphere, it's instinct.

Dave: All these weird kids, all these punk rockers and really weird kids. If you go and find out what job their parents do, they are all doctors and lawyers who have been to public school. Say someone like Lenny was your dad, he's not going to let his kid go out with orange hair and 12 earrings in his nose.

Lenny: Yeah, he's right. I was talking to this kid last week. She had a pair of drawers on, stuck right up her bum. She had a bra on with all studs in it, and she had orange and green Mohican hair and funny glasses. I said, 'Do your mum and dad know you look like that?' She then says, 'My dad's a doctor...' They were rich people, they came from Hampstead.

See, I think they just turn like that to rebel against

their parents. Where we have had the bad life in this world, we guide our children differently. My kids, please God, will never ever turn into that. Don't get me wrong, I think I'm a smashing guy now because now I can see where I'm going and that's the way I'm going to go.

Interviewer: I've been told that you're a bit of a sex symbol in the West End.

Lenny: Thank you very much, a lot of the people reckon I look like Tom Cruise. Funny enough, I have that menacing face.

Dave: He's quite cuddly, really.

Lenny: I am quite cuddly, I shouldn't really be bothering with being cuddly as what we are talking about is two different things, but I'm a character, and that's it.

(Interviewer asks Lenny about a bare-knuckle fight.)

Lenny: We used to shut the gates, come in here, say like someone would bring £20,000 and bring a gypsy, and they would be two-handed and I'd be two-handed and we would have a bare-knuckle fight. We would then cut the bid up and fight. There would also be bits of string hanging there and we used to train in there. It was like something out of the New York Bronx. This is what it's all about, hard training.

Interviewer: What sort of training did you do?

Lenny: I used to get up at six every morning and go for a six-mile run. See, people don't know all this, they just think you go and have a bare-knuckle fight. I used to train for two hours, six-mile runs, come in here, go on the bags and then my friend Kenny

187

used to lay the fights on. We would have a bare-knuckle fight in here and some of them were bad… I done a lot of damage to a lot of people, but yet again it was for a living.

Dave: I saw Lenny training once in a car breaker's yard, just to build up some adrenalin. He had a fucking big pick-axe handle and he started beating up a car, ripping doors off, just to let a bit of anger out. How many people do you know who could beat up a Cortina?

Lenny: You have got to leave out the evilness… Dave then starts winding me up, and says that Cortina is old. I then said to Dave, 'I could have still done a new Cortina,' but we didn't have one, you know it's just our life.

Interviewer: Tell us about the fight when you bit that bloke's ear off.

Lenny: Well, I had a fight with a gypsy and, when he turned up here, I said to the guy, 'What do you want?' He said, 'I just want a straightener,' that's a stand-up fight with no kicking or nothing. So I said, 'OK then, so we went in there and we was having a tear-up and all of a sudden I've got in close and he's nutted me. Funnily enough, that's how I've got this scar here. He's nutted me and I couldn't understand; it was supposed to be a straightener.

Anyway, it's done my nut. I nutted him, I kicked the life out of him, bit his throat, bit half his ear off, and I suppose it sounds evil, it sounds mad, but we were two big guys having a fight; it was either him or me and it fucking wasn't going to be me. So I

188

done the business… we do all we have to do to win.
Anyway, I won the fight, I nicked the £20,000 and I
went home and bought my wife a nice car and I
went away for ten days. Ain't it a lovely way to make
a living?

Tell them about the time you hit someone with a
stool, Dave.

Dave: I was on this show with Lenny and he's a hard
act to follow, you know what I mean, a fucking hard
act to follow, mate… I went out and people were
leaving because Lenny had finished. I had a tear-up
with a bloke named Buster somebody and I battered
the fucking life out of him, I mean, I can't do all the
funny business like the ducking and diving and all
that bollocks, but I was winning so well. I could
afford to be flashy in front of everyone. I knew I'd
won, and if you're that close to someone then it
don't matter how many judges are putting points
on. I knew who's winning. I could look at him and
see I was hurting him. I knew I'd fucking beat the
geezer, it was a points decision.

I was standing there in my corner, there was a
bucket there and a stool, and the ref in the middle
then goes, 'And the winner is…' I was just about to
put my hand up and he puts up the other geezer's
hand. So I've looked over and, as he's looked round
at me, he gave me a right look. So I've grabbed the
stool and I done him with it. I done him really bad;
his corner men came over and then my corner men
came in and there was a huge row in the ring.
There were some television people filming there. I

189

don't know who they were, they were filming Lenny.
Lenny: It was good. I'll tell you why it was good…
they come to see me fight because they know I am
an animal and they know there's going to be
murders and villainy in the ring. This kid's come
along and the kid's done the same thing, so I said to
the promoter, 'When I fight again, put this kid on
the show.' 'Why's that then, Len?' 'Because he's just
hit this geezer with the stool… what will happen
now is, instead of selling 30 seats last time, this time
he'll sell 230, get that kid on the bill next time. I
said I want kids like that… remember, we are not
with the British Boxing Board, we were fighting for
a few quid and fighting to win – end of. If you have
got to, hit someone with a stool; if you can't get a
stool, then hit them with the referee. If they want to
watch boxing, then go to the Albert Hall.

They are still talking about our fights and they
happened a few years ago… I mean, the shows are
over now because all the characters are retired and
moved on to better things, but that's what it was like
in those days.

RICHARD LITTLEJOHN SHOW (1)
*(Chat-show host and TV critic Richard Littlejohn is joined
in the studio with Sharron Davies, Paul Ross and boxing
trainer Frank Maloney. Lenny had just finished filming
his part in the Bruce Willis film* The Fifth Element.*)*
Richard: Now, we are going to meet a man who
made his name as a bare-knuckle fighter, an
unlicensed boxer, he was once dubbed 'the hardest

man in London', and who am I to argue with him? You probably know him, like I do, as Eddie Davies, the gang boss in ITV series *The Knock,* which goes out on Sunday nights. Please welcome, with the greatest possible respect, Lenny McLean.

(Lenny walks on and shakes hands with Richard and the other guests.)

Richard: Welcome, nice to see you, how are you? I have got to ask you this. I've got the *Radio Times* here – you were a boxer but now you're an actor – it says, 'Eddie Davies is played by Leonard McLean...' have you gone all luvvy on us?

Lenny: No, I'll never go luvvy, but I want to be a bit posh now that I'm on the television. It's a better world, isn't it? You hit someone on the street and they want to give you five years... do it on the television, and they want to give you five grand.

Richard: Tell me about how you got into acting. How did the part in *The Knock* come from?

Lenny: Well, I'll tell you what happened. All my life, I have been involved in the other world. I bumped into Mike Reid one day and said, 'Mike, you're not even a good actor, you just play yourself.' Mike then said to me, 'Len, you got to get into the game and play yourself,' and that's what I done. I made a few enquiries, got my Equity card and went for a casting.

Richard: It's normally quite difficult to get an Equity card, how did you go about persuading them?

Paul: (Laughing) He asked them... who's going to say no to him?

Lenny: What I actually did, I went down there and I

191

sung to them, I sung 'Please Don't Say No', and they give it to me. And I like the acting, it's fantastic. I went for a casting on *The Knock* and I met the director and casting guy and they didn't want me, even though I played the part well, but behind the scenes I heard how I got the part.

Paul Knight, the producer, said, 'I want to give Lenny a chance,' and it's people like him, if they give more people like us a chance, we can come from our world and get into that world.

Richard: Do you think you'll be a little bit typecast... you have come on there as a sort of underworld gang boss?

Lenny: Well, I play the part well, don't I? I have been rehearsing for 30 years.

Richard: What other parts do you fancy... Hamlet or something?

Lenny: I could do Hamlet – 'All right, my son, you coming down?' I don't suppose I'll ever do Hamlet.

Richard: Do you think, if you got into the acting lark earlier, your life would have been different?

Lenny: Yeah, I think so, I mean it's like if I had got into the acting, I think I would have been a good actor, because if you want something, you put your blinkers on and say you want that and you get it... you have got to go for it.

Richard: I got told you just worked with Bruce Willis.

Lenny: I worked with Bruce Willis on his latest movie called *The Fifth Element*; he's the nicest guy you could ever wish to meet, because, when you meet the big stars, they are so down to earth. He had a dressing

room downstairs; he had a wine cabinet, a colour
TV, a bed, a shower, it was beautiful. There were also
a couple of stars next door and they had the same. I
was stuck up in the loft... I had a chair, a table, and I
thought to myself, I think they are taking the piss,
but I didn't want to say anything because if people
like us raise our voice, they think, We should never
have cast him. So I thought, Say nothing, because it's
a $60 million movie and I'm with all the top stars, so
I thought I'd make out I'm a top star.

So I came out of my dressing room and went
downstairs. Someone then said to me, 'You are
supposed to stay in your room.' I said, 'I'm going to
sit down here.' I was now outside Bruce Willis's
dressing room. So he comes back after one of the
shoots, he's smothered in blood-like make-up. He
then says to me, 'Listen, I want to tell you a joke.' I
said, 'Hold up, let me just ask you something... how
much are you getting for this?' Bruce replies, 'You
aren't half nosey, but I'm going to tell you because
you are so big, I'm getting $20 million.' I said,
'That's a bit more than me.' Bruce then says, 'What
you getting?' And I said, 'Four-and-a-half grand...
you don't want to swap dressing rooms, do you?'

We then had a good laugh; he told me a couple
of jokes, fantastic, I won't tell you because it's a
family show, and he then went back into his
dressing room and I went back to mine.

I thought, I don't know, I've got to nick his
dressing room... when he went out for the next
shoot, I went in and had a shower.

Richard: Well, maybe if he had seen what I'm going to show now, he'd have given you up his dressing room without any problem at all. This is a film of the *London Programme* made of you fighting unlicensed.

(They show a clip of Lenny's third fight with Roy Shaw.)

Richard: Well, I wouldn't have liked to have been on the end of that... how long ago was that?

Lenny: I was a younger man then and plus there was 30 grand on the table and I had to have that money.

Richard: Thirty grand just for that fight?

Lenny: You say 30 grand just for that fight. I mean, we were two powerful guys. You say to someone then, would you like to fight Lenny or the other guy, and they will say no. But that's how we got our living.

I used to go to Derby Day and fight bare-knuckle. I used to go to car places, fight bare-knuckle, and I would smash my hands to pieces.

Richard: So you've differentiated between unlicensed and bare-knuckle... you had gloves on then. What are the rules in unlicensed boxing?

Lenny: No, no, I used to say to the guy, 'How do you want it, you want an all-in or a straightener? It's up to you.

Richard: What you mean 'all-in'? Everything goes – kicking, biting and butting?

Lenny: Everything, but the thing is, we didn't interfere with the public. We don't interfere with the bloke up the bus stop; we are two big powerful guys fighting the toughest guys all over the country.

I went to America in 1986 on my own… they were seven-handed at the airport, they picked me up in New York and took me to the Plaza. They put me on the fourteenth floor. The next day, I went to Glamours Avenue in a bottle warehouse where they stood bottles up and I fought their toughest guy in New York bare-knuckles. I broke that hand and I broke my thumb… they give me my bit of dough and I went back to the hotel on my own. I thought to myself, I've got two broken hands; if they come back for the money I won't be able to hit them, so I thought what I'd better do is wait at the airport. So I waited at the airport for eight hours, fell asleep, got on the plane, got home, went to the hospital, plastered my hand up, got home, give my wife the money, went to bed. My two kids come in and said, 'Daddy, have you been fighting again?' I'd been halfway around the world.

Richard: *(To Frank Maloney)* I don't know if you have ever been to an unlicensed fight, but that looked more ferocious than any fight I have ever seen. How would these guys fare if they tried to fight professionally?

Frank: Well, I saw Lenny fight on these unlicensed shows… he fought one at Yorkshire Grey and I went to it. If someone had got hold of Lenny when he was younger, I think he could have been a great fighter.

Lenny: *(Interrupts)* I am a good fighter.

Richard: *(Reading a viewer's fax)* If you were younger and you had gone into the professional game as opposed to the route you took, would you be up there instead of Lennox Lewis competing against Tyson?

Lenny: You could never say that, but all I can say is, if there were more people like this chap here [Frank] guiding young kids into the boxing, there would be less people around like me. I mean, I have had a violent life, it wasn't a life I chose, it was a life I done to get a living. I've known violence for 40 years. I've been shot twice; left for dead; I've been stabbed; I've been nicked for a murder I never done. I've been minding the roughest, toughest pubs in England. I've had 20,000 bar-room brawls. I've got pins in my hands and it's not a life I chose, it's a life that came my way.

Richard: You have taken a lot of punishment... you've dished out... what's the worst thing you have done to anyone?

Lenny: In one of my bare-knuckle fights, I bit a guy's nose off. *(The crowd start gasping in shock.)* But listen, you have got to understand...

Richard: (Interrupts Lenny and says to former Gladiators *presenter Sharron Davies)* Sharron, you have gone green. I mean, you like the fight game, could you stomach watching that?

Sharron: I'm terrible, actually, watching it it was quite rough on *Gladiators,* but they didn't bite anybody's nose off.

Lenny: But you're a lady.

Richard: I wonder what they'd call Lenny if he was on *Gladiators.*

Paul: Sir. *(The audience starts laughing.)*

Lenny: Sharron, she's a lady and she's doing something now for the children, which is fantastic, but I come from the real world, where you know you had to be the Guv'nor to get anywhere.

Sharron: Well, it's a way out, isn't it?

Lenny: Well, thank you, it's a way out... I'll tell you what's happened, people don't understand. They come to me now they have read the article; they are doing my life story. It took me 11 years to get my movie where it's come now. I had a phone call yesterday, we have got the £10 million for the movie. My book comes out in three months... it was written by Peter Gerrard, one of the top writers in the country, and I says to him, 'What do you think of the story?' And he said it would be a bestseller. It's fantastic. We know it's violent as that's the life I was in.

Paul: (Reading a fax) Barbara from Bethnal Green thinks you could build on your acting career as she thinks that you would make a great James Hewitt.

Lenny: (Laughing) Who's he?

Sharron: (Reads out another fax) How would he fight Tyson?

Lenny: Well, let me tell you, when I was a younger man, say like when I was in my twenties – I'm not giving myself a gee – I was Mike Tyson with no gloves on. I was mustard, but you had to be, you had to be and that's how I got a living, and I was good.

Richard: You were known as 'the hardest man in London'... did that mean people were always coming and you had to keep proving yourself?

Lenny: Yeah, I was always fighting minding a club, you'd get a little firm in ten-handed, they have had five lots of scotch, then six, they walked in and it was, hello, now they have had ten lots of scotch and they are looking at you and they want to fight you. And I'm looking at them and I say, 'Don't you dare, because I will kill you.' But I want to get away from that life now and I really fancy the acting.

Richard: Lenny, you're the Guv'nor.

Richard Littlejohn Show (2)
(A few years after appearing on Richard's show, Lenny was invited back to promote his new book. Even though he was very ill at the time, as Peter Gerrard explained in his book Tribute, *there was nothing that was going to stop Lenny appearing with Peter. They were also joined by the Minister of Sport Tony Banks. Lenny then gave Richard a very emotional interview.)*

Richard: He was dubbed 'the hardest man in Britain', he graduated to TV stardom, and he was the booze runner in the hit series *The Knock.* He's now facing his ultimate battle... here to tell us more about it, would you welcome the Guv'nor, Mr Lenny McLean.

(Lenny walks on with a walking stick looking immaculate as ever. He then starts shaking hands with Richard.)

Lenny: I'm a bit tired today.

Richard: Last time we met, you were in *The Knock...*

now you have been mixing with some real hard
men, haven't you – Vinnie Jones. He was here last
week with his film.

Lenny: Nice man, Vinnie, good man.

Richard: You have got the book out called *The
Guv'nor.*

Lenny: That comes out in July... it was scheduled for
September.

Richard: You are a man in a hurry at the moment,
aren't you, Len?

Lenny: Well, they don't know if I'm going to be alive
in September, so they are bringing it out in July.

Richard: Is it as bad as that?

Lenny: I've got cancer in the head, brain, cancer in
the lung and I'm paralysed down one side.

Richard: I'm sorry to hear that, mate.

Lenny: But I will fight to the end, and I shall go out
like a man.

Richard: Good for you... I can't imagine you being
frightened of anything.

Lenny: No, I'm not frightened of no man or beast.
The Guv'nor doesn't mean to say you could fight
this guy or fight that guy, it's what's in here *(points
at his heart)*. When they told me I was going to die,
what I done was get all my affairs in order and go
like a man. That's why it's called *The Guv'nor.* And
I'm a strong man and I don't remember coming in
and I won't remember going out.

Richard: How did you find out you were ill? How did
you react?

Lenny: I took my wife on holiday and I couldn't lift a

case and I had to ask this man who was 70 could he lift the case. I said to my wife, 'This isn't right, I'm the Guv'nor. That man's 70 and he's moved my case.'

So, when I come back, I went to the hospital and done a scan. They said you have cancer of the brain, cancer of the lungs and I was paralysed down one side.

Richard: Lenny, tell me this. I was talking earlier with Tony [Banks], and you were an unlicensed boxer. I've seen film of you fighting that the people who now have that footage will not let us show it on television any more because they say it is frightening. They wouldn't let us show it again today. Do you think the kind of punishment that you took in bouts you fought in have contributed to your illness in any way?

Lenny: I think anyone who tries banning boxing today is an idiot. What it does is get kids off the street that wind up in prison; it puts them on a tunnel that's going to put money in their pockets. You hear about kids from the East End who have got little brains but they can fight. That's his only chance to get his big house and get out of the jungle, and if he's in the jungle he will end up in prison. So, if only one guy dies out of a thousand, you have got to take that percentage, because, if you ban it, it will go underground.

Richard: But the fights you were in, Lenny, were underground.

Lenny: Yeah, but I'm a one-off, see, don't forget, I'm

a one-off; there is 20,000 street fighters out there not getting a tenner. I'm a one-off, I'm the Guv'nor, I'm a one-off.

Richard: Well, you won a lot of money fighting in America, I remember… wasn't there a story, didn't you tangle with the Mafia? Tell me what happened there.

Lenny: Some businesspeople arranged for me to go to America… I met some people at Kennedy Airport, they took me to the Plaza. I met some businesspeople and had a bare-knuckle fight. I broke both my hands, went back to the hotel and said to my pal, 'I think we better wait at the airport in case they come back with guns to get their money back.'

So we sat at Kennedy Airport for ten hours, went back to London. I gave him three grand, took the wife home £26,000, and the kids come in and said, 'Dad, have you been fighting again?' I'd been halfway around the world. See, I'm a one-off.

I'm not giving myself a gee because I'll be dead in six months. What I'm saying is this – you cannot ban boxing because what happens to the young kids, how are they going to get their few quid?

Richard: What has really been the most difficult fight of your life? Forget your illness for now… what's the nastiest, most vicious fight you have ever been involved in?

Lenny: A gypsy fight, where I had a bare-knuckle fight on a caravan site. I won the fight and, when I went back the next day for the money, they tried shooting me… it was just aggravation all my life.

Tony: (To Lenny) My dad died of cancer, it really cut me up badly, but, Lenny, you have got to fight it, you are right, it's in there *(points at his heart);* you have got to fight it hard.

Lenny: It's like running a marathon every day… you feel knackered. When I got asked to come on here, I come on here because the guy who's writing the book, Peter Gerrard, he's a great writer, and he said, 'Can you come on here?' I said, 'I will crawl on there.' You know, to give this book a gee, because this book isn't about a gang who go and interfere with the ordinary public or the guy at the bus stop, it's about one man's fight against tough guys.

Richard: Any regrets, Len?

Lenny: No, I shall go out like the Guv'nor.

(The camera then pans to an emotional Peter Gerrard and members of the audience.)

Richard: Well, I'll tell you what, mate. I hope you live to see it become a bestseller. This man is a fighter, he's the Guv'nor, ladies and gentlemen… Mr Lenny McLean.

(Lenny then waves to the audience and nods his head as they clap him.)

7
Life and Soul

Now and again, Lenny would take a break from all the aggravation of the fighting game and door work. Lenny used to like a party. He would also help out in any way, shape or form with a lot of charity work. He always turned up immaculate and put a show on for all the other celebrities; you could always count on Lenny to be there. Throughout the last year, I have interviewed several people who have partied with the Guv'nor in a few different places.

The first interview I did was when I bumped into a boy from my home town who had been present at some of these parties with his father. Here's what they had to say about the time they met Lenny McLean.

CARWYN AND PHILLIP FRYZER
In the middle of the Nineties, I saw a documentary on the TV featuring the bare-knuckle fighter Lenny McLean. I thought

to myself, This man is awesome, and I've got to meet him. Also at the time I was interested in the Kray Twins and I had started writing to Reggie Kray.

My father Phillip and I then got invited to a party on a boat on the River Thames for the Krays' sixtieth birthday party. While being a member of the Krays' fan club, I was in touch with a bloke named Gary Piper and he started telling me about the parties going on in London which Lenny McLean and Dave Courtney usually attended. We then received an invite for a charity show which Reggie was organising for some little boy who had muscular dystrophy.

So we turned up for this party, not realising that it was in Lenny's pub. Twin brothers named George and Andrew were running it at the time for him. It was a cracking pub with photos of boxers everywhere.

Once there, we started noticing various celebrities such as Charlie Kray, *EastEnders* actor Steve McFadden (Phil Mitchell) and a load of others. After a while, I noticed Lenny walking into the pub and talking to the bouncers on the door. He had an immaculate suit on. I went and told my father straight away. Throughout the night, he seemed really busy talking to people, but I thought to myself, I've got to meet this man and maybe have some photos as well. So I saw Lenny going to the toilet and I said to my father, 'I'm going to meet him now... see if he'll have a chat with us.'

So I walk in the toilet as Lenny's having a piss and says to him, 'All right there... you're Lenny McLean.' Lenny then goes, 'Yeah,' looking at me puzzled. I was then a bit dumbstruck. I thought to myself, What the fuck do I say now then? He doesn't know me from Adam. So I say to him, 'Any chance I can have a chat with you?' He replies, 'No problem.'

So he finishes his piss and we start chatting by the doorway. We then started blocking the doorway, so Lenny says, 'Come on, we'll go up the back for a chat and some photos.'

So I call my father and we go up the back of the room for a chat. Lenny then started talking to us as if he had known us ages. We talked about him boxing and bouncing and he was really getting into his stories. He mentioned his bare-knuckle fights and that he'd never lost in the street and no one could ever beat him. He then started growling a little, and, just by looking at the sheer size of him, I don't think anyone could. The man was fucking massive, and no fat on him, just huge. He had no tie on and his neck was bulging out of his shirt.

After talking to him for a while, we left him to carry on mingling. We then had our photos taken with a few gangster celebrities but one of the ones I really wanted turned us away as you could see he had no time for us.

Now there was a bouncer on the door named Phil who my father had met a few times in previous parties. So my father says to him, 'Is there any chance you could sort it out with this bloke so we could have a few photos taken with him?' Minutes later, he's posing for photos with us.

After a while, Lenny came flying over to us and we start chatting again, so he then says to us, 'Come over by here and have a photo because it's lighter.' He then actually lifts one of the tables with food on from the buffet out of the way so we could have a good photo. My father couldn't believe how much he was going out of his way to be nice to us. So, as I'm about to pose for the photo, my father says, 'Spar up then, boys.' Lenny then goes into a boxing stance; I thought to myself, Oh fucking hell, as Lenny's throwing punches near me. My father says to Lenny, 'Throw a right, Len.' I quickly added, 'He's only joking, Len.' I then took a photo of Lenny with my father and only then could I actually see the size of his hands – they were nearly twice the size of my father's. Lenny signed a few autographs for us and we went our separate ways, after we had thanked him for being so nice to us.

We carried on drinking and we ended up being one of the last there with Charlie Kray and the twins that were running the place.

All we can say is, he was sound as a pound and went out of his way to be nice to us. We were two Welsh boys and he couldn't do enough for us. We remember the day like it was yesterday and the photos still hang on our wall to this day.

ANDY GRAVENOR

I first met Lenny McLean at a party to celebrate the sixtieth birthdays of the Kray Twins. The party was on board a boat moored on the River Thames. I had been sent an invite by Reggie Kray and met his brother Charlie at the party.

A bit later on in the evening, Charlie took me over to a large well-dressed man standing by the bar. Charlie then said, 'Andy, this is a good friend of mine – Lenny McLean.' I had heard of Lenny, but never seen him before except for a couple of his fights on video… his fights against Roy Shaw were legendary. His reputation went before him and it was a fearsome reputation at that. I also knew he had not long come out of prison and had got a 'not guilty' on a murder charge. He looked intimidating and had a very firm handshake, but, as he said hello, his face broke out into a smile, and I now felt a lot more at ease.

I had a chat with him for a while and he mentioned getting into acting after speaking to the TV star Mike Reid from *EastEnders*. He was very friendly and was not a bit put out. When I asked if we could have a photo together, he said, 'Do you want a nice one or a nasty one.' So I asked for a nasty one, but, when he put his arm around my neck and squeezed, I thought my neck would snap. I then choked out the words, 'I want a nice one.' Lenny started laughing and asked me was I OK before we had our photo taken. When I had the photo printed and I seen it, he still didn't look too nice, but I still treasure it.

I met him again at another party a while later, and again he was very friendly. I also saw him at Ronnie Kray's funeral but didn't get the chance to speak to him. I was never mates with Lenny, but he was always very friendly and welcoming whenever I met him and spoke to him.

When I saw him on film, I felt like I was watching my friend on the screen, because that was the way he made you feel. My big regret is not going to Lenny's funeral. I received a few phone calls from a couple of friends asking me if I wanted to go, but I was unable to, due to personal circumstances at the time. I wish I had been able to go and pay my final respects to a great man.

SCOTT MYTTON

I first became interested in the London scene in the early Nineties, after watching the film *The Krays*. From that moment on, I had a fascination for any well-known face who had built up a reputation for themselves. I met Lenny McLean at The Guv'ner's public house in Stepney, on Saturday, 15 April 1995. Reggie Kray had organised a charity night that I'd been invited to for a kid with muscular dystrophy. I had made lots of friends in London and I was really looking forward to a good night out with the lads.

At the time, I had read an article in a newspaper concerning Lenny, which stated that he had taken on 18 men, nine of whom he had put in hospital and the other nine had run away. He looked quite a big man in the newspaper, but I still wasn't completely convinced.

However, when he walked into the room that night, I was amazed at how big he really was. He was huge and, when he gripped my hand to shake it, I thought he was going to break some bones. Then I thought back to the newspaper article and I suddenly became convinced that it was possible what he had done to those 18 people.

There were a lot of people at the party in The Guv'ner's that night, but I can remember thinking that, if everyone in the room were lined up to fight him and I was at the back of the queue, I would have turned around and run the other way.

I never really got to know Lenny that well, but it was still an honour to have met him. Unless you met Lenny, you couldn't possibly imagine just how big he really was and that's a night I will remember for the rest of my life.

DAV OWENS

I'd never been much of a reader, so I don't know how I found myself in the paperback section of a motorway service station. Maybe it was the prospect of nine hours on a coach travelling between Glasgow and Merthyr that forced such drastic measures; after all, there's very little that you could call scenery within sight of the fast lane of the M6, but either way I found myself browsing through the biographies that sat four deep on the shelves. I mean, I'd tried reading before, of course, and not just the books we were forced to read at school – it was just that my attention span was so short that by the time I'd turned the page I'd forgotten what I'd just read. Books had never been so much a story, more like ink on paper.

For a non-reader in a bookshop, there is an obvious dilemma before you even begin the selection process – which section do you go to? I wandered aimlessly around looking for inspiration when my gaze was met by the sinister, menacing glare of a black-and-white photograph that drags me back to childhood images of newspaper front pages. Of course, I'd seen the picture a hundred times before... who hasn't? David Bailey's portrait of the Kray Twins is one of the most famous photographs of the Sixties.

I picked up the book and started to read the liner notes. I then realised how little I actually knew about the Twins; they were in prison for a long time... they ran protection rackets in 1960s' London... they'd murdered someone... and, a few years ago, they were headline news in both newspapers and on TV when they were released to attend their mother's funeral. The title was *The Profession of Violence* and such was its mysterious appeal that I was soon at the counter paying for a book for the first time in my life.

Back on the bus, I opened up my new acquisition and started to read, before encountering my second dilemma of the day. Five days' hard drinking in Glasgow over an international rugby weekend had taken its toll, and a combination of my better judgement and one hell of a hangover told me that, if I attempted anything more ambitious that looking at the photographs, it was likely to result in my breakfast being worn by anyone within six feet of me.

With this firmly in mind, I put the book in my travel bag where I would hopefully forget about it until I had reached home and had slept for at least ten hours. In fact, that's where it remained for the next week or so until I found it nestled in among sweaty socks and beer-encrusted shirts when I finally remembered to clear out my bag.

I thumbed through it once again, easing myself in gently by taking another look through the photographs. Then a giant step – I read the Introduction. It was unusual. Rather than suffering from the instant amnesia I had previously encountered whenever I was within reach of a book, I actually found myself looking forward to turning the page, wondering what was coming next.

Congratulating myself on successfully navigating the entire seven pages of the Introduction, I decided to push the boat out and go for gold. There was no stopping me now from exercising my newfound skill and, with all the enthusiasm of a regular at the local library, I launched myself into Chapter One.

After reading for half-an-hour or so, I put the book down momentarily to get myself a drink and glanced at the clock. That couldn't be right... it was four hours since I'd started reading!

I picked the book back up and looked at the page number... 140. I'd been oblivious to all that was happening around me and had quite literally 'lost myself in a good book'.

The damage was done now so I carried on, and on, and on. It was only when my eyes burned so much that I could not continue that I decided to take some sleep, and it says much of John Pearson's literary skills that the first thing I did the next morning was to carry on where I had left off the night before.

It is a sad fact of life that those who live their lives on the 'wrong' side of the law are consistently more interesting than your average law-abiding citizens, and perhaps sadder still that John Pearson could succeed where at least half-a-dozen English teachers had failed, in teaching me the pleasure that could be attained by reading. The damage had well and truly been done and, after finishing the full complement of 326 pages in a little over 12 hours, I found myself hungry for more.

A visit to my local bookshop followed in the hope of finding more accounts of the extraordinary lives of these fascinating characters. The only problem was that this was in 1985 and the titles were very few and far between. However, over the years, a steady collection has been built up and, through the pages of the various volumes, more and more interesting characters emerged, and it transpired that my appetite for reading about acts of villainy and violence had been well and truly whetted.

In 1992, a trailer for a TV documentary caught my eye. *World in Action* claimed to be giving the most candid insight ever into the shady world of unlicensed fighting and, on the due date, I sat down to enjoy what promised to be an enthralling hour's entertainment. Although I was expecting some violent scenes, nothing had prepared me for what was to follow.

Unlicensed promoter Reg Parker reminisced about a guy whom he regarded as 'the godfather of unlicensed boxing'. 'Nobody else could walk in his shoes,' he claimed... Lenny McLean. The shot cut to some amateur footage inside the ring at an unlicensed show, a huge guy with huge shoulders, huge hands and a huge moustache strutted around the ring clearly aware that it was his show and that he was in charge. He then turned to face his opponent's corner and, clenching both fists, leaned over and bellowed at his adversary, Brian 'Mad Gypsy' Bradshaw. The aggression and hatred that oozed from him would have been enough to make any sane person jump over the ropes and make straight for trap two in the nearest gents' toilet.

They met at centre ring for what turned out to be very short preliminaries. As the referee was about to tell them what, if any, were the rules, 'Mad Gypsy' leaped up and did what must surely be the most regrettable thing in his entire life. He stuck the head in! The following 30 seconds or so remain the most vivid visions of pure uncontrolled violence and aggression I have ever witnessed. 'Mad Gypsy' was punched unconscious, punched while unconscious, picked up and punched to even further unconsciousness, before finally being stamped on and kicked across the ring. It is disturbing to think of what would have happened had the half-dozen or so people not jumped upon Lenny to stop the onslaught.

At work the next day, it was the sole talking point. I continued to collect true-crime books and, in particular, books relating to the Krays. Several sources of information had been found and one or two good contacts, and it was through one of these contacts that I received an invitation in late 1993 to a party being held aboard a boat moored on the Thames. The party was to celebrate the Twins' sixtieth birthday and, as well as our host for the evening – Charlie Kray – there was a promise of a number of celebrities and 'faces'. The day was one to remember.

In the afternoon, a guided tour was given around the East End by the late Laurie O'Learie, a childhood friend of the Twins and a true gentleman. It took in all of the sites I'd been reading about for the past ten years, and Laurie provided a great insight into the lives of Reg and Ron from the ages of five years upwards.

It was in Laurie's company that I spent much of the time at the party and, among others, the guests included Helen Keating, Garry Bushell and an up-and-coming actor called Derek Martin – relatively unknown at the time but famous now as cabbie Charlie Slater in *EastEnders*.

On the upper deck there stood a huge guy in the company of about four or five others. I vaguely recognised the face, but could not put a name to it. The first thing to strike you about him was the sheer size; he exuded an enormous presence and the body language of those around him left you in no doubt as to who called the shots.

For reasons unknown, I resisted the temptation to ask Laurie who he was – maybe it would be a show of my lack of knowledge for not recognising someone who was undoubtedly of high standing within such circles.

On my return home the next day, I scoured the pictures in my collection of books so that my curiosity could be satisfied. Imagine my horror when I discovered that it was none other than 'the Guv'nor' himself… Lenny McLean! I was gutted. He looked much older (far older, in fact, than his 44 years), and the moustache… that huge, menacing moustache had disappeared. At six foot three inches, over 20 stone and with a face that made him look every inch the hardest man in England, it is difficult to imagine how anyone could fail to recognise Lenny, but I had managed it effortlessly. What a missed photo opportunity! Still, I guess I'll have to make do with a picture of a pre-fame Charlie Slater.

The next year or so made me even more determined to meet the Guv'nor, and I figured my best chance would be when I'd heard that Lenny had opened The Guv'ner's pub in Cleveland Way, Stepney. The trek was again made from South Wales to London's East End on a sunny Sunday morning and I was surprised to find The Guv'ner's almost empty, especially since it had only been open just over a week.

Behind the bar serving were both Jamie and Val McLean, beneath a pair of Lenny's huge gloves. It is unclear whether they hung there as a feature or as a reminder as to whose gaff this was, should anyone be tempted to start trouble. A deterrent in similar style to the 'Beware – I Live Here!' messages that are found in people's front windows attached to photographs of Alsatian dogs.

A guy who was painting the flat above sat at the bar, and I bought a drink and wandered around viewing the newspaper cuttings that adorned the walls. After an hour, it was obvious that there was going to be a no-show from The Guv'nor himself.

It was at Ronnie Kray's funeral that my chance finally came. As I stood outside the gates to St Matthew's Church, the cars were pulling up and face after face poured out. I watched as a huge figure unfolded himself from the back of a Bentley – Lenny McLean. He walked towards me and stood about ten feet away waiting, as others got out of their cars. Should I?

'Lenny!' I called and he turned with that furrowed brow of his that indicated both displeasure and curiosity at the same time. I held out my hand for him to shake if he so wished and he took a few steps over, grabbed it firmly for a second, before turning away and heading into the church with the rest of the mourners.

It was a surreal day all round; the awesome spectacle of Ronnie's horse-drawn hearse moving slowly and silently through Bethnal Green, standing just a few feet away from Reg Kray, seeing Charlie Kray, Mad Frankie Fraser, Charlie Richardson, Johnny Nash, Freddie Foreman and Tony Lambrianou at close quarters. But the day, for me, will be remembered primarily for one thing – meeting the Guv'nor!

Steve Wraith first got involved with the London scene after writing a letter to Reggie Kray. He then started doing security for some parties all over London. Throughout the years, he became good mates with the Krays. His book called *The Krays, the Geordie Connection* was finally released last year. He even has his own website and video out of the same name. Here he recalls the times he met Lenny McLean.

STEVE WRAITH

I often look back over the last 15 years and still really can't believe that I got so involved with the people that we all read about and, in some cases, dedicate our lives to. My fascination as a schoolboy was, of course, the Kray brothers. I read the gripping *Profession of Violence* by John Pearson and was hooked. I wanted to have the flash suits, the snooker hall and the famous friends and, as I grew older, I forged a friendship with the most notorious crime family this side of the Atlantic.

Through my association with Ronnie, Reggie and Charlie, I had the honour to meet one of their long-time friends, Lenny

McLean. It was 1994 and I had been asked by Dave Courtney to take care of the security arrangements at one of the infamous Kray parties, which were held every couple of months at venues up and down the country. I agreed and assembled a squad of six of the best to take care of things. The venue was a pub called The Guv'ner's in East London, and I was to meet up with the Guv'nor himself… Lenny McLean.

The pub was looked after by two brothers who I knew quite well, George and Andrew Wadman. I had a lot of time for them, and it was George who introduced me to Lenny that night. I am never overawed by meeting anyone – nothing could top meeting Ronnie Kray in his Savile Row suit and all in Broadmoor – but Lenny was a legend. He was a giant of a man. I'm no dwarf – six foot two and counting – but his shape seemed to fill the whole room. His handshake was as you would imagine – vicelike but without being intimidating. He had a deep, almost croaking voice and, as we chatted, I discovered a wicked sense of humour. We talked only briefly that night about who I was and where I was from and why I was there. I was getting the once-over by the Guv'nor, but it was to be expected.

At the end of the night, he shook my hand again and thanked me and the lads for a job well done. With the party over and the guests dwindling home, I sat with the lads and Lenny in the company of Charlie Kray and Tony Lambrianou, and we finished off the scotch before saying our goodbyes.

It was not until the following year and under less happier circumstances that I met the big man again. 1995 saw the death of Ronnie Kray, and the wake following the funeral was held at The Guv'ner's. The handshake was still firm and strong but this time the words, 'Steve, how are you, mate?'

filled the air. I was honoured that he remembered my name after a year, but I dare say he had checked my credentials out that first night we met.

We talked about the day's events and about how pleased Ronnie would have been with the turnout. As the night grew to its conclusion, a lot of people started taking photographs of the chaps in the yard behind the pub. I stood back as the flashlights pinged, when suddenly that deep voice bellowed, 'Steve, c'mon, son, get in here…' I didn't need to be asked twice.

I never got the chance to meet up with Lenny again before his untimely death, but followed his acting career with great admiration. The man was a real gent, a legend, and someone who I was proud to call my friend.

8
Door Rage

Lenny had started work on the door at a very young age in his home town of Hoxton. Night after night, the trouble would come and Lenny started building a reputation as a fighting doorman. Many challenges came and Lenny overcame all of them.

Lenny then made his way to the Camden Palace and, by tht time, had already made a name for himself. It was in the Camden Palace that Lenny took a new up-and-coming doorman under his wing and became friends with him for the rest of his life. That bloke's name was Mick Theo.

Mick has appeared in Lenny's other books and Lenny would always talk very highly of him. I had an address for Mick two years ago and left him various messages but he never got back to me. I was then given his mobile number by someone as I neared the completion of this book. This was the ideal interview with which to finish the book. I told him I'd really like to include him and he agreed, so we then set up an interview.

After another long journey, I finally got to North London and met Mick in his mate's restaurant. Mick turned up in an immaculate suit and we went and sat down. Here's what he had to say about his friendship with Lenny McLean.

MICK THEO

I first started bouncing when I was about 17 years of age in a place over in North London. While doing security and doing the doors all over the place, I started hearing the name of Lenny McLean mentioned regularly on my travels. I was working for Scorpion Security at the time and we'd go round cleaning places up. I then went to the Camden Palace looking for work and they took me on board.

I was introduced to Lenny who was the main man there at the time. Straight from the off, Lenny took a liking to me and we became really close friends. The place was a good venue; any problems, Lenny would always be up front. There wasn't that much trouble there, it was basically kids just pissed up and they would then end up having Lenny McLean on their case.

Upstairs in the Camden Palace was a restaurant and Lenny and I used to have our breaks together all the time and we became very close to each other. For instance, we would be up in the restaurant eating steak and chips and all the trimmings and, as we were about to munch into it, we would get a buzz from downstairs off one of the doormen and they would then have to wait until me and Lenny came down. There would be about ten men working, but they would have to wait until Lenny came to lead the gang into wherever the problem was, like a team marching in and all ready for action.

I was a competitive bodybuilder at the time in a big way and trying my best to become British Heavyweight Champion, which I went on to achieve in 1990. Once Lenny and I became good friends, we started training together regularly as well. We used to go to a place called Slim Jim's in Greenwich; it wasn't really a boxing gym, it was a weights gym; part of the floor was wood and we used to make our own ring up so we could move about with the gloves on. There were a few bags up as well. No one in this gym would dream of getting in there with Lenny and having a tear-up or even having a friendly spar. Obviously, with me being so close to Lenny, he had his film *The Guv'nor* coming out, and we talked about me having a part in the film as a boxer and he was going to show me how to box.

I actually invested in the film after he talked me into it. Lenny was trying to raise money from everywhere, but it's a hard old game, especially if you haven't got the backers. So Lenny tried really hard; I would have given him ten out of ten for trying to get the film off the ground. Some film producers were asking Lenny for money all the time to get his movie going. I gave Lenny 20 grand at the time.

I went up Pinewood Studios a few times with him. As time went on and nothing was happening, I said to Lenny, 'Look, Len, to be honest with you, I can't see this film happening, no disrespect but I'd like my money back.' He gave me my money back and nothing ever came of the film, which is a shame.

Going back to the training, to go from bodybuilding to boxing was really hard as you're carrying 19½ stone of muscle and even trying to hold your gloves up alone was hard. Lenny carried on showing me some moves and I trimmed down a little bit. Not having the experience of a pro boxer, all I would do with Lenny in sparring was hold my hands up and protect my face and head which was leaving all my rib cage open. Lenny stopped me this once and says, 'Son, you're all open underneath, bring your hands down a bit, and just tuck your chin in, I could punch you all day long until the cows come home.' I said to him, 'Len, leave me as I am, mate, I know what I'm doing.' He's then pushed me in the corner and smashed me straight in the ribs, breaking them and winding me and I've gone down. As I'm on the floor trying to get my breath back, he's grabbed hold of me by the elbows and lifted me back up and says, 'Come on, son, only 30 more seconds.' I'm trying to breathe and tell him at the same time my ribs have gone. I think he was teaching me a lesson and, by fuck, it didn't half work. Anyway, it taught me a lesson and I rested my ribs for a month or so and then jumped straight back in there with him.

We used to have some good little tear-ups. A few times he used to drop his hands and say, 'Don't fucking do it this way, do it that way,' and I'd put one over the top and hit him. This one day, though, he didn't like it and he just lost it; he chased me round the gym, he wanted to give it to me; there were a couple of other people who worked with us in the club training there that day and they had to stop him from getting at me. He had lost it completely, he had just snapped, even though I was his best mate.

He was a lovely man but if you said the wrong thing or done the wrong thing then he would just see red; he would lose it proper, and knock you out.

Going back to the Camden, we had a few fights in there but they weren't really bad tear-ups. It was more of a rougher area and we had a lot of shit going on in there.

This one night we were in the Camden Palace and there was me, Lenny and another four doormen. Now we used to take the cash in boxes to a night safe across the road. This one night, we got robbed – this geezer came up with a shooter, took all the boxes and let one go and then he shot off into the night. I think a lot of people didn't like Lenny but they couldn't show him as he would have given it to them.

Once I was doing the doors, I was a bit like Lenny... I'd go straight in and wouldn't give a fuck about anything, just do my job. At times, people who I worked for said I was too heavy, but I was just doing my job. I must have been in the Camden for about four years and then I finished there.

I then went to a place called Rah Rah's in Islington which the Adams used to have. I wasn't working and Lenny had phoned them up and told me to get down there as there was a job for me. I then worked there for a while. Lenny then moved on to The Hippodrome and I ended up going in there with him.

The Hippodrome was a bit different to the Camden Palace as you would get a lot of tourists going in there; you wouldn't get that much trouble there as it was a nice place. The reason Lenny had left the Camden Palace for The Hippodrome was because this big leisure group owned both venues. They also owned another big club called Limelight around the corner to The Hippodrome. So Lenny basically would walk round with the manager of The Hippodrome to The Limelight, show his presence and they would then come back to the club.

There were quite a few of us working in The Hippodrome – there was John, Connie, Brian, Steve and a few up-and-comers, but it was just me and Lenny from the Camden Palace.

Lenny and I used to go for our little breaks together

around the corner in China Town. We'd eat many meals there and go for little walks and then head off back to work. In The Hippodrome, we had this little office room to the left of the entrance and we would use it for meetings or for eating Chinese food.

Now, Lenny would hardly be seen unless there was trouble in the venue. If there was trouble then you would see him putting his gloves on and then he would walk in and sort it out. Now this one night the manager has come in and told Lenny that one of the waitresses is being bothered by a couple of big guys. So Lenny's gone out there to see what's happening. As he's walked out of the office, the waitress has told Lenny that they are harassing her. So Lenny says, 'Where are they?'

Lenny starts to walk into the club and these two blokes are walking out towards him. Now, these two blokes even made Lenny look small. Lenny was standing on a step below, so these blokes looked even taller again. So Lenny says, 'Have you been harassing the waitress?' The one then says to Lenny, 'What the fuck's it got to do with you?' Lenny says, 'Do you know who I am?' And the one replies, 'I don't give a fuck who you are.' Before the bloke could finish his sentence, Lenny's hit him with a right hand, dropping him; he's then turned and hit his mate with a left hook, dropping him as well. Both men knocked out with one punch each. He then started growling at them and said, 'Don't know? Should have known.'

Normally, Lenny would lose it and tear into them on the floor as well, but on this particular occasion for some reason he didn't. He started shouting at the doormen, 'Get them fucking out of here now.' The doorman replies, 'Len, I can't, they are too heavy.' Lenny says angrily, 'Roll them out. Roll them.'

The blokes must have been about 25 stone each. Lenny kept laughing and saying to all of us all night, 'Don't know... should have known... don't know... should have known...'

I'll never forget the night when Gary Humphreys stripped off and started pissing on the dance floor. Obviously, at the time we didn't know what character this person was. Lenny's got hold of him and given him a slap and we chucked him out.

I was there on the night it all happened and had seen everything. I was awoken the next morning by this little clock radio; it's gone off and the first thing I'm hearing is this news flash saying, 'Hippodrome bouncer hits member of the public and he's died...' So I've rung Lenny up straight away and said, 'Len, have you heard the news?' I think he knew what was coming next but he said, 'What... what... what?' By now he was panicking, so I said to him, 'Len, that bloke from last night, he's dead.'

I think he was in shock. He thought I was winding him up. The next thing you know, they are trying to do Lenny for murder. The full story came out in the end, that, after we had chucked Humphreys out, he had then gone up the road to a casino and he had had a run-in with the police. It all came out in the end in Lenny's favour; the case then got dropped from murder to manslaughter, and finally to ABH.

The only way I could describe Lenny is, what he done, he done, and he done a good job when he done it. If there were problems north, south, east, west, he'd sort it out on the phone. He'd say, 'I'm fucking big Lenny McLean... Do you know who I am?'

I've been there many times, just a phone call to sort

trouble out, that's the power he had. A lot of people wanted to know him because they were frightened of him.

We were in The Hippodrome a few times and people would turn up to see him and we'd be sitting there in this meeting and, the minute they started talking crap and nonsense in his eyes, he would tell me to get them out of there before he'd hurt them. I watched many people trying to get to know Lenny because he was Lenny McLean and he was dangerous. They didn't want to know him because he was a nice bloke, because he would never show them that side of him; Lenny was always on his guard.

Lenny did like money, though. We'd go out and collect a debt together and, if there was ten grand involved, he'd get six and I'd get four; he'd always get more. We done a few debt jobs over the years, but just his presence used to do the job. He was a straight guy, but it was just the power he had and reputation; over the phone alone, debts used to get paid nine times out of ten.

Being with Lenny, you'd never have any problems, because people would think they had to deal with Lenny as well as Mick Theo, and it's always been that way.

A lot of people classed Lenny as a bully, but what is a bully? You're on a door doing a job. Lenny used to strike first and make sure and, being a big man, he usually knocked them out. He could lose it a few times when they were out cold, when it didn't need it, but there must have been a screw loose or something. I think it had all to do with the way he got brought up and was abused as a kid. His stepfather used to beat him up, which turned his son into big Lenny McLean, which was an animal.

A nice memory I have of Lenny is walking down the road or

whistling to himself in the car 'Always look on the bright side of life…' He loved that tune. His picture of me and him in the Camden Palace hangs in my office in work to this very day.

Once Lenny left The Hippodrome after the jail incident, I also moved on and opened up my own chain of mobile-phone shops. I opened my own wine bar and then moved on to the nightclub that I have got to this present day.

I think, when Lenny came out of jail, he was a changed person. I could see a different Lenny McLean. He started using his brain and I think he was now a man. You get to a point in life when you have got to start thinking straight because you'll probably end up getting nicked and 100 per cent of the time you are just doing your job, you're getting paid to protect a club, and the police want to nick you, and that proved that with Lenny.

Lenny then went on to work in Cairo Jack's, which was also owned by The Hippodrome. I still kept in touch with him regularly. He phoned me up this one day and asked me would I be at the opening of his pub called The Guv'ner's. As I was the British Heavyweight Bodybuilding Champion he wanted me to lift John Huntley and a Page 3 girl on my shoulders for a photo for the local newspaper. It was good exposure for his pub and we all had a good night.

I seen Lenny fight 'Mad Gypsy' Bradshaw a few years earlier. A lot of people were ringing Lenny up and saying, 'What's happening, Len?' I don't know how many times Lenny would reply, 'He's challenged me and I'm going to fucking knock his head in.'

Anyway, the fight went ahead and the rest is history. I think a lot of people just wanted to fight Lenny to prove a point. They were nobodies but just wanted to say they had fought Lenny McLean; they were never going to beat him or get anywhere.

I also kept in shape by doing boxing training and even opened up my own gym. Some of my fighters then started boxing on another mate of mine, Alan Mortlock's, unlicensed shows.

One of my good mates, the boxer Scott Welch, then asked me to go down for a part in the movie *Snatch* a few years later in which he was starring with Brad Pitt. There were about 30 guys going for the part of Mad Fist Willy. I done a little casting shoot and I got the part.

Another time, I had this club called Bentley's which was a wine bar and I had some fruit machines in there. Lenny kept saying to me, 'I've got a mate who does fruit machines and I'll get him to put one in your place.' This is about a year before he got cancer. So I kept saying, 'Yeah, yeah, yeah…'

Anyway he kept pulling me up on it and asking, 'What's happening with this fruit machine… are you going to have my machine in there?' Fruit machines in clubs can earn a couple of grand a week.

Now, even as close as I was to Lenny, he still insisted that I take my machine out and put his in and he could earn all the money on his. So I said to him one night, 'Len, it isn't happening, mate… I've got a fruit machine, I don't need two.' He just lost it on the phone with me, the air turned blue as he was screaming down the line.

So I stayed away from his house for a few weeks and Val rung me up and said, 'Mick, what's the matter, we don't see you…' I said to Val, 'Val, look, he wants to put a fruit machine in my business. Now my machine takes a few grand a week and it pays my rent and wages and bits and pieces… have a

bit of respect, I'm not going to let him take the piss out of me.'
Val then says, 'You know what he's like, Mick, come round, he
misses you; he hasn't seen you for a while.'

So I've gone round this one day with it in the back of my
mind being prepared that it might kick off because of the
words on the phone. I thought to myself, Fuck it, I'm going to
stand up to him. So I walked in his front room and he said,
'All right, son?' And I said, 'You all right, Len?' He then said,
'Sit down.' I thought to myself, Here we go. He looks at me
and says, 'You caught me on a bad day that day, you know,
like guitar strings, when they are supposed to be all tuned in,
one of my strings weren't tuned in that day.' There wasn't
much I could say back to that.

Later on in life, when the nice person came out of Lenny
and the big bomb was gone from exploding, and his life was
coming normal, that's when cancer hit him.

He had now moved to Bexleyheath. He had bought his
own place, was doing it up and getting ready to enjoy his life
and his new movie career and he finds out he's got cancer. I
think Val broke the news to me that Lenny had got cancer. I
had an argument with him again and Val had phoned me up
and asked me to go round as Lenny wasn't too well and he
was missing me.

So I went round and spoke to Val and she explained it all
to me. I then spoke to Lenny about it and he said, 'I'm fighting
it, son.'

And he did, he fought it until the end. It got to the point
near the end that Lenny was moving around on a stick. I
used to go up and pick him up and take him out. He had
slowed down a lot and put a bit of weight on from the tablets
he was taking. Val would ring me up and ask me to take him

out. We used to love going out to eat together, he loved his food. My wife and I and Val and Lenny used to go out a lot; he loved his Chinese food.

Len gave Val and his kids everything; he'd buy his kids new cars and he would look after them. He was a good family man and husband. I was very close to Val and Jamie and Kelly. I saw them grow up from a young age. I've been there for his family and I'd go around at Christmas with presents. Lenny then faded away slowly and that was the end of a legend.

I regarded Lenny as a father figure to me. He was the Guv'nor of what he did. We were always there for each other, through thick and thin. He was a lovely man. If people knew the other side of him, they'd have a shock. Good guy, always laughing and cracking jokes and being a practical joker.

He was a good man, Lenny. I miss him a lot.

In the past two years, I also collected these comments from different people who had met Lenny as he was working on the door.

RUSS TALLISS

It was around 1990 or 1991, I cannot remember exactly. Anyway, a few weeks before, there was a programme on the TV about boxing and what would happen if it was banned. They had some footage of the Bradshaw fight in which Lenny was headbutted and then took his revenge. I was shocked at the savageness of it and it stayed with me for weeks. All I can remember was the name Lenny McLean and the Guv'nor.

It took me back to the times when I was about ten and we were living in Forest Hill and I can remember my dad taking me to a café and leaving me there while he and some other men went to watch boxing on Shooter's Hill Common or Deptford at a pub. He never spoke about it, only that it was different to that on the TV.

Anyway, with this programme still fresh in my mind, I and a few mates decided to go to The Hippodrome. It was as we were walking up to the door that I saw Lenny and the programme flashed in my mind. The sheer size of him was unreal but, while my mates ponced about deciding whether to risk getting in, I went up to Lenny and explained that I saw him on the TV and it was just amazing. He then took me inside the foyer where we had a long chat about boxing and fighting in general. It was the fact that there I was, a nobody, chatting to this animal of a man, yet he was talking real sense.

After what seemed like a hour (actually about 15 minutes), he let me and my friends in for free and finished with the words: 'Behave, you lot.' We did not need telling, although I had to explain who he was to a couple of my mates.

We stayed until around 2.00am and, when we left, he remembered me and shook my hand. We never went there again but the events will always be with me – he was a real genuine man, no front, no bullshit and certainly no fear.

SIMON HARRIS

I met Lenny when he worked on the door at the Camden Palace. We used to chat to him while we were queuing up to get in. At first, we did not realise who he was, he just came across as a decent bloke. It was only when I saw a programme on TV that I recognised him as the doorman we spoke to.

In the interview, he said he did not consider what he did [bare-knuckle] as violent. At the end of the day, the guys in the ring were being paid for it and knew the consequences. His perception of violence was mugging some old dear for the contents of her purse. He had a great outlook on life, in my opinion, and did what he did to get by.

As I said, I met him only a couple of times to chat to while we queued up to get in, but I never saw him have to deal with anyone. I guess his presence alone was enough to put anyone off doing anything stupid. I was really shocked when he died as he had a great future ahead of him in films. I read his book and it confirmed to me that he genuinely was a decent bloke, provided you did not cross him. I am surprised that he was not included in Kate Kray's book *Hard Bastards*, but that may just be down to the fact she could not interview him.

MARTIN DONAGHEY

I saw Lenny McLean working at the Camden Palace many years ago. I got drunk and misbehaved a little bit, but just one look from Lenny and I had to go home. No words spoken by Lenny, just a stare... pure power.

JERRY

In around 1983 or 1984, I had the dubious honour of being ejected by legendary London bouncer Lenny McLean a couple of times at the Camden Palace. There used to be a free night on a Wednesday, and there'd be all these 'Mods' there, it was a pretty lively place. I was only about 17 at the time so it was hard work getting in past Lenny. There was another three or four others on the door as well; they were a magnificent-looking mob, even just Lenny himself.

I'd started fighting with this other young lad over some girl and they came and threw me out. They were absolute gentlemen and escorted me out. After seeing them in action a few weeks earlier in a huge brawl against some Mods, I was a bit worried as they were fearsome that night.

When I got chucked out the second time, they were exactly like gentlemen again. I'd fallen asleep very drunk and woke up in a hallway thinking I was in the bathroom. Next thing I know, I'm being manhandled out. I thought to myself, I'm in trouble here, but they just got me to the door and told me to sod off.

TONY DUBENS

I knew Lenny McLean for a while and met him many times. I knew Lenny when he was bouncing; at the time he was downstairs at Cairo Jack's. I was introduced to him by the boxer Bruce Wells. I found him to be extremely interesting, humorous and courteous, particularly to the ladies. I was very sad when he died, and I paid my respects at the funeral.

Lenny was an incredible man, with a massive stage presence. He would walk into a room and all eyes would be on him, not just because of his size, but he was so brave and outgoing and extrovert. He carried himself so high, you knew the man was something just by looking at him. When he entered a room, he usually barked comments or conversation as if he wanted people to notice him. He'd have a comment for everyone he passed in a room or on the street, things like, 'All right, beautiful?' to a passing girl. Not to make a pass, but just to make her feel special. That probably was a gift, to make people feel special and important. He loved being in the company of nice people, but, if he didn't like you because you were drunk, mouthy, leery or cheeky, you wouldn't be in his company another second.

There's something else I remember quite well. Bruce Wells, a very well-known and respected fighter in his day, and a true gentleman, went to visit Lenny to deliver a message for me. Lenny, at the time, was in the basement of a bar, and Bruce entered the bar on the ground floor and asked a couple of guys at the bar if they knew where Lenny was. The two guys obviously didn't know who Lenny was and started taking the piss, and going out of their way to be rude. Bruce eventually found Lenny downstairs and told him what had happened. Lenny marched upstairs and began to approach them. They became stiff with fear. Lenny grabbed them both by the scruffs of their necks, and used their heads as battering rams to open the fire escape door and throw them out. They may think twice before they bully a pensioner again. This was typical of Lenny, who would always act to defend those too weak to protect themselves.

BRENDAN SEALY

On planning a night out with a couple of friends, the missus and I decided to go to London. We thought we wouldn't worry about the expense and have a cracking night. So I booked a limo from Wycombe and we all started to get ready for the night out.

While getting ready, I saw an ad on the telly for the Brit Awards and, being a bit of a scammer, my brain started ticking over and, before you knew it, I had printed off four Brit Award passes on my mate Rob's computer.

Now picture this – these passes were printed off on normal paper and stuck on cardboard from a crisp box and we put shoe laces from Rob's daughter's shoes into little holes. We put them around our necks and off to London we went. The plan worked and we got into all the top clubs in London easy. We then went to this one club called Brown's and there was this huge queue outside with all these celebrities. So off my brain goes again, I pull a taxi over and we all got in and drove round the block. We pulled up outside the club and I jumped out and ran up to the doorman and said to him, 'Don't let anyone see me with these two birds.' Looking a bit confused, he must have thought I was somebody famous. He then grabbed two of his mates and moved some of the barriers down towards the taxi and ushered us all straight in.

I'm at the bar and it's buzzing with all these celebrities. We head upstairs to the VIP room. After a while, I managed to sneak us all into the VIP room. We were in and out the VIP most of the night.

We then left Brown's and made our way to The Hippodrome a bit later in the night and the bouncer on the door says, 'Sorry, we are full.' He was having none of it. By now, Rob and I were also up for it as we had been drinking all night.

Next thing you know, this huge bloke walks over and with a rumbling voice says, 'On your bikes, boys, we are full.' I looked up and says, 'Here, mate, I'll give you double if you let us in.' He then says, 'Now what the fuck is in here so bad you want to pay double for?' I said to him, 'Fuck knows… I'm just having a ball and we are pissed as farts.'

By now, we didn't give a fuck and thought this is the part where we get chucked out. The next thing we know, the bloke says, 'Come on, in you come.'

Well, fuck me, I could not believe it. This bloke had shovels for hands and could have done us no problem at all, but no, he says, 'Come on in.' He then put his arm around me and says, 'What the fuck are you doing with a torn crisp box round your neck?'

Well, I'll be fucked, my pass had turned round and you could now see what it was. So I said to him, 'I made these earlier to get in everywhere...'

He then started laughing like fuck and said to me, 'You are a fucking loony... get in here and enjoy yourself and if you play up I'll toss you and your mate out the nearest window.'

What a geezer, I thought; he let us in, gave both the girls a big kiss and cuddle like he had known them for years and didn't even charge us and, on top of that, he took us to the bar and got the barmaid to give us all a drink.

Well, this bloke – or should I say gentleman, because that's what he was – was the one and only Lenny McLean. What a gent, he spent nearly all the night talking to and looking after us. He knew exactly what our game was but he didn't want to spoil it. So he just made it better. Trust me, we spoke and laughed for ages and anyone else would have been angry at what we did to the bouncers, but he loved it and made a point of rounding the night off and making it one of the best nights of our lives.

He told me about some of his fights and things that had happened to him and I couldn't believe what I was hearing. This man could have done me and Rob together, but he just wanted us to have a good night. What a superstar and clever man; he knew his job better than any bouncer in London but still was a perfect gent.

God rest you, Lenny ... you touched a tiny piece of our lives that night and we will never forget you and your massive impact.

9

To Bexley and Back

After reading the book *Stilks* by Stellakis Stylianou, I noticed a couple of mentions of Lenny McLean's name in it. I had the chance to tell Stilks that I ran the Lenny McLean website at a book launch party, but didn't think the time was right. A mate of mine then told me he had lined up an interview with him for a book he was doing about doormen called *Bouncers*. He asked me if I would go with him. I thought to myself it would be an excellent chance to get some stories for the website and this book.

So off we went again, out of the house by five and on our way up to London. Stopped off at the services for another piss-poor breakfast, but who gave a shit? I wasn't paying for it; the food was always down to my mate. That was the set-up. I get him to London and he pays for the food and, for the first time in over 30 journeys, we had been on time. We arrived in Crayford without getting lost once.

Stilks turned up and met us in his Mercedes and took us to

his mate Max's house. Max was another bouncer who had been in the game more than 20 years and also appeared in the book *Bouncers*.

Not long after meeting Stilks, my mate explained that I ran the Lenny McLean website. Stilks then started talking about Lenny and I was thinking to myself, I wish I had a tape recorder. I was trying to take it all in so I could write it out when I got in later.

A bit later, Stilks started impersonating Lenny. Now, as you know, I've never met Lenny, but all of a sudden I was getting a feeling what Lenny was like.

After my mate had done his interview, Stilks and his mate Max took us to dinner at a Chinese restaurant. On the way there, Stilks pointed out where Lenny used to live. The thing was, we were in a car and couldn't really stop. These were the places I'd been looking for, for a long time, and they were just passing me by.

After dinner, we went back to Max's house for another cup of tea and Stilks told me a bit more about Lenny before we left to go home. The hardest part now was trying to get down what he had said. About a year later, I got hold of Max's phone number and explained to him about this book. He then put me in touch with Stilks, who arranged for me to go and stay with him and to do some interviews. Stilks gave me a guided tour around Bexleyheath and then we sat down and we had a chat about Lenny. Here's what he had to say.

STELLAKIS STYLIANOU

I started working in the Music Machine, which was then named the Camden Palace. I had just missed working with Lenny because he was moving on to somewhere else and I was his replacement. I was just learning the door game and he was in his prime. Lenny said to a mate of mine that I would one day make it to the top of my game. I then started seeing him about when I was going to gyms.

I was in this gym one day and there was a few of us there training, and they had this speedball. So Lenny's on this speedball and he can't get the rhythm going on it. So my mate says to Lenny, 'Do you want me to show you how to use it tidy, Len.' Lenny moves to the side and leaves my mate go on it. Lenny then turns to my mate laughing and says, 'For fuck's sake, mate, you're not much better than me.'

Lenny then goes over to the counter and says to this other boy who was about to start training, 'Do you fancy a run, son?' The boy looks at Lenny and says, 'Yeah, why not, Len?' Lenny then flips him 20 pence and says, 'Here you are, son, run down the shops and get me the *Sun* newspaper.' The boy's face was a picture.

Another time, Lenny was bouncing with this other doorman that I know. The doorman was having shit off these four blokes. He then starts screaming for Lenny's help. Lenny hears him and runs in and knocks the four of them out cold.

I remember when Lenny decided to leave Slim Jim's to go to Reg Parker's gym. Lenny decided to take the sunbed with him; he thought it was his sunbed. He put it under his arm and left with it.

Lenny didn't like paying for things either. I had this good friend who was a pro boxer and a right face; he used to sell clothes on the market. Lenny used to go up to him and say, 'What have you got today?' Lenny would then take the clothes off him, try them and wouldn't pay for them.

I remember another time Lenny had gone for a job playing a boxer in a TV advert. Lenny had turned up and there must have been about another ten actors looking at playing the part. They all had to wait in this room and go in one at a time. Lenny then said to all of them, 'I think it's in your best interest that you all leave.' By the time it came for Lenny to go in for the part, nearly all of the actors had left and Lenny ended up getting the part.

I used to see Lenny quite a bit when I used to pop down to T's nightclub to see Reg Parker, who was also working on the door with Lenny. Lenny would always greet me with a handshake and ask how I was. Also, while I was working at the Camden Arms on a Sunday night, which wasn't far from his house in Bexleyheath, Lenny would be in the car park buying jellied eels off the stall outside the pub.

My good mate Nick Netley had been Lenny's bodyguard at the 'Mad Gypsy' Bradshaw fight. Nick was a very hard, fit man; he was training for Britain's Strongest Man at the time and was about 21 stone of lean muscle. Lenny was a big man but Nick was bigger again. Lenny wasn't a very well-liked man in some of those fights and he used to wind the crowds right up. Nick Netley brought Lenny into the ring and the crowd would just part when they saw Nick coming through. I don't know if you've seen a video of Lenny fighting 'Mad Gypsy' Bradshaw, but Nick is the bloke in the white T-shirt who jumps in the ring to pull Lenny off Bradshaw. He was the only bloke who could handle Lenny in those days. There's a photo of Nick in Lenny's book, *The Guv'nor*, bringing Lenny into the ring.

NICK NETLEY

I only met Lenny about a dozen times. A mate of mine had pulled out of being in his corner for the 'Mad Gypsy' Bradshaw fight. There must have been about 50 per cent gypsies in there and we thought it was going to kick off. I was in my prime at the time and didn't give a shit about the crowd. I must have been about 21 stone. I was in the back of the changing room and warming Lenny up on the punch pads. Lenny's hands were in a right mess from all the years of fighting. Lenny could half dig and was hitting my hand back with his big punches.

I then lead Lenny to the ring. I could see that Bradshaw's eyes were all glazed and then he went and stuck the nut in Lenny. I could see Lenny wiping his head to see if he had been cut and I thought to myself, Lenny's going to fucking kill him.

Lenny destroyed Bradshaw and then started stamping on him. I thought, If I don't get in there, Lenny's going to finish him. Lenny was still irate by now and still kicking him. I then went down under Lenny's big swings and rugby tackled him up against the ropes. We finally managed to get Lenny out of the ring and there was no trouble in the crowd.

But you had to watch what you said with Lenny around as he would lose it quite easy. I never really had a chance to see the other side of Lenny as there was always someone round us. It was like he was trying to play his tough-man image at all times. We trained a bit together and he always trained really hard, the same as me; there would be no talking, we would just get on with it.

We were up in Slim Jim's the next day after the Bradshaw fight and we were just talking about the fight. I then said to Lenny, 'If I hadn't been there to stop you last night, you would have killed that bloke.' He then looked at me with this stinking stare as if to say, 'What? You could have stopped me?'

I first came across Reg on a TV documentary about unlicensed boxing from the late 1980s. Reg had organised one of Lenny's most talked-about fights in unlicensed boxing. He had promoted Lenny's fight with 'Mad Gypsy' Bradshaw in 1986 at the Yorkshire Grey pub. On the documentary, Reg had said, 'There's only one Lenny McLean, there will never be another Lenny McLean. Lenny McLean was the Godfather of unlicensed boxing, and there will never be another one; you couldn't compare, couldn't walk in his shoes.' Stilks then set up an interview for a Sunday morning. On the way to the interview we passed the Yorkshire Grey pub which had now been turned into a McDonalds. We arrived at Reg's gym called Shapes, which he had run for over 21 years. I was introduced to Reg and we had a cup of tea and a chat. Here's what he had to say about Lenny McLean.

REG PARKER

I first met Lenny when he came to train in my gym. This must have been around 1984. I'd heard about him for years and seen a few bits about him on the TV. He was a very strong man. I used to help him out quite a few times when he was on the big weights. We also used to have a pro boxing gym next to the weights room; it's now been turned into a cardiovascular room. I sparred with him quite a few times, but, every time you sparred with him, he'd have to deck you.

Lenny trained quite a lot in the boxing gym. Another one

of my mates used to hate it when Lenny turned up, as he always ended up getting bashed up.

I'd had a couple of unlicensed fights myself when I was younger and, when Lenny came along, I thought it was an ideal opportunity to promote my very own shows. We had a good chat and I made him top of the bill at the show. I lined him up a fight with a bloke named Bryan Bradshaw, nicknamed the 'Mad Gypsy', who had fought about half-a-dozen fights and was undefeated.

The fight was held in the Yorkshire Grey pub in Eltham. About 500 people had crammed themselves into the Harrogate Suite. If we had held this a couple of years later in the Ritzy, we would have had about 2,000 people there. Various cameramen were there on the night and Lenny destroyed Bradshaw in seconds. It took a couple of people that night to calm Lenny down. A lot of people thought Bradshaw was dead; he had swallowed his tongue and the referee had pulled it out. It looked like he had been run over by a train.

Lenny was on a good high after the fight. He came up to me afterwards and we had a drink I paid him his money and he went home.

Lenny also used to work on the doors for me down at T's nightclub. We used to have a good laugh there. I remember this one night down there, this young bloke had come to talk to him. The bloke was going on to Lenny about how he couldn't stand bodybuilders and that he was a boxer and this and that. Lenny then tells him right off and tells him that he was a bodybuilder as well. The bloke's face was a picture. I saw Lenny knock a few people out down in T's nightclub when I was working with him. He was also a very comical bloke. He could either be comical or frightening. He could sit

243

there and have you laughing for hours telling you stories. I have always got on great with Lenny and that's the way I'll always remember him.

LES MARTIN

I have been around the London scene for well over 40 years. I had known everyone from that era, including the Krays, and was good mates with Charlie Kray.

Lenny was a real good bloke. The bloke was massive, really huge. I used to go up The Guv'ner's pub quite a bit when the Wadham boys were running it. I was absolutely gutted when I heard he had died. I went to the funeral which went really well. I got interviewed by the *Daily Mirror* at the funeral and I told them that, if Ronnie Kray had a nightclub in heaven, then Lenny's on the door. The next day, it appeared in the papers. I still have the cutting to this day.

BILLY DONOGHUE

Lenny was a really nice bloke. Him and my father were really good mates. I went round his house one day when I was younger and he was out the back in his garden doing a bit of sunbathing. He liked his smoking and was always doing roll-ups. This wasp then starts flying around by us and Lenny could see I was absolutely petrified. He jumps up as quick as lightning and squashes the wasp in his bare hands as I just looked on shocked.

Another time, Lenny had got me a start in this nightclub playing my music. Now, the music I was playing was not the type the owner wanted there. So I told Lenny and he made a phone call to the owner of the club and told the owner that, from now on, they play my music.

One night, I went out and I popped round to The Hippodrome in the West End. Lenny was on the door that night and spotted me. He made a point of calling me to the front and lifting me up over the other people there into the club.

Boxing fanatic Eric Guy has the biggest collection of boxing videos in Great Britain. Eric himself had over 33 amateur fights before having a crack at the unlicensed scene where he ended up undefeated. There's nothing this bloke hasn't seen in the boxing world and he has a book out soon on his escapades. Eric recently appeared in *Footballer's Wives* playing a bare-knuckle fighter. Here's what he had to say about the couple of times he met Lenny.

ERIC GUY

A couple of years ago, we had Roberto Duran over here staying at this health-centre gym called Profiles. Gary and Martin Kemp were doing some training over there at the time; I knew them from years ago and they asked me would I train them for a bit. So I trained them for the day and they then asked me did I want to get involved in training them for this *Krays* film they were going to do.

The film then got put off for a while and then, when it was put back on, they had gotten John H Stacey to do the job. Anyway, they rung me up and told me they were filming the boxing sequence and did I want to come along as a guest. So I went over there and Charlie Kray who had been at that training set took me over and introduced me to Lenny. Charlie said, 'Oh, Lenny, this is Eric…' and, as I put my hand out to shake his, his big hand enveloped mine and he said, 'Hi, my name is Lenny.' I then said, 'Fucking hell, you're a big fucker, aren't you?' I then had a good chat with him.

Lenny ended up appearing in a scene in the film while the Kemp brothers are fighting. I then saw him down the West End in The Hippodrome while I was with Lennox Lewis and Maloney.

I then got into the unlicensed scene myself and, one day, I went down to a place he used to work in Commercial Road. Dave 'The Bomb' Haye was in his office with him and he mentioned to Lenny that I was fighting that night in Ilford. Lenny says to me, 'How are you feeling?' I said, 'I'm feeling all right, I've been training hard and all that.' Lenny then says to me, 'Come on, then, stand up and shape up and let's have a look at you.'

So he stands in front of me and says, 'Yeah, yeah, you look good...' and all of a sudden he throws four punches towards my face. None of them hit me, but the last punch his finger caught me in the eye.

Now, you know when you get that split-second of anger... I could have gone two ways. I could have let my anger out and smacked him one like most people would have in that situation, or bite my tongue. I took the second one and bit my tongue. I said, 'Fucking hell, Len,' and Lenny said, 'Anyway, you're looking good, son.' I invited him to the fight but he was too busy; anyway, I went on to win that night.

I caught up with Mark in a gym he runs in Crayford. Mark was a pro boxing trainer, training people like Julius Francis. Mark was in the middle of training one of his new prospects named Freddy Luke. In between rounds, he sat down with me and here's what Mark had to say about his good mate Lenny McLean.

MARK ROE

The first time I ever seen Lenny was in 1979 when he fought a guy called Cliff Fields. My mate, Danny Fontalio, who was an ex-pro boxer, refereed the fight. Lenny had been doing really well but just ran out of steam.

Then, a little while after that fight, I used to train in a gym called Slim Jim's which was down in Greenwich. Lenny was only about 15½ stone at the time and we started weight training together, and his physique improved rapidly. He was ever so strong. We became pretty close as training partners and friends. I done a little bit of pad work with Lenny, and a lot of the other guys, but with Slim Jim's we didn't have all the room in the world and just made space. But more time was spent after the weights sitting down in the foyer outside drinking tea, and Lenny would be doing his roll-ups.

Another time, Lenny was training in the gym and he must have had about five plates on each end of this bar; there must have been over 500 pounds on this bar and Lenny calls out to Boy George's brother, Jerry O'Dowd, 'Come on, hit me.' Lenny's walking round, psyching himself up. Jerry says, 'I'm not hitting you.' Lenny then says to this other guy, 'Come on, you hit me.' The bloke hits Lenny across the face. Lenny then says, 'Come on, hit me harder.'

So the bloke hits him harder. Lenny then goes down on the bench like the Incredible Hulk and lifts the weight. Lenny jumps up and says, 'I'll teach you to fucking hit me,' and gives the bloke a clip. Jerry O'Dowd turns to the bloke and says, laughing, 'That's why I didn't hit him.'

Another day, Lenny was pummelling away on this bag and this big bloke went up to him to have a moan at him because he had been fucked off out of a club. Now that's the last thing Lenny wanted to hear when he was training, so Lenny clumped him one and the bloke went over; he then disappeared and no one's ever seen the bloke since.

Another time, I was with Lenny and we were leaving the gym and a traffic warden was putting a ticket on to Lenny's car. Lenny shouted at him, 'Oh, do you like hospital food? Because the Greenwich Hospital is just round the corner there.'

The guy looked at Lenny and tore it up in front of him, so he carried that bit of an aura about him, but, if you knew him and got on with him, there was no intimidation at all.

A couple of years ago, I used to do a bit of healing work and Lenny knew that. So this one day, Lenny asked me would I do a bit of healing on his bad hand. He then asked me would I do it now and again… it was just something he believed in, and he reckoned his hand had never been as good after I touched it.

One day, we were in the shower in Slim Jim's and he said to me, 'Here you are, boy, do us a favour, put that dressing on my backside…' and I turned round and he had this hole in his arse where I think he had been stabbed or shot. I was thinking to myself, He's just trained with that injury, he must have been in so much pain, but he hadn't let on.

I saw Lenny have a few other fights. I went to the one at Eltham when Lenny fought the gypsy kid. The majority of fights Lenny had he won.

I remember when Lenny fought Dave York over at Woodford. Dave had been a schoolboy champion as a kid. I think Lenny was carrying him throughout the fight as Dave was way out of condition, but I think Dave got a bit excited in the fight and stuck the nut into Lenny, so Lenny said to have some of this and started nutting him back and that was the end of it, he got rid of him. As much as anyone can say love or hate him, everyone went to see him fight because they knew it was going to be exciting.

I think Lenny done a few people favours; you have only got to look at where Frank Warren is today and he could probably say he owes it all to Lenny McLean.

I did a couple of nights with Lenny while he was working in the Camden Palace. Basil, Big Brian was all working there as well. If you knew Lenny and then you got on well with him, then you could go up there any time and he'd treat you as a really normal person, but anyone he didn't like or he thought was a threat, he'd fuck them off out of there, don't matter who they were, and I seen that happen quite a few times.

I went up the Camden Palace quite a few times for a drink and a bit of food. I took my wife up there one night and we went upstairs to sit down to have a meal. Lenny would sit by us and have a bit of food. He would then start flexing his chest and his pecs would go up and down; he then turned to my missus and says, 'I bet you can't do that with those…' We'd all burst out laughing as he was always making jokes like that, but you could get on with Lenny.

I think the people who run him down are the people who opposed him, because they were the people he could never get on with, but most people he would treat as any normal person. The one thing about Lenny is, most people would make him out to be some big strong guy, who didn't have much in the brain, but it wasn't like that. I would say he was one of the guys who didn't really suffer fools. That's the way it was. We were talking once and these two guys were sitting there and they kept asking silly questions. He turned round and said to me, 'You can't educate a mug and that's what these two are here.'

This one time I was talking to Lenny and I had just come away from my first wife. I was going through a bad time and I was saying to Lenny that I didn't know what I was going to do, as my head was all over the place. He then said to me, 'Well, if she done to me what she done to you, I'd pour a saucepan full of hot oil over her belly and then chuck her off the balcony.' I started laughing and said to him, 'I wouldn't go that far, Len.' He said, 'No, she'd have to be taught a lesson,' and carried on talking normal.

I remember another night up the Camden and there was this guy sitting on this couch and Lenny asked him to take his feet down, please, and he told Lenny to fuck off. Lenny got hold of him and must have hit him down five or six times. I don't know what the bloke was on but he kept getting back up, but I don't think the bloke would have looked the best the next morning, but one thing Lenny could do was punch. Throughout the years I knew him, he hardly changed but just got bigger.

It was such a shame in the end as he started doing all right for himself with the acting.

I think that the reason he didn't get a few of those bits and pieces years ago was that he was so intimidating. Lenny always wanted to be in control; even if he was in a club and he wasn't in charge of the place, he wanted to appear like he was.

It was a little bit sad to hear the way that he went because he used to be so strong. He was always polite and well mannered. I remember Lenny would always turn round and say, 'Be a winner… if you want to make your mark, you have got to be a winner,' and that's probably the best advice you can give anyone.

Don Austin first started on the doors around 1977 at the legendary Music Machine (now called the Camden Palace). He had first started working on the docks when he was a kid earning the nickname 'The Docker'. After having a go at the unlicensed game himself, Don turned his talent to training kids at the Thomas a'Becket gym in the Old Kent Road. Later on in life, he went into politics and ended up becoming the Mayor of Greenwich. Don also does a bit of acting in his spare time as well.

I met Don over a cup of tea and here's what he had to say about Lenny McLean.

DON AUSTIN

I first met Lenny around 1978 in a nightclub called Virgo's – it's demolished now – over in the East End of London. He was working on the doors there and we both got chatting to each other. I was also fighting unlicensed as well at the time. I had three fights, winning them all. I knew my limits and packed the boxing game in.

I then started training and working on the doors with him as well. I seen him fighting loads of times on the door; he could be physically terrifying when he wanted to be.

I got to know him really well. I know he had a fearsome reputation, his physical presence was quite frightening, really, but I speak as I find, and I really liked the bloke. But then, if you look at the life he had growing up, you can understand it. I honestly believe, if someone had got hold of

251

Lenny when he was about 17 years of age, I think the least he would have been was British Heavyweight Champion. I told him that many times over.

OK, I think he would have had trouble with boxers like Joe Bugner and Billy Aird, who were clever and well skilled, but I think Lenny had more heart for a row than anybody else.

I remember when Joe Bugner boxed Muhammad Ali and it went the full 15 rounds. It was reported that Bugner done 20 lengths of the pool after the fight; there was a lot of criticism going round saying he could have tried a bit harder in the fight. Now, if that was Lenny McLean, he would have gone in and it would have been a row from the opening bell… it would have been shit or bust.

I remember I was on the door with him once at the Camden Palace and he had gone downstairs for some reason. Now, I was on my own on the door and these three big blokes turned up and are swearing and chucking their weight about. So I says to the blokes, 'Hold up, lads, you are not coming in.' I thought, I'm on my own, but I'm going to go down fighting. I then heard one of the bar girls saying, 'I'll go and get Lenny.' Next thing I know, Lenny runs in and says to me, 'What's the matter?' By now the three of them had seen Lenny and legged it out of the club and were nowhere to be seen. I then said to him, laughing, 'Thanks for turning up, Len,' but, to be honest, I think I would have ended up in hospital if he hadn't turned up so quick.

Another night, I was talking to some Scottish blokes from Glasgow outside the Camden Palace and Lenny came out and I introduced them to him. Lenny then says to them, 'Who's the hardest man up in Glasgow?' One of them replies with some Scottish name like 'Alex McIntosh' or

'McLeesh'. Lenny says, 'Yeah, that's him, I went up there and knocked him out in three rounds… we had a right big bet on it that day.'

We used to train a lot in a gym named Slim Jim's in Greenwich. This one time I was training with Lenny and I had a phone call saying that my aunt, who was about 93 at the time, had been robbed by some blokes posing as workmen. They had robbed her of £40 quid. Lenny was tamping [irate] and said to me, 'Here you are, give her £100.' He was a very soft-hearted person; he could be hard man when he wanted to, but very soft-hearted as well. He could be a very funny person as well.

Later on in life, I got involved in politics and this one night I took the Mayor of Sevenoaks up to the West End to see this play. We then went along to The Hippodrome as I knew Lenny was working there. Lenny charmed her and she was quite taken in; he was a proper gentleman.

I went to see Lenny fight a few times; he'd fight all the hard nuts.

The thing is, when you're a big doorman with a reputation like Lenny's, you become like the marshal; everybody wants to shoot him down. A lot of people reckoned Lenny was the best street fighter you'll ever meet in your life, and I wouldn't argue with it. I didn't go and visit him while he was in prison as it would have taken a visit away from his family. I can't speak highly enough of him, really, he always had my back and we became good friends. I thought he was a terrific guy.

While I was up in London staying with Stilks, I had the chance to do a few nights on the door with him and his mate. His mate had also worked on the doors with Lenny in the past. Here's what he had to say.

LENNIE MULLANE

Around 1992, I was working for this company called Scorpion Security. My missus was pregnant and I was working on the doors to get some extra money. This bloke named Leroy, who I used to work with in this club called Stars, phoned me up and asked me would I cover this bloke for a couple of weekends. The place was a club in the West End called Cairo Jack's. It had a downstairs to the place as well.

So he gave me all the details and I made my way there on a Friday night.

I walked into the club and I noticed this big bloke near the front door. As he turned round, I realised it was Lenny McLean. I'd heard about his reputation for years. I thought to myself, This bloke is fucking huge. I was only 24 at the time and he was a lot older than me.

So I goes across and says to him, 'Hi, Lenny, I'm working with you tonight.' He then shakes my hand and says, 'What's your name, son?' So I says to him, 'Lennie, Lennie Mullane.' He says to me, 'Are you taking the fucking piss, son?' I then replied, 'No, Len, I'm Lennie Mullane and you're Lenny McLean.'

This broke the ice and we both had a good laugh about it. We had a really quiet night except for the few odd scuffles. Throughout the night, we talked about the everyday things that went on in life. We talked a bit about his fights, and the way he came across to me was he was only fighting because of the money. He seemed a real family man. I found him to be a really nice bloke.

This one bloke then comes out of the club and says to Lenny, 'I wouldn't like to have a clump off you.' Lenny turns to me and says, 'I bet he fucking wouldn't.' I worked the following week again and it was more or less the same, really quiet.

It was nice to have worked with him and to see him go on to star in *The Knock* and then later on in life in the movie *Lock, Stock and Two Smoking Barrels.*

10
Meeting the Guv'nor

Throughout his life, various people crossed Lenny's path. It may have been in a gym, a boxing ring, on the door of a club or even just walking down the street one day. I'll leave this chapter to those people to do the talking.

Dave Lea is one of those people – he now resides in Los Angeles, works in the film industry as a fight-coordinator, action actor and choreographer to many of Hollywood's top actors. I caught up with Dave who had just finished working on his latest project, a Michael Bay movie called *The Island* starring Ewan McGregor and Scarlett Johansson. Dave also has his own website at www.daveleastunt.com.

DAVE LEA

I first met Lenny McLean on a trip to London where I was attending the movie première of *Batman Returns*. I was told by a close friend of mine that Lenny was interested in meeting with me. Lenny had wanted to see me in regards to his movie called *The Guv'nor*. I had just been to a Page 3 model party and was on my way to the West End with two of the models who I had worked with previously in London. I parked my car on the street near The Hippodrome and told the ladies that I wouldn't be long and to just sit tight and wait for me.

I had never met Lenny, I had only heard or read about him. It was business for me. So I arrived at the door and there were these two guys who were huge and looking down at me (mind you, there was a step up to the entrance). One then says to me, 'What do you want, mate?' I replied, 'Hi, my name is Dave Lea and am here to see Lenny.' The big doormen then replies, 'Hang on there, mate.' Next thing I know, out came this huge guy. He's stood there, this mountain of a man, three times bigger than the front of Harrods.

Lenny told me that he had heard of my work in action movies and was interested in discussing the fight scenes for his movie *The Guv'nor*. As we were chatting away, I noticed that there were two guys harassing the two ladies in the car, so I said to Lenny, 'Hang on a second, Len.' As I approached the two guys and told them to back off from the car, they got a little bold and stupid and, the next thing I know, Lenny stepped up and took care of the situation. One went flying against the wall and kind of went to sleep. The other took a slap in the face and did a full flip and landed on his ass, looking very confused. Lenny then said to me to run along before the police turned up. There must have been about a thousand people around there who saw it, as it was pretty late and in the West End.

We started meeting in a few of the pubs in the West End

to discuss things about the movie. I started noticing two sides to the man, a side of the man that not many people would get to see. We would discuss his film *The Guv'nor* a lot and he really wanted me to be the one to do the fight scenes. I would give him different ideas how we could make it more realistic as there was around six major fights, and it was important to get a different flavour to each fight. This wasn't *Kung Fu Theatre* or *Ninja Turtles* – can you imagine big Lenny doing one of those fancy run-up-the-wall flip-over kicks? I don't think so.

This one day, we were in a wine bar in Wardour Street, and yet again we were discussing his movie and his book. It must have been about six o'clock in the evening. There were three blokes in the corner who looked like office guys and they were getting really loud. We could no longer hear ourselves speak. Lenny then shouts to them, 'Oi, I'm fucking talking over here.'

Everything goes quiet for a bit. It then starts getting louder again and, by now, Lenny's had enough. He smashes his hand down on the table which makes a big bang; he then holds his huge fist up and says, 'Do you want some of this?' He turns to me and says, 'A couple of glasses of wine and they think they are something.' The guys were then as quiet as mice.

I'd speak to Lenny regular about the film on the phone from America. He was really trying his best to get it going. He had given me the script hoping that someone might take it up.

I had been on the set of *Demolition Man* with Sylvester Stallone one night. It must have been about three in the morning and we were in between shots on the set. I started having a chat with him and I was telling him about Lenny and what he was like. I told him he was the real deal with a heart of a lion. He seemed really interested in what Lenny had done in his life.

On another trip to London, I went down to Pinewood Studios with Lenny to meet with the producers. Lenny then asked me did I want to meet Reggie Kray, as Lenny had been telling Reggie about me and Reggie wanted to meet me to discuss some business with him. Reggie hadn't been happy with the way *The Krays* film had turned out and there was another film in the pipeline and he wanted to discuss the project with me. It was going to be a follow-up to *The Krays*.

Lenny picked me up and took me with him on the visit. On the way, Lenny pulled into an off-licence to pick up a small bottle of shorts for Reggie.

Reggie was pleased to meet me. It felt strange meeting Reggie Kray; he was very polite and well dressed. Me and Lenny stayed for a few hours. It was funny seeing the big man Lenny sneaking Reggie a small bottle of shorts under the table as both of them shared in this 'Don't let the screws see us' moment. My feeling was they couldn't give a damn – Lenny or Mr Kray that is. I mean, what were they going to do? Give Mr Kray extra time? It seemed to me that Lenny and Reggie were in charge of the visiting room and all that went on.

Reggie then gave me an envelope with a poem in it which I found to be of interest due to the quote he had signed on it. As me and Lenny were leaving, Reggie mentioned that he was having a private wing party afterwards, in honour of the visit. One can only imagine how many good reasons you can have in prison to have a drink. It was funny to hear, mind you; it seemed Mr Kray had enough influence to maybe have got me and Lenny an evening pass to the wing.

On my return to Los Angeles, I kept in touch with Mr Kray and, on hearing the sad news of his death, I sent a fax to the hospital with my condolences. I will say, on meeting Mr Kray, he was very articulate and, to be honest, for a man to have been locked up for so long, he had this excitement in him when we discussed a possible Kray sequel. In fact, the day after my visit, I was staying at my sister's house in Essex. It was early morning and she stumbles into my room and says stuttering, 'Dave, Reggie Kray is on the phone for you.' I forgot to tell her I had given Mr Kray her number. She handed me the phone from her shaking hand with a very stunned look in her eyes; it was quite funny at the time, and still is. Mr Kray had called to say thanks for coming to visit him and that he was going to send a package to me and he wanted to know where to deliver it.

So, by now, my sister is thinking, Package? What next? We will have the Sweeney knocking on the door.

Reggie then sent me two of his books to read. Don't women panic, though? It was only Reggie Kray calling her home.

I kept in touch with Lenny even though I was back and forth to America with work. I always kept his *Guv'nor* filmscript with me and always tried my best to get it off the ground. I spoke to quite a few people in the mix in Hollywood. They found Lenny's story very interesting. I had also worked with director Guy Ritchie on a Madonna video and had asked Guy about his work on *Lock, Stock and Two Smoking Barrels*. We then talked about Lenny, and Guy told me that Lenny was quite interesting to work with. He told me he was in his element in front of the camera.

I still kept in touch with Lenny on the phone right up until he passed away. I was very sad when my sister rung me and told me the bad news. It's a shame the film never took off, as he wanted to get it on the big screen so much. It was a pleasure to have known the big man and I hope his movie gets done, and done the best way possible.

Everyone has a story to tell – me, even you – but maybe Lenny is looking down from up there, and maybe he's still working the doors. Just that the doors may resemble the Pearly Gates, and he is shouting down, 'Oi, you lot, stop fucking around and get my movie made, it's well overdue.' And I don't think he will rest until it is on the silver screen.

In knowing Lenny, he, like many of us, was on a journey in life and every journey has its destination. For many of us on that journey, we may encounter 'turbulence'. Sure, Lenny may have been a product of his environment, and yet he fought his way up and out. My belief is, Lenny may have had the toughest fight ever in the end. I would like to think he didn't lose; maybe he found what we all are searching for – peace – and, in doing so, gave it to those family and close friends. Even those who are reading this, including myself, we are all on a journey in search of something.

Hey, Lenny, I hope someone is reading this and calls 'Action!'

Billy Cribb's memoirs finally came to light in 2004 when his book *Tarmac Warrior* was released. Billy had appeared in the banned *Bare Fist* documentary which Lenny starred in. I caught up with Billy over a cup of tea.

BILLY CRIBB

I first met Lenny myself at this airport in NYC where he had both hands heavily bandaged and was as bored as me waiting for a plane back to the UK. He was pacing up and down and growling at everyone who even looked his way for a second; he wasn't a patient man by any stretch of the imagination.

We had a chat for a while over a coffee, which I remember tasted like shit. Those Yanks think they have the coffee market sewn up, but you can't beat a good cup of instant, can you? We talked about the fight scene in the UK, which is how I got to hear about the Kings pub where they were putting on unlicensed fights, and couldn't wait to give it a look. We also talked about the fight he had just had over there in which he had broken some of the smaller bones in his hands. He blamed his corner for that, which I have to agree with; they need to know their job when it comes to taping and bleeding. If they get it wrong, it could fuck up the fight for you big time. The fighter is so keyed up he often can't feel if something is wrong because you're fighting on pure adrenalin.

Lenny McLean got me through that time and helped me get out of the fight world. I did a documentary with Lenny called *Bare Fist* which, while still banned, will eventually be released.

Lenny leaned on me one day and made me promise to pack the game in. He said, 'Son, you've got a lot to offer those kids who need you [I now counsel drug abuse and young offenders] don't let them down.' I replied, 'OK.' He said, 'OK is no good to me, I can't spend that – promise me.' So I made the promise. He said, 'Good boy,' like I was a kid, then he took hold of me and squeezed me like a little doll under his huge arm. I am only five foot four to his massive frame.

Without Lenny, I would still be fighting and may even be dead. Believe me, Lenny was a man with a big heart. Don't let the roaring fool you. Like me, what else can you do without a good education? You have to go for the gold. Lenny, thanks from my four girls, for giving them their dad back.

TONY FERRY

I remember the first time that I saw Lenny McLean was at a boxing event at Woodford Football Club. A friend of mine, Lee White, was also on the bill that day. Lee and I used to drink in a pub called the Hare & Hounds on the Purley Way. I hadn't known Lee for that long, but several of us from the pub travelled up with Lee's other friends and family by coach to watch him fight that day. It was an afternoon event, either on a Saturday or Sunday. I think it was organised by Terry Downes.

The ring was set up on the football pitch; there were wooden benches all around and a large marquee behind the ring. We were all searched by two hefty doormen with no necks on the way in. This was when I got my first glimpse of Lenny. He was just inside the entrance. I did not know who he was, as it was my first time to go to that sort of event. He was huge, with staring eyes, someone you definitely wouldn't want to get on the wrong side of. I think it was one of Lee's other mates who then said that it was Lenny McLean.

Anyway, we got a beer and sat down to watch the fights. We were about three rows from the front of the ring. There were around ten or twelve fights on the bill. Some were lightweights, which were very fast. Then some big guys were on, which were a lot slower. I think Lee was light-heavy, a stocky lad. I'm sure he won on the day, but I'm not 100 per cent sure.

Then came the fight that everyone had come to see.

Lenny McLean was fighting this huge bloke named 'Man Mountain' York. They both entered the ring; there was a mixture of cheers and boos, and chants for Lenny. Lenny easily had the most support.

I think it only lasted a round. I remember seeing Lenny sticking the nut on York. The referee didn't seem to be able to control the fight. Lenny really went into him, trying to kick, stamp, anything to take him out. This caused a commotion with the crowd. I think a few of York's supporters tried to get into the ring at Lenny. Then Lenny's lot were trying to get at them and, within a few minutes, the whole place erupted and everyone was fighting.

Lenny and his corner men left the ring to go to the changing rooms and some of the crowd was trying to leave... it was unbelievable. I had never witnessed anything like this; there were benches and bodies flying everywhere and, as we were trying to leave, the huge beer tent collapsed. You could see the canvas moving because of the people underneath. We just wanted to get back to our coach to safety as we had Lee's mum and a couple of others with us. I thought we were going to get a bashing one way or another.

As we left the ground, we made our way up a 100m-long driveway to the coaches. We had to wait at the top of this driveway for our coach to turn up. Things then seemed to have quietened down a bit. There was a small pub or club right outside the ground at the end of this driveway. We were part of a crowd of about 80 or more people.

Time seemed to be passing very slowly and we were all very nervous and uneasy; you could just sense something was going to happen. All of a sudden, there was this loud roaring noise, the pub doors then burst open and Lenny came out with a chair in each hand, running towards us shouting and hollering that he was going to kill us all. Lenny starts shouting, 'Who wants some?'

By now, there were other people leaving the ground as well at the top of the driveway. Lenny and a handful of others then chased us. I've never seen so many people running for their lives.

Luckily, at this moment our coach pulled up in the car park across the road and we all got on it as fast as we could. I could feel my heart coming out through my chest, and we never felt safe until the coach had pulled away. I don't know if something had happened in the pub or if he thought the crowd that had gathered at the top of this driveway were waiting to have a go at him (which they weren't). He was obviously pissed off, going by his reactions. It was a funny sight to see all them people running from one man. We all needed a few beers when we got back to Croydon that night, I can tell you. I have never forgotten that day, and have been interested in Lenny ever since.

I would have loved to have met him in person as I think we would have got on well.

LAURENCE ELVEY

I met Lenny this one night when I was working in a nightclub in Romford. Lenny had popped in to see the owner, just as I was struggling to drag this bloke out. When the bloke suggested a toe-to-toe with me, I agreed. I then had a real tough fight and only just won it.

I shook hands with the bloke and off he went. Little did I know that Lenny had been watching all of this. Lenny came up to me as I was wiping the blood from my face and said to me, 'You did well, my son, keep up the good work, you're a good lad.'

Later, when he was leaving, he pulled me to one side and said, 'Keep your chin up, son, there's always people keeping an eye out for you.' He then shook my hand tightly, winked and left.

I remember Len when I saw him like it was yesterday. He was this big, I mean natural, hard, big bloke, that stood firm and solid. He looked like a brick shit-house, a look that would scare any terrorist, nonce, madman or hard man. This look was a look that told 1,000 stories. The leather skin, the big shovel-like hands that held mine like they were tiny baby's hands. His look when he congratulated me for taking on a loud-mouthed punter that had offered me out in public – me, the little guy, out of all the other doormen. I agreed, took on this local thug and taught him a lesson that left me in a lot of pain. But I proved my point. It made me feel special; it made me feel like I'd achieved something unique.

The short time, the few minutes that I saw him, was like a lifetime. His words sunk deep and carved a path for my future years, whether it was on the door or afterwards in my present years. I never knew Len was there, but he said I did well and it was nice knowing that Lenny thought I was a good kid.

DANIEL ROCHE

I first met Lenny about nine years ago when I was having breakfast in this café in Hoxton. He walked in and sat down right by us. He was a very good friend of a lady called Alice, who was also a good friend of my father's. Being only 14 years old at the time, I was obviously very taken by the size of Lenny, but, as soon as I was introduced to him by my father, I was put at ease very quickly.

I remember Lenny telling me not to drink Pepsi but to always drink Sprite, 'as it won't rot your teeth'! I found Lenny to be very polite and very funny. My dad also met Lenny on a number of occasions at parties which were held in the downstairs of the café.

To this day, I can remember how polite and friendly Lenny was to everyone in the café, even though it was only a brief meeting, and very few words were exchanged; everyone knew or had heard of Lenny McLean.

JONATHAN JAMES

In the beginning of the Eighties, I was working as a bodyguard for the singer Steve Strange. Steve had taken over the Camden Palace in London and the place was doing really well. I turned up this one night as I had to meet Steve inside. The doormen were huge and there were quite a few of them there. The main one on the door refused to let me in. I then tried explaining to him that I was Steve's bodyguard. He then said to me, 'You must be the prettiest bodyguard in London,' and then he let me in.

Once I was inside, I went and saw Steve. Steve said to me, 'Lucky you didn't start on him, as that's Lenny McLean.' Now, to be honest, I hadn't heard of him and just thought he was an ordinary doorman. After Steve started telling me stories about him, I realised how lucky I was not to have said anything to him. I always got on well with Lenny after that first meeting.

LEE CRYSTAL

I remember years ago when there was a local carnival held in Victoria Park. Lenny and a few of his mates came up with the idea of putting on a fighting booth for the public. People would come and pay money and have a go at Lenny. All the money was going to charity.

They set up a little ring with four ropes and Lenny took on all challengers. A mate of mine at the time, who had never had a fight in his life, jumped in and had a go at Lenny. Lenny was showboating and moving around; by now everyone was in stitches laughing at the both of them.

After a while, Lenny caught him on the chin and he's gone down. Lenny's looking over him and one of my other mates at the side comes running in with this bucket of ice-cold water and chucks it straight over him. My mate jumps up in shock, not knowing where he was. Everyone, by now, has nearly pissed themselves laughing. We moved on as Lenny took on the next challenge without a care in the world.

ROBBIE BUTLER

I first heard of Lenny when I was a kid after getting hold of some of his fights. I was living with my cousin Jimmy in London a few years later, and Jimmy introduced me to him. I went round his house and we had a good chat in his kitchen.

Another day, I was in his house with Jimmy, and Lenny was winding me up. He says to me, 'What would you do if that dog started shagging your leg?' I replied, 'I'd fake an orgasm, Len...' We then all started laughing.

I was standing on his doorstep this once after I had been training down at Charlie Magri's gym. Lenny says to me, 'What's Charlie Magri think about Lenny McLean?' I replied,

'He thinks you're sound, Len, you're a good fella.' Jimmy was already in Lenny's house and was stood behind Lenny as I was talking to him. Lenny then says, 'Nah, nah, nah... what does Charlie Magri think about Lenny McLean?'

I was a bit confused by now and told him the same answer again. I could see Lenny was now getting louder and more aggressive and I was getting a bit worried. Jimmy then came out and whispered to me, 'Say he's nuts...' Lenny asked me one more time and I replied, 'Len, he thinks you're a fucking raving lunatic.'

Lenny then started smiling and says, 'That's it, son.' Lenny then gave me a kick up the bottom, messing about as I was leaving.

I seen Lenny in a temper this once and it was like the blood just drained from his face. Normally, most people go red when they get mad. He seen someone down the road and he started telling us this little story and he was going mad.

I was also boxing at the time for West Ham Boxing Club. Lenny rung me before my first fight and said, 'What you've got to do, Robbie, is be calm all day, and then, as soon as you get in the ring, start hating him, absolutely hate him, imagine he's smacked your mother in the mouth, go over there and fucking destroy him.' It was a good bit of advice and it worked a treat.

I then went down Cairo Jack's this once and had a cracking photo done in his office; the photo still hangs on the wall in my own boxing gym.

Lenny McLean was a very funny man, a blinding bloke. He kept me out of serious trouble. I learned a lot from him and I'm very grateful.

PHILLIP WRIGHT

I had heard of the name Lenny McLean quite a lot as I was from the East End of London. I was in the Carpenter's Arms in Stepney one day with a crowd of my mates. Lenny walked in with one of his mates who I didn't know but he looked a bit tasty as well. We knew he'd walked in before we saw him because of the change of atmosphere. That was the presence Lenny brought with him. The hairs on the back of your neck stood up.

We were getting a bit boisterous and loud but a long glance from Lenny was enough for us to move on.

We had a great fighter on the Isle of Dogs called Deci Richards (pronounced Deeshey); he was another from the Lenny mould, a 1,000-yard stare that would scare you to your boots. We heard rumours that he and Lenny were going to get it on; I don't think they ever did, but I would have loved to have seen that.

I also heard that Lenny was going to fight Jamie Reeves, the monster of a geezer from Sheffield who won the World's Strongest Man. I don't think that happened but, again, that's one fight I would have loved to watch.

LENNY JONES

About 15 years ago, I used to travel from Wales to the East End of London delivering scrap. I had met a lot of people from London and I had heard the name Lenny McLean mentioned a few times. I had seen him in various newspapers and he was a legend back then.

So, this one day, after dropping off a delivery, me and a few of my mates made our way to a pub called The Duke in the East End. As we were having a drink, I noticed Lenny

McLean over in the corner of the pub and he had a little gang with him, a couple of them looked just like hangers-on. So I said to my mates, 'I'm going over to meet him and have a chat.' They all start panicking. Anyway, I thought, Fuck it. So I went over and said to him, 'You're Lenny McLean, aren't you?'

He looks at me and says, 'Oh, you're from Wales.' He then puts out his hand and starts shaking mine, nearly crushing it. You could see by just looking at him he was ready to go, he looked awesome and you could see he was really in his prime. I couldn't believe how wide he was in real life, as I had only seen him in newspapers.

I could see his mates were looking at me as I was chatting to Lenny. Anyway, we chatted for a while, then I went back and told my mates what he had said. I never had the chance to meet him again.

Another contributor I managed to meet up with was Brian Varney, an ex-booth fighter now living in the Welsh Valleys, who had worked up in London a few years ago.

BRIAN VARNEY

I remember the time I met Lenny McLean pretty well. I had been doing a bit of work up in London on the tunnels near the Vauxhall Bridge. I was working for this company named Theissens who did the concreting sections on bridges.

I had gone into this pub on my dinner hour for a pint and a pie. I sat at the bar minding my own business when these two pretty big blokes walked in and one sat either side of me. Now, I could see straight away they were trying to intimidate me, so I just ignored them. I then ordered another drink off the barman and, as he was passing my change to me, one of the blokes sticks his hand out in front of me and takes my change off the barman. I thought to myself, I'm fucked here, but I'm going to give it a go.

So I shot both on the bull's-eye – I elbow the one to the right of me as hard as I could; I then elbow the other one on the other side as well. Next thing, I'm standing up trying to fight them; one of them hits me with a right hook straight on the chin. Now, fighting one man is hard enough but, when you are up against two, it's a totally different ball game.

I was still a bit dazed from that right hook, when, all of a sudden, this big bloke with a rough-looking face comes from the side and flattens the one; he then turns and flattens the other one as well. I swear I don't know where the bloke came from. He then started shouting and growling at them and the two men got off the floor and shot out the door. You could see that they knew him.

I thanked the man for his help and he then said to me, 'That's all right… do you know who I am?' So I said, 'No, but I can see that you're a seasoned fighter.' He said to me while laughing, 'Where are you from, you?' So I said, 'Up north, originally.'

He said, 'I thought so… I'm the Guv'nor, Lenny McLean.' I said to him again, 'Thank you, Mr McLean, for all your help.' He then looked at me laughing and said, 'You don't have to call me "Mr".'

We shook hands. Now, my hands are big but his eclipsed mine and must have been the biggest pair I have ever seen. He then invited me any time to go and have a drink with him in London. I'm not sure, but I think he had his own pub at the time. Let's be fair, the bloke had never met me in his life and had come from nowhere to help me and make me feel really welcome.

I then found out he had a book out a couple of years ago and had been taken ill. I never got round to having that drink with him as I moved on with work, but you could never meet a nicer person in your life.

ALGEE HAMMOND

Back in the Eighties, I decided that, although I was fairly fit at the time, I wanted to go to a gym and do a bit of weights, as I was quite into the bodybuilding look. I contacted a mate of mine named Les and he asked me to come to Slim Jim's in Greenwich and train with him and his mates. Some of them were doormen in the well-known clubs in the West End and Camden.

I started going to the gym and met all the characters that knew Les and some new people that trained at the gym. While training for about six weeks there, I kept hearing the name Lenny McLean mentioned. I had heard of him before as a lot of people I knew were into boxing and unlicensed boxing and, as everybody knows, Lenny McLean was the Guv'nor (well, everyone except yours truly).

One day, I went down to the gym and started doing some weights. At approx 10.30am, I heard a gruff voice say, 'All right, Kenny, my son.'

I turned round and there was Lenny McLean. Although I had never met him before, nobody had to tell me it was him, a huge big man and a face as scary as you can imagine. Kenny, who worked at the gym, said, 'Hello, Lenny.' Lenny looked around the gym and there was me not far behind him, and a couple of other people training. As he looked at me, I thought to myself, Fuck me, do I ignore him or do I nod and get on with my training? I opted for the nod and left him alone – best bet option.

From that day on, I started to see Lenny quite a lot down the gym during the daytime and, through some of the people I trained with, got to know him. Don't get me wrong, I was never a good friend of Lenny's, just someone that knew him down the gym, and we had mutual friends.

As the months passed, I was getting right into the weights; my mates were all into boxing training, which I also enjoyed, but I liked the idea of building my muscles up a bit.

One day, Lenny walked into the gym and spotted me doing the weights on my own. As he was into the weights as well at that time, he came up to me and said, 'You want to train with Lenny?' I can't remember if I was excited to train with him or shit scared to refuse, but I said, 'Yes,' and we started to do some angled bench presses. I can remember being quite full of myself training with the Guv'nor, Lenny McLean, as I felt when people started to come into the gym, they would think, That's Lenny's mate… (sad bastard, I know, but, when you're young and into that scene, it's not often you get friends with the Guv'nor of his trade – it was a buzz).

I soon realised that being Lenny's training partner was not all it was cracked up to be, especially when he started loading 20-kilo discs on the bar. I thought to myself, Fuck me, I don't lift that much in all my sets together. Lenny got under the bar and started doing ten reps with 120 kilos. I am standing just above his head spotting him, thinking to myself, Shit, if he needs help to lift this off his chest then I won't be able to lift it. And as my bollocks were about six inches from that big bulldog face I was even more worried.

275

I got down to the bar and said to Lenny, 'I don't think I can lift this much.' He replies, 'Are you a man or a boy?' Not to make myself look a complete prat in front of him and everyone else in the gym, I grasped the bar and lifted it off the stands. Not too bad, I thought to myself, then, as I started to lower the bar, I felt the excitement, bravado and, more importantly, my pride pouring out of my overloaded lungs. I dropped the bar to my chest and Lenny realised that I could not lift the weight and he pulled it off me and put it back on the stands.

We done a few more weights and then he said he was going to do some bag work. Thank fuck for that, I thought. I then said, 'Cheers, Lenny, thanks for training with me.' He replied, 'That's all right, boy.' That was my first real one-on-one with Lenny, apart from the odd conversation over a protein drink in the main area.

I got to talk to Lenny a lot after that; I had heard a lot of things about him – some good, some bad – but he was always all right with me, although we never did the weights together again. I wonder why.

I must admit, some days he would come into the gym and didn't look very happy, so caution was taken not to talk to him until he talked to me. I don't think he would have got the hump and got violent, but caution is the order of the day for self-preservation, especially with someone who was as big and hard as Lenny.

One day he came into the gym and I was on the light bag doing some bag work. He walked over to the heavy bag next to me; I nodded and he nodded back, but he didn't seem too happy. I thought, OK, eyes front, shut your mouth, Algee. He started to jab the heavy bag around, then all of a sudden he mumbled something and really started to give it to the bag. I was trying to control the light bag so it didn't swing in his way. As I glanced at him I could see that familiar screwed-up face, the look that says, 'Don't mess with me.'

As I was hitting the light bag on my best behaviour, a young bloke, about 17, opened a window not far from Lenny. Lenny just stopped in his tracks and turned to the poor unsuspecting kid and screamed, 'Shut that fucking window.' The young man stood there frozen with fright and I couldn't help but notice that his grey jogging bottoms had a wet patch right on the crotch. I wanted to laugh but Lenny might have thought I was taking the piss, so I made my way to the skipping ropes a bit sharpish. The kid managed to shut the window and disappeared up to the changing room.

Another time in the gym, there was quite a few of the usual daytime crowd and the atmosphere was quite jolly, piss-taking and all that. A young bloke called Steve was looking out the window and decided to wind Lenny up – he was only about ten stone and would take the piss with Lenny a lot; I think he only got away with it because of his size and he also had a great personality. Lenny had just got a new car and was chuffed with it; he used to have a Mini, although he did look a bit daft in it, with the size of him, but fucked if I was going to tell him.

Anyway, Steve turned to Lenny and said, 'One of those sailors out there has just kicked your motor, Lenny.' I thought to myself, Shit, that's the wrong thing to tell him, Steve. Lenny moved like a whippet with a banger up its arse, flying down the stairs of the gym and on to the street. As soon as he reached the street, he started to scream at the sailors.

We were all looking out of the windows and I must say I've never seen half-a-dozen men run so fast in all my life. I don't think he got hold of any of them – good job, really, or there would have been a ship leaving dock with half its crew missing that night. He came back into the gym with the right hump. Steve, realising he'd been a doughnut for saying it, quietly slipped up to the changing room.

This is one of a couple of instances I witnessed Lenny losing it but, to be truthful, most of the time in the gym he was all right with everybody and he used to enjoy his after-training sessions in the main area, having a protein shake and a roll-up and a good chat with all those who would listen.

He did like an audience; it must have been the actor in him. Also, for a tough, hard man, he had a very dry sense of humour.

As I said, I wasn't a close friend of Lenny's, just someone he knew down the gym, but, as someone I've met in my life, I will never forget him, simply because characters like that only come along once in a while. I suppose he done things wrong in his life, but I knew nothing of them, only hearsay. So I respect him for the fact that he was good at what he did, lived life to the max and was respectful to me.

RICK

I was fortunate enough to meet Lenny McLean, if only for a while, when training at Slim's in Greenwich, but what an impact. I can still see him in the sauna while we were sweating our bollocks off, fully attired in tracksuit and towels, shadow boxing and saying, 'How do I look, Rick?' Such a man, I will remember him for ever.

MEETING THE GUV'NOR

KENNETH JONES

I remember Lenny from years ago when I used to live in Bethnal Green. The bloke was an absolute animal and reminded me of a young Mike Tyson. There was no chance in hell that anybody was going to beat him on the cobbles. He was just so big and powerful and would go at any man and just wouldn't lose.

DARIUS HURLEY

I now live in Chicago but am originally from Edmonton. My uncle Terry Hurley used to know Lenny really well. I remember him telling me once how Lenny had gone with him to collect a debt from a bloke in Finsbury Park and the punter had lost control of his bowel movements when he took one look at Lenny. I personally can't think of anyone who looks scarier than Lenny when he was in his prime.

TERRENCE T OLDHAM

Lenny was a wonderful man who respected all who respected themselves. I had the privilege to meet Lenny on numerous occasions and found him very polite. My memories of this 'man's man' are for ever. Until we meet again, much respect – you fought on until the end. God bless you, and God bless your family.

DERICK MCQUIGLEY

Lenny was a true gentleman, vicious but fair, and always good to his own, not like some of these toe-rags these days. I had the honour of associating with Lenny on many occasions back in the good old days. His passing was a sad loss. Lenny was always a gent, like me, a member of the old school.

LEE RICHARDSON

I'd heard a lot about Lenny when I was younger and then I went and saw him fight 'Mad Gypsy' Bradshaw with a couple of my mates. I was only a young kid at the time and I went backstage after the fight and Lenny said to me, 'All right, son,' and he put his arm around me. It had quite a lasting impression on me. I then met him again at a boxing do when my dad, Charlie Richardson, came out of jail.

Frankie Fraser was staying with us once and me, Frankie and my dad watched all Lenny's fights.

Lenny used to come around our house in New Cross. He used to tell me stories all the time and, because I was a kid, I was always fascinated. Charlie would say to Lenny, 'Come on, take the kid with you.' So, by the time I was 15, I was 'suited and booted' and working with Lenny. Lenny would say to people, 'Have you got the money?' and the next thing you know we would be on our way to the bank. Just one look at Lenny coming towards them and people would be chucking the money at him; he was a monster of a man.

I saw Lenny slap a few people on collecting jobs and he's knocked them down. That's usually all it took and he'd get the money. Lenny always got the money.

Whenever I went to a nightclub I'd go straight to the front of the queue and he'd say, 'All right, Lee... If you need anything, let me know,' and he'd then give me a big hug.

He'd then take us to the VIP section, get us bottles of champagne and introduce us to some birds. I remember Lenny saying, 'Come on, girls, this is a part of my firm. Do you know who his old man is?' It used to put me right on the spot sometimes, but I'd laugh it off.

I saw Lenny kick off a couple of times in the Camden

Palace. Once, this bloke tried pinching the radios from the club and he took them out in the car park. Lenny caught him and said to him, 'You're going to wash all these cars, or I'm going to fucking hurt you, it's as simple as that.' Me and my mates stood with Lenny laughing as we watched this bloke wash all the staff's cars.

Another time, Lenny caught this bloke selling Jack and Jills [pills] in the pub. Lenny didn't hit him hard, though, he just gave him a back-hander to wise him up before he threw him out.

I saw him pick this one bloke up in this nightclub by his neck with one hand and drag him across the dance floor and told him to say sorry to this woman he had chucked a drink over. Lenny then says to the bird, 'Go on, slap him.' The woman slaps him then Lenny goes and chucks him out.

Another time, Lenny tried getting into Brown's nightclub and the doormen wouldn't let him in because his name wasn't on the guest list. Lenny says to them, 'You're having a laugh, ain't you? Now get out of my way.' Both the bouncers put together weren't the size of Lenny and he went straight past them. A couple of my dad's mates were in there and we all got on well and had some champagne. We then moved on to this poker club. Now, I can't play poker and neither could Lenny, so I'm drinking whisky and Lenny's drinking tea, and we had a good laugh and a good night.

One day, Lenny was around our house in New Cross. He and my dad had a bench-press competition in the back garden. Now Charlie isn't as big as Lenny but he couldn't half bench press. As we are putting the weights on the bars, Lenny shouts out, 'Got any more?' He said to me and my mates, 'Push down on each side.' He then starts pushing the bar and us up and down together. I thought the bench was going to snap. Lenny had amazing power.

Another day, Lenny had got chucked off the film set of *The Krays*. He had helped this girl into the ring being the gentleman that he was and she went into a right mood and said, 'Thanks, but no thanks.' Lenny was in one hell of a temper and he gave her a mouthful. They threatened to close the whole set down unless Lenny left.

Lenny was the first person to take me up to Pinewood Studios. We went up there and we were talking about his film being made. Lenny and I both belonged to the same acting agency called Central Casting.

Once we went to this mansion in Hertfordshire. Lenny and I were doing this film up there. It was based in the Seventies and I was playing a luggage boy, and Lenny was playing a minder or something. After taking ages to get there, Lenny and I turned up and they had all these different parts cornered off. They had these people doing a scene where they were jumping up and down and crossing their legs like dancers; Lenny and I started laughing and the security has come at us. The guards said to me and Lenny, 'You can't go in there.' Lenny replied, 'I'll go where I fucking want.' Anyway, we got chucked off the set. Lenny said to me, laughing, 'Fuck them… I'll do my own film.'

I also appeared in a couple of newspaper articles with him over the years, and Lenny had written a little bit about me in his book, *The Guv'nor*, I thought that was really nice of him.

I then lost touch with Lenny but caught up with him a few months before he died. I didn't even know he was ill when I saw him. He looked as strong as an ox. I had a shock when my dad told me that he had passed away.

He was a character, it's just the way he was. There's only one Lenny McLean.

You could see a dark side of him and then you could see a very nice person. He used to make me laugh all the time with his little stories. He didn't take shit off no one and, at the same time, loved his family.

He was larger than life with a heart of gold and could fight like a lion. He was a good bloke – I miss him.

Alex Steene's son Greg has been involved in the fight game for well over 25 years. He was a former boxer himself, having fought for Battersea in the amateur ranks. He then started promoting and has done over 150 shows since. Along the way, he has also managed four world champions. He is currently the General Secretary for the Professional Boxing Promoters' Association.

GREG STEENE

I used to know Lenny McLean really well. He used to come round to my dad's office in the West End regular. My dad and Joe Pyle used to be business partners and they used to promote Roy Shaw. Lenny came up to our office with his uncle Bobby Warren one day and made the challenge to fight Roy. Roy was the original Guv'nor at the time.

The match was then set up and I was asked to be the timekeeper for the fight. I was right up there where the action was taking place; it was one hell of a fight. From the first bell, Lenny came steaming in and Roy done everything to hold on and soak the punches up. Lenny was catching him really hard, only, because Roy had so much experience, he was able to hang on. I think anybody else that day would have gone over. How Roy was actually standing nobody knows, he took so many punches that first round.

Lenny ran out of steam after throwing so many punches. Roy then came back but Lenny was so strong; Lenny had taken loads of punches but he wouldn't get knocked out.

Both men were pretty tired going into the fourth round. It got to a point where the referee stepped in and stopped it in the fourth round after Roy asked him to. We had a chat with Lenny backstage and he was hugely disappointed. The bout had also been a winner-takes-all; it was a lot to put yourself through to come out with nothing, but that was the way they did it in them days.

A couple of months later, Lenny started coming to our office regular trying to do a deal for a return fight. Lenny used to say to me, 'It's a great responsibility being the Guv'nor.' You couldn't really have a day off; if Lenny was under the weather, he couldn't go out through his front door, because, if he did, he'd get some little Herbert coming along wanting to have a go. It's like he couldn't say to them, 'Hang on a minute, come and see me next week.' He was the Guv'nor, he couldn't have a day off; he had to be there every day, ready to take on all-comers.

I went to a lot of Lenny's fights. His best fights were against tough street fighters; the ones who gave him the most problems were former professionals. I remember when my dad had a letter off Muhammad Ali saying that he wouldn't mind fighting Lenny if he ever came to Britain.

My dad used to mention Lenny's name to a lot of people. I remember my dad telling me one story how he had gone to prison to visit Lenny. My dad knew one of the top screws there in this prison and the screw arranged for my dad to go in. Lenny was feeling down there that day. The screws brought Lenny into this room and my dad was sitting there; it wasn't even visiting day.

Dad had taken a load of fags in and gave them to Lenny. Lenny couldn't get over how my dad had got in there. They chatted for hours and Dad really cheered him up.

I seen Lenny a few times on the door at The Hippodrome; he was well in charge. All Lenny had to do to most people was growl at them and that was enough.

I went to the funeral to pay my respects; there was a lot of the chaps there. My dad and I were good friends with Lenny all through his life, we liked him a lot.

11
The Legend Lives On

It's now over seven years since Lenny was taken away from this earth. There's not a day that goes by that his family don't think about him. I spent many hours speaking with Val on the phone with her recalling various memories, many of which were brought to light a few years back in the brilliant book *Married to the Guv'nor*. So I asked Val if her kids would like to contribute something to the book.

Their hardest task was where to begin. They probably had enough memories to fill over ten books. As well as contributions from Jamie and Kelly, there's also a contribution from Karen Latimer, Kelly's best friend, who spent a great deal of time with the McLeans and was like another daughter to Lenny.

I had the privilege of meeting Jamie in a café in the East End of London, and he offered me these thoughts about his dad.

JAMIE MCLEAN

Seven-and-a-half years have now gone past and there is not a day that goes by when I don't think about my dad. It upsets me so much; even after all this time, I found it hard to put pen to paper.

All I want to say is that you have to respect a man like my dad, because of all his achievements. The book, the film and his television work made his family safe and secure... everything he'd ever done was for his family.

He was a true man who opened up a new style of biography and autobiography – that of the normal person with a story to tell. My dad was the original. His book gained so much respect and interest that it reached the number-one spot in *The Times* bestseller list. Thanks to *The Guv'nor*, the likes of Roy Shaw did their books, and for that they should be grateful to my dad.

Many a time, people have shown me quotes in other books where the author has put my dad down. Really, you have to see these people as cowards as they never said these things to his face but, then again, I suppose they think that by including my dad's name it makes it more interesting and sells more books.

Me, my mum and my sister try to move on without him, but it is so difficult because we loved him so much. We are coming up to Christmas knowing, once again, how much we'll miss him and how hard it will be, because he loved Christmas so much, probably more than us kids. That shows you the sort of man he was. I am proud to be my father's son.

KELLY MCLEAN

My dad. It's hard to know where to start; he was so proud of me and Jamie. He hated the fact that he had to leave us and our mum, that's all he spoke about; he was more worried about leaving us than dying.

I've never known such a brave man. He laughed his way through his illness – perhaps that's what kept him so strong. My dad had so much ambition; he came from nothing and fought his way up to where he wanted to be on the television, and the big movie screen, and not forgetting his number-one bestselling book. He made us so very, very proud.

It's now been over seven years since Dad passed away and not a day goes by without me thinking of him. My dad has left me, Jamie and my mum with lots of good memories. Take his impressions, for instance – Elvis, Burt Reynolds, Mike Reid and not forgetting George Clooney. I told Dad I liked Clooney and he was always taking him off after that; these are very funny memories of Dad.

No one really knew my dad, not like we did. No one saw the real him, the family man, the way he laughed and joked and messed around at home.

My dad loved Christmas, all of us sitting together around the table. You could never put a present under the tree for him, as he would rip it right open. I had to leave my presents round at my friend Karen's house, they were safer there.

My dad was the most generous person you could ever meet. Me, my mum and Jamie never wanted for anything. He loved giving us all the things he never had; he worked hard for what he achieved and he did it all for Mum, me and Jamie.

On 28 July 1998, a big part of us was taken away. My dad should still be here, he was taken out of our lives far too young, and he had so much to live for.

I miss him every single day, we all do; some days I laugh, some days I cry. I think of all the things he should be here for and that really upsets me. Me, my mum and Jamie needed him with us a lot longer. We were not ready to say goodbye so early.

It keeps me going believing there is somewhere else; that way I know we'll all be together again some day. He made me so proud of him, he achieved everything he set out to do… people that live to be 80 wouldn't have fitted in what my dad did in his 49 years.

Through his illness, my dad was so strong; he was still the man Jamie and I grew up with. When my dad passed away, he was 18 stone – cancer never took anything away from him, he had his strength, his wit, but, more importantly, his dignity. He didn't wither away, he went when he was ready, with all of us by his side.

I love him so much and miss him terribly, a man I'll always be proud to call my dad.

KAREN LATIMER

What a man! I've known Lenny McLean for the best part of my life. I was friends with Kelly and Jamie and, as we got older, Kelly and I became best friends. I was always in Kelly's house, and Val and Lenny welcomed me into their home and treated me like one of the family. Lenny treated me like another daughter; if ever I needed him, he was always there.

I remember this one time I was still at school. I had a little evening job in a chemist down Roman Road. There was a bunch of boys and girls in their twenties that used to come in and knock things off the shelves and pick on me. As I was only young, I was really scared. So every night, Lenny would meet me from work and walk me home. Lenny used to put his hand on the back of my neck and lead me home… it brings a smile to my face just thinking about it now.

I used to love Lenny picking me up because I usually finished work at around seven o'clock, but Lenny would usually get to me about half-five. So I always got out early. I would say, 'I don't finish 'til seven, Len,' but he would turn up. It's not like my boss was going to argue with him.

Lenny had such a great sense of humour, so dry and witty. He had sayings most people never heard of. He could always make you laugh; even when Lenny was ill, he never stopped joking.

On this one occasion, Val and Kelly weres out shopping and they had been gone about an hour. All of a sudden, Lenny starts clenching his chest and falls back in his chair. I screamed at him, 'Len, Len,' but nothing happened. I phoned Val, panicking like mad. Val said to me, 'He's getting you at it… put him on the phone.'

So I leaned across and puts the phone to Lenny's ear and Val says, 'Len, we're on our way home with pie and mash…' Lenny suddenly opens his eyes and says, 'Lovely, babe.' He just wanted to see my reaction. You'd never have believed he had lung and brain cancer; luckily, Val knew him so well!

Lenny, through his illness, was so strong. They say you never beat cancer – well, Lenny did, he died the man he always was, strong and proud.

I feel blessed to have been part of his life, part of his family.

I miss him so much, he's someone I'll never forget. I'll always have a story to say about Lenny and remembering him always brings a smile to my face.

12
The Show Must Go On

They say every story has an ending, but I just can't see it yet. After collecting and hearing all the interviews while writing this book, I feel like I now know Lenny even more than before, even though I have never met him. For every bad story there was a good one.

Some days, I'd travel hundreds of miles to be told that he was a bad one, and this, that and the other. Then other days, I'd get told that you would never meet a nicer bloke. So who's telling the truth? I honestly still don't know, but will continue to research until I get the final picture.

It's now over six years since my brother Steven and I started the website. As of now, we have a brand-new website up and running and we will continue to run it and give the fans of Lenny a chance to see some of the stuff they would never have seen anywhere else.

I believe that Lenny's tales will go on for ever and, as a few people told me, there will never be another Lenny McLean.

He was truly a one-off who was taken away from this earth far too soon. Lenny knew that his book was going to number one – it had to, as it was unlike any other at the time. Also, with the technology of the internet these days, more people are only now hearing the name of the Guv'nor, Lenny McLean. So, for some people, the show has just started.

When I see some of the messages left on the guestbook from countries worldwide, I think to myself, That's the same message I was leaving six years ago. So who knows what we are going to be reading in another six years from now. Perhaps someone else will get addicted like me and they might be bringing a book out too.

I finally had to bring down the shutters on this book as the stories were coming in thick and fast. Where do you decide to stop? I could be there in another year's time and the stories could still be coming in.

Hopefully, by the time this book comes out, things will have started moving with the film and Lenny would have got what he wanted most in life, to see his name up in lights in the West End. He fought so hard to get that film made and his family will have the chance to see his dream come true.

I have had my ups and downs while writing this book but things are sent to try us and I have overcome all of them so far. I don't know what Lenny would have thought about this book personally. I'd like to think that he would have loved it, as he loved people talking about him. A very good friend of Lenny's told me that, if he'd been here, then he would have said, 'Well done, son.'

I have tried answering the questions I have been asked throughout the years and, from what I've seen and heard, Lenny, in my eyes, will always be… the Guv'nor.

Copyright Notices